YOUR PERSONAL
HOROSCOPE
2023

JOSEPH POLANSKY

YOUR PERSONAL HOROSCOPE 2023

Month-by-month forecast for every sign

Thorsons

Thorsons
An imprint of HarperCollins*Publishers*
1 London Bridge Street
London SE1 9GF

www.harpercollins.co.uk

HarperCollins*Publishers*
1st Floor, Watermarque Building, Ringsend Road
Dublin 4, Ireland

First published by Thorsons 2022

3 5 7 9 10 8 6 4

© Star ★ Data, Inc. 2022

Star ★ Data asserts the moral right to be
identified as the author of this work

A catalogue record of this book is
available from the British Library

ISBN 978-0-00-852035-9

Printed and bound in the UK using 100%
renewable electricity at CPI Group (UK) Ltd

MIX
Paper from
responsible sources
FSC™ C007454

This book is produced from independently certified FSC™ paper
to ensure responsible forest management.

For more information visit: www.harpercollins.co.uk/green

The author is grateful to the people
of STAR ★ DATA, who truly fathered
this book and without whom it
could not have been written.

Contents

Introduction

Welcome to the fascinating and intricate world of astrology!

For thousands of years the movements of the planets and other heavenly bodies have intrigued the best minds of every generation. Life holds no greater challenge or joy than this: knowledge of ourselves and the universe we live in. Astrology is one of the keys to this knowledge.

Your Personal Horoscope 2023 gives you the fruits of astrological wisdom. In addition to general guidance on your character and the basic trends of your life, it shows you how to take advantage of planetary influences so you can make the most of the year ahead.

The section on each sign includes a Personality Profile, a look at general trends for 2023, and in-depth month-by-month forecasts. The Glossary (*page 5*) explains some of the astrological terms you may be unfamiliar with.

One of the many helpful features of this book is the 'Best' and 'Most Stressful' days listed at the beginning of each monthly forecast. Read these sections to learn which days in each month will be good overall, good for money, and good for love. Mark them on your calendar – these will be your best days. Similarly, make a note of the days that will be most stressful for you. It is best to avoid booking important meetings or taking major decisions on these days, as well as on those days when important planets in your horoscope are retrograde (moving backwards through the zodiac).

The Major Trends section for your sign lists those days when your vitality is strong or weak, or when relationships with your co-workers or loved ones may need a bit more effort on your part. If you are going through a difficult time, take a look at the colour, metal, gem and scent listed in the 'At a Glance' section of your Personality Profile. Wearing a piece of jewellery that contains your metal and/or gem will strengthen your vitality, just as wearing clothes or decorating your room or office in the colour ruled by your sign, drinking teas made from the herbs ruled by your sign or wearing the scents associated with your sign will sustain you.

Another important virtue of this book is that it will help you to know not only yourself but those around you: your friends, co-workers, partners and/or children. Reading the Personality Profile and forecasts for their signs will provide you with an insight into their behaviour that you won't get anywhere else. You will know when to be more tolerant of them and when they are liable to be difficult or irritable.

In this edition we have included foot reflexology charts as part of the health section. So many health problems could perhaps be avoided or alleviated if we understood which organs were most vulnerable and what we could do to protect them. Though there are many natural and drug-free ways to strengthen vulnerable organs, these charts show a valid way to proceed. The vulnerable organs for the year ahead are clearly marked in the charts. It's very good to massage the whole foot on a regular basis, as the feet contain reflexes to the entire body. Try to pay special attention to the specific areas marked in the charts. If this is done diligently, health problems can be avoided. And even if they can't be completely avoided, their impact can be softened considerably.

I consider you – the reader – my personal client. By studying your Solar Horoscope I gain an awareness of what is going on in your life – what you are feeling and striving for and the challenges you face. I then do my best to address these concerns. Consider this book the next best thing to having your own personal astrologer!

It is my sincere hope that *Your Personal Horoscope 2023* will enhance the quality of your life, make things easier, illuminate the way forward, banish obscurities and make you more aware of your personal connection to the universe. Understood properly and used wisely, astrology is a great guide to knowing yourself, the people around you and the events in your life – but remember that what you do with these insights – the final result – is up to you.

A Note on the 'New Zodiac'

Recently an article was published that postulated two things: the discovery of a new constellation – Ophiuchus – making a thirteenth constellation in the heavens and thus a thirteenth sign, and the statement that because the Earth has shifted relative to the constellations in the past few thousand years, all the signs have shifted backwards by one sign. This has caused much consternation, and I have received a stream of letters, emails and phone calls from people saying things like: 'I don't want to be a Taurus, I'm happy being a Gemini', 'What's my real sign?' or 'Now that I finally understand myself, I'm not who I think I am!'

All of this is 'much ado about nothing'. The article has some partial truth to it. Yes, in two thousand years the planets have shifted relative to the constellations in the heavens. This is old news. We know this and Hindu astrologers take this into account when casting charts. This shift doesn't affect Western astrologers in North America and Europe. We use what is called a 'tropical' zodiac. This zodiac has nothing to do with the constellations in the heavens. They have the same names, but that's about it. The tropical zodiac is based on the Earth's revolution around the Sun. Imagine the circle that this orbit makes, then divide this circle by twelve and you have our zodiac. The Spring Equinox is always 0 degrees (Aries), and the Autumn Equinox is always 0 degrees Libra (180 degrees from Aries). At one time a few thousand years ago, these tropical signs coincided with the actual constellations; they were pretty much interchangeable, and it didn't matter what zodiac you used. But in the course of thousands of years the planets have shifted relative to these constellations. Here in the West it doesn't affect our practice one iota. You are still the sign you always were.

In North America and Europe there is a clear distinction between an astrological sign and a constellation in the heavens. This issue is more of a problem for Hindu astrologers. Their zodiac is based on the actual constellations – this is called the 'sidereal' zodiac. And Hindu astrologers have been accounting for this shift all the time. They keep close tabs on it. In two thousand years there is a shift of 23 degrees, and they subtract this from the Western calculations. So in their system many a Gemini would be a Taurus and this is true for all the signs. This is nothing new – it is all known and accounted for, so there is no bombshell here.

The so-called thirteenth constellation, Ophiuchus, is also not a problem for the Western astrologer. As we mentioned, our zodiac has nothing to do with the constellations. It could be more of a problem for the Hindus, but my feeling is that it's not a problem for them either. What these astronomers are calling a new constellation was probably considered a part of one of the existing constellations. I don't know this as a fact, but I presume it is so intuitively. I'm sure we will soon be getting articles by Hindu astrologers explaining this.

Glossary of Astrological Terms

Ascendant

We experience day and night because the Earth rotates on its axis once every 24 hours. It is because of this rotation that the Sun, Moon and planets seem to rise and set. The zodiac is a fixed belt (imaginary, but very real in spiritual terms) around the Earth. As the Earth rotates, the different signs of the zodiac seem to the observer to rise on the horizon. During a 24-hour period every sign of the zodiac will pass this horizon point at some time or another. The sign that is at the horizon point at any given time is called the Ascendant, or rising sign. The Ascendant is the sign denoting a person's self-image, body and self-concept – the personal ego, as opposed to the spiritual ego indicated by a person's Sun sign.

Aspects

Aspects are the angular relationships between planets, the way in which one planet stimulates or influences another. If a planet makes a harmonious aspect (connection) to another, it tends to stimulate that planet in a positive and helpful way. If, however, it makes a stressful aspect to another planet, this disrupts that planet's normal influence.

Astrological Qualities

There are three astrological qualities: *cardinal*, *fixed* and *mutable*. Each of the 12 signs of the zodiac falls into one of these three categories.

Cardinal Signs
Aries, Cancer, Libra and Capricorn
The cardinal quality is the active, initiating principle. Those born under these four signs are good at starting new projects.

Fixed Signs
Taurus, Leo, Scorpio and Aquarius
Fixed qualities include stability, persistence, endurance and perfectionism. People born under these four signs are good at seeing things through.

Mutable Signs
Gemini, Virgo, Sagittarius and Pisces
Mutable qualities are adaptability, changeability and balance. Those born under these four signs are creative, if not always practical.

Direct Motion

When the planets move forward through the zodiac – as they normally do – they are said to be going 'direct'.

Grand Square

A Grand Square differs from a normal Square (usually two planets separated by 90 degrees) in that four or more planets are involved. When you look at the pattern in a chart you will see a whole and complete square. This, though stressful, usually denotes a new manifestation in the life. There is much work and balancing involved in the manifestation.

Grand Trine

A Grand Trine differs from a normal Trine (where two planets are 120 degrees apart) in that three or more planets are involved. When you look at this pattern in a chart, it takes the form of a complete triangle – a Grand Trine. Usually (but not always) it occurs in one of the four elements: Fire, Earth, Air or Water. Thus the particular element in which it occurs will be highlighted. A Grand Trine in Water is not the same as a Grand Trine in Air or Fire, etc. This is a very fortunate and happy aspect, and quite rare.

Houses

There are 12 signs of the zodiac and 12 houses of experience. The 12 signs are personality types and ways in which a given planet expresses itself; the 12 houses show 'where' in your life this expression takes place. Each house has a different area of interest. A house can become potent and important – a house of power – in different ways: if it contains the Sun, the Moon or the 'ruler' of your chart; if it contains more than one planet; or if the ruler of that house is receiving unusual stimulation from other planets.

1st House
Personal Image and Sensual Delights

2nd House
Money/Finance

3rd House
Communication and Intellectual Interests

4th House
Home and Family

5th House
Children, Fun, Games, Creativity, Speculations and Love Affairs

6th House
Health and Work

7th House
Love, Marriage and Social Activities

8th House
Transformation and Regeneration

9th House
Religion, Foreign Travel, Higher Education and Philosophy

10th House
Career

11th House
Friends, Group Activities and Fondest Wishes

12th House
Spirituality

Karma

Karma is the law of cause and effect which governs all phenomena. We are all where we find ourselves because of karma – because of actions we have performed in the past. The universe is such a balanced instrument that any act immediately sets corrective forces into motion – karma.

Long-term Planets

The planets that take a long time to move through a sign show the long-term trends in a given area of life. They are important for forecasting the prolonged view of things. Because these planets stay in one sign for so long, there are periods in the year when the faster-moving (short-term) planets will join them, further activating and enhancing the importance of a given house.

Jupiter
stays in a sign for about 1 year

Saturn
2½ years

Uranus
7 years

Neptune
14 years

Pluto
15 to 30 years

Lunar

Relating to the Moon. See also 'Phases of the Moon', below.

Natal

Literally means 'birth'. In astrology this term is used to distinguish between planetary positions that occurred at the time of a person's birth (natal) and those that are current (transiting). For example, Natal Sun refers to where the Sun was when you were born; transiting Sun refers to where the Sun's position is currently at any given moment – which usually doesn't coincide with your birth, or Natal, Sun.

Out of Bounds

The planets move through the zodiac at various angles relative to the celestial equator (if you were to draw an imaginary extension of the Earth's equator out into the universe, you would have an illustration of this celestial equator). The Sun – being the most dominant and powerful influence in the Solar system – is the measure astrologers use as a standard. The Sun never goes more than approximately 23 degrees north or south of the celestial equator. At the winter solstice the Sun reaches its maximum southern angle of orbit (declination); at the summer solstice it reaches its maximum northern angle. Any time a planet exceeds this Solar boundary – and occasionally planets do – it is said to be 'out of bounds'. This means that the planet exceeds or trespasses into strange territory – beyond the limits allowed by the Sun, the ruler of the Solar system. The planet in this condition becomes more emphasized and exceeds its authority, becoming an important influence in the forecast.

Phases of the Moon

After the full Moon, the Moon seems to shrink in size (as perceived from the Earth), gradually growing smaller until it is virtually invisible to the naked eye – at the time of the next new Moon. This is called the waning Moon phase, or the waning Moon.

After the new Moon, the Moon gradually gets bigger in size (as perceived from the Earth) until it reaches its maximum size at the time of the full Moon. This period is called the waxing Moon phase, or waxing Moon.

Retrogrades

The planets move around the Sun at different speeds. Mercury and Venus move much faster than the Earth, while Mars, Jupiter, Saturn, Uranus, Neptune and Pluto move more slowly. Thus there are times when, relative to the Earth, the planets appear to be going backwards. In reality they are always going forward, but relative to our vantage point on Earth they seem to go backwards through the zodiac for a period of time. This is called 'retrograde' motion and tends to weaken the normal influence of a given planet.

Short-term Planets

The fast-moving planets move so quickly through a sign that their effects are generally of a short-term nature. They reflect the immediate, day-to-day trends in a horoscope.

Moon
stays in a sign for only 2½ days

Mercury
20 to 30 days

Sun
30 days

Venus
approximately 1 month

Mars
approximately 2 months

T-square

A T-square differs from a Grand Square (see above) in that it is not a complete square. If you look at the pattern in a chart it appears as 'half a complete square', resembling the T-square tools used by architects and designers. If you cut a complete square in half, diagonally, you have a T-square. Many astrologers consider this more stressful than a Grand Square, as it creates tension that is difficult to resolve. T-squares bring learning experiences.

Transits

This term refers to the movements or motions of the planets at any given time. Astrologers use the word 'transit' to make the distinction between a birth, or Natal, planet (see 'Natal', above) and the planet's current movement in the heavens. For example, if at your birth Saturn was in the sign of Cancer in your 8th house, but is now moving through your 3rd house, it is said to be 'transiting' your 3rd house. Transits are one of the main tools with which astrologers forecast trends.

YOUR PERSONAL HOROSCOPE 2023

Aries

THE RAM

Birthdays from
21st March to
20th April

Personality Profile

ARIES AT A GLANCE

Element – Fire

Ruling Planet – Mars
   Career Planet – Saturn
   Love Planet – Venus
   Money Planet – Venus
   Planet of Fun, Entertainment, Creativity and Speculations – Sun
   Planet of Health and Work – Mercury
   Planet of Home and Family Life – Moon
   Planet of Spirituality – Neptune
   Planet of Travel, Education, Religion and Philosophy – Jupiter

Colours – carmine, red, scarlet

Colours that promote love, romance and social harmony – green, jade green

Colour that promotes earning power – green

Gem – amethyst

Metals – iron, steel

Scent – honeysuckle

Quality – cardinal (= activity)

Quality most needed for balance – caution

Strongest virtues – abundant physical energy, courage, honesty, independence, self-reliance

Deepest need – action

Characteristics to avoid – haste, impetuousness, over-aggression, rashness

Signs of greatest overall compatibility – Leo, Sagittarius

Signs of greatest overall incompatibility – Cancer, Libra, Capricorn

Sign most helpful to career – Capricorn

Sign most helpful for emotional support – Cancer

Sign most helpful financially – Taurus

Sign best for marriage and/or partnerships – Libra

Sign most helpful for creative projects – Leo

Best Sign to have fun with – Leo

Signs most helpful in spiritual matters – Sagittarius, Pisces

Best day of the week – Tuesday

Understanding an Aries

Aries is the activist *par excellence* of the zodiac. The Aries need for action is almost an addiction, and those who do not really understand the Aries personality would probably use this hard word to describe it. In reality 'action' is the essence of the Aries psychology – the more direct, blunt and to-the-point the action, the better. When you think about it, this is the ideal psychological makeup for the warrior, the pioneer, the athlete or the manager.

Aries likes to get things done, and in their passion and zeal often lose sight of the consequences for themselves and others. Yes, they often try to be diplomatic and tactful, but it is hard for them. When they do so they feel that they are being dishonest and phoney. It is hard for them even to understand the mindset of the diplomat, the consensus builder, the front office executive. These people are involved in endless meetings, discussions, talks and negotiations – all of which seem a great waste of time when there is so much work to be done, so many real achievements to be gained. An Aries can understand, once it is explained, that talk and negotiations – the social graces – lead ultimately to better, more effective actions. The interesting thing is that an Aries is rarely malicious or spiteful – even when waging war. Aries people fight without hate for their opponents. To them it is all good-natured fun, a grand adventure, a game.

When confronted with a problem many people will say, 'Well, let's think about it, let's analyse the situation.' But not an Aries. An Aries will think, 'Something must be done. Let's get on with it.' Of course, neither response is the total answer. Sometimes action is called for, sometimes cool thought. But an Aries tends to err on the side of action.

Action and thought are radically different principles. Physical activity is the use of brute force. Thinking and deliberating require one not to use force – to be still. It is not good for the athlete to be deliberating the next move; this will only slow down his or her reaction time. The athlete must act instinctively and instantly. This is how Aries people tend to behave in life. They are quick, instinctive decision-makers and their decisions tend to be translated into action almost immediately. When their intuition is sharp and well tuned, their actions are powerful and successful. When their intuition is off, their actions can be disastrous.

Do not think this will scare an Aries. Just as a good warrior knows that in the course of combat he or she might acquire a few wounds, so too does an Aries realize – somewhere deep down – that in the course of being true to yourself you might get embroiled in a disaster or two. It is all part of the game. An Aries feels strong enough to weather any storm.

There are many Aries people who are intellectual. They make powerful and creative thinkers. But even in this realm they tend to be pioneers – outspoken and blunt. These types of Aries tend to elevate (or sublimate) their desire for physical combat in favour of intellectual, mental combat. And they are indeed powerful.

In general, Aries people have a faith in themselves that others could learn from. This basic, rock-solid faith carries them through the most tumultuous situations of life. Their courage and self-confidence make them natural leaders. Their leadership is more by way of example than by actually controlling others.

Finance

Aries people often excel as builders or estate agents. Money in and of itself is not as important as are other things – action, adventure, sport, etc. They are motivated by the need to support and be well-thought-of by their partners. Money as a way of attaining pleasure is another important motivation. Aries function best in their own businesses or as managers of their own departments within a large business or corporation. The fewer orders they have to take from higher up, the better. They also function better out in the field rather than behind a desk.

Aries people are hard workers with a lot of endurance; they can earn large sums of money due to the strength of their sheer physical energy.

Venus is their money planet, which means that Aries need to develop more of the social graces in order to realize their full earning potential. Just getting the job done – which is what an Aries excels at – is not enough to create financial success. The co-operation of others needs to be attained. Customers, clients and co-workers need to be made to feel comfortable; many people need to be treated properly in order for success to happen. When Aries people develop these abilities – or hire someone to do this for them – their financial potential is unlimited.

Career and Public Image

One would think that a pioneering type would want to break with the social and political conventions of society. But this is not so with the Aries-born. They are pioneers within conventional limits, in the sense that they like to start their own businesses within an established industry.

Capricorn is on the 10th house of career cusp of Aries' solar horoscope. Saturn is the planet that rules their life's work and professional aspirations. This tells us some interesting things about the Aries character. First off, it shows that, in order for Aries people to reach their full career potential, they need to develop some qualities that are a bit alien to their basic nature: they need to become better administrators and organizers; they need to be able to handle details better and to take a long-range view of their projects and their careers in general. No one can beat an Aries when it comes to achieving short-range objectives, but a career is long term, built over time. You cannot take a 'quickie' approach to it.

Some Aries people find it difficult to stick with a project until the end. Since they get bored quickly and are in constant pursuit of new adventures, they prefer to pass an old project or task on to somebody else in order to start something new. Those Aries who learn how to put off the search for something new until the old is completed will achieve great success in their careers and professional lives.

In general, Aries people like society to judge them on their own merits, on their real and actual achievements. A reputation acquired by 'hype' feels false to them.

Love and Relationships

In marriage and partnerships Aries like those who are more passive, gentle, tactful and diplomatic – people who have the social grace and skills they sometimes lack. Our partners always represent a hidden part of ourselves – a self that we cannot express personally.

An Aries tends to go after what he or she likes aggressively. The tendency is to jump into relationships and marriages. This is especially true if Venus is in Aries as well as the Sun. If an Aries likes you, he or she will have a hard time taking no for an answer; many attempts will be made to sweep you off your feet.

Though Aries can be exasperating in relationships – especially if they are not understood by their partners – they are never consciously or wilfully cruel or malicious. It is just that they are so independent and sure of themselves that they find it almost impossible to see somebody else's viewpoint or position. This is why an Aries needs as a partner someone with lots of social graces.

On the plus side, an Aries is honest, someone you can lean on, someone with whom you will always know where you stand. What he or she lacks in diplomacy is made up for in integrity.

Home and Domestic Life

An Aries is of course the ruler at home – the Boss. The male will tend to delegate domestic matters to the female. The female Aries will want to rule the roost. Both tend to be handy round the house. Both like large families and both believe in the sanctity and importance of the family. An Aries is a good family person, although he or she does not especially like being at home a lot, preferring instead to be roaming about.

Considering that they are by nature so combative and wilful, Aries people can be surprisingly soft, gentle and even vulnerable with their children and partners. The sign of Cancer, ruled by the Moon, is on the cusp of their solar 4th house of home and family. When the Moon is well aspected – under favourable influences – in the birth chart, an Aries will be tender towards the family and will want a family life that is nurturing and supportive. Aries likes to come home after a hard day on the battlefield of life to the understanding arms of their partner and the unconditional love and support of their family. An Aries feels that there is enough 'war' out in the world – and he or she enjoys participating in that. But when Aries comes home, comfort and nurturing are what's needed.

Horoscope for 2023

Major Trends

This year is an eventful year, both for the world and for you personally. Three long-term planets change signs in 2023, which is highly unusual. Pluto will move (temporarily) out of your 10th house of career into your 11th house. He will hover between the two houses this year, and next year too. Saturn, your career planet, will leave Aquarius, where he's been for over two years, and move into Pisces on March 8. And Jupiter, which is now in your own sign, will move into your money house on May 17. The cosmic chess board is being rearranged.

The year ahead is prosperous, Aries. With Jupiter in your sign until May 17 he will bring the high life – the good life. There will be more travel. More importantly, you will live on a higher standard than usual. More on this later.

Saturn's move into your spiritual 12th house on March 8 indicates an important career shift. The career becomes more idealistic. You'll be more involved in charities and altruistic activities. You need to feel that your career – your life work – is important for the planet. It is a time to be more disciplined in your spiritual life and practice. More on this later.

Mars, the ruler of your Horoscope (and a very important planet for you) will be 'out of bounds' for a very long time this year – from January 1 to May 4. This shows that personally you're outside your normal orbit, outside your normal boundaries.

This is not an especially strong love year. With all the long-term planets in the Eastern sector of self, 2023 is a 'me'-oriented year. Of course, the short-term planets will energize the Western, social sector, particularly later on in the year – but the social sector will never dominate this year. Details on this later.

Pluto's move into your 11th house (from March 24 to June 12) is merely a foretaste of things to come. This transit impacts on friendships, although not necessarily on romance. Friendships were tested over the past two years, but soon they will get a serious, long-term testing – 20 to 25 years. The whole social circle will completely change in the coming years.

Your main interests this year will be the body and image (until May 17); finance; career (until March 24 and from June 12 onwards); friendships, groups and group activities (until March 8 and from March 24 to June 12); and spirituality.

Your paths of greatest fulfilment this year will be the body and image (until May 17 and from July 18 onwards); and finance (from May 17 onwards).

Health

(Please note that this is an astrological perspective on health and not a medical one. In days of yore there was no difference, both these perspectives were identical. But these days there could be quite a difference. For a medical perspective, please consult your doctor or health practitioner.)

Health is good this year. The long-term planets are either making harmonious aspects or are leaving you alone. Of course, during the year the short-term planets can cause some stress, and your health and energy could be less than usual at these times, but these are temporary things, not trends for the year.

Good though your health is, you can make it better. Give more attention to the following – the vulnerable areas of your Horoscope this year (the reflex points are shown in the chart opposite):

- The head and face. These are always important for you, Aries. Regular scalp and face massage will not only strengthen the given areas but the entire body as well (there are meridian lines that go to the rest of the body). Craniosacral therapy is also good for the head: the plates in the skull need to be kept in right alignment.
- The musculature is also always important for Aries. You don't need to be Arnold Schwarzenegger, just to have good muscle tone. Good muscle tone will keep the spine and skeleton in right alignment. Muscle tone also seems to be a factor in physical balance. So, regular physical exercise is excellent – each according to their age and stage in life.
- The adrenals are another important area for you, and the reflex points are shown opposite. The important thing is to avoid anger and fear – the two emotions that stress them out.

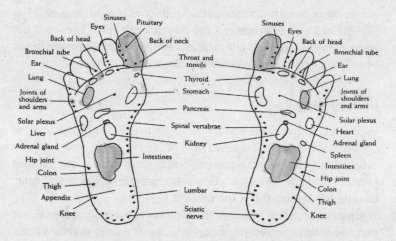

Important foot reflexology points for the year ahead

Try to massage all of the foot on a regular basis – the top of the foot as well as the bottom – but pay extra attention to the points highlighted on the chart. When you massage, be aware of 'sore spots' as these need special attention. It's also a good idea to massage the ankles and below them.

- The lungs, arms, shoulders, small intestine and respiratory system. Mercury, the ruler of these areas, is your health planet, and so these areas are always important for you. Regular arm and shoulder massage is always good. Tension tends to collect in the shoulders and needs to be released.

Jupiter will be in your sign until May 17. While this is a happy transit in general it does have some caveats. Weight will need to be watched. (This is the natural consequence of living the good life.) Women of childbearing age are also extremely fertile during this period, and pregnancy would not be a surprise.

Mercury is a fast-moving planet (only the Moon moves faster than him), so, as our regular readers know, there are many short-term trends in health that depend on where Mercury is at any given time and the kind of aspects he receives. These are best covered in the monthly reports.

Mercury will be in retrograde motion more than usual this year. Generally, he retrogrades three times a year but in 2023 it will be four times – from January 1 to the 17th; April 21 to May 14; August 23 to September 14; and December 13 to the end of the year. These will not be good times to undergo tests and procedures as the results might not be reliable. Best to reschedule these things, if possible.

Home and Family

Your 4th house of home and family is not prominent this year – it is not a house of power. This tends to the status quo. You seem basically satisfied with the present home and family situation and have no need to make dramatic changes. (This will change in a few years' time, though, but for now this is the way it is.)

A parent or parent figure in your life becomes more spiritual this year and seems involved in your spiritual life. It is likely that the karmic relationships between you and this person will be revealed this year, and over the coming years. (Sometimes, instead of spirituality, they resort to alcohol or drugs – but this also comes from spiritual urges: a desire to transcend this world.)

Your family planet, the Moon, is the fastest moving of all the planets. Where the other fast short-term planets will take a year to move through your chart, the Moon will move through it every month. This leads to short-term trends in the home and family life that depend on where the Moon is exactly and the kinds of aspects she receives. Again, this is best covered in the monthly reports.

Moon phenomena are short lived. Eight times in any given month she will re-stimulate eclipse points, causing emotional disturbances or shake-ups at home. Eight times in any given month she will make stressful aspects to the long-term planets Saturn and Uranus. This also causes upheavals and high passions – especially in a parent or parent figure. But the trends of the year as a whole are as have been described.

If you're planning renovations to the home or major repairs, March 26 to May 21 are good times. If you're merely redecorating in a cosmetic kind of way, May 7 to June 5 and June 21 to July 23 are good times. These latter periods are also good for buying art objects for the home.

A parent or parent figure is likely to move this year – it looks happy. If he or she doesn't move there could be renovations in their home that have the same effect as a move. He or she could acquire an additional home, or gain access to an additional home. If the parent figure is of childbearing age, a pregnancy could happen. Siblings and sibling figures in your life have a stable family year tending to the status quo. Moves are unlikely. The same is true for children and children figures, but they are probably contemplating moves, which could happen down the line. Grandchildren (if you have them) or those who play that role in your life are not likely to move this year. They need to work out emotional issues.

Finance and Career

As we mentioned earlier, the year ahead is a prosperous year for you, Aries. Jupiter in your sign might not bring money per se, but it brings an elevated lifestyle. You live 'as if' you were rich. The cosmos supplies for this. More importantly, Jupiter will move into your money house on May 17 and will really start to prosper you in a tangible way. Assets you own will increase in value. Happy financial opportunities will come (perhaps from foreign lands or through foreigners). Earnings will increase.

Uranus has been in your money house for many years now. This transit has brought much experimentation to the financial life, as well as excitement and surprises. Earnings could have been sky high or ultra low; there has been much volatility here. Now, with Jupiter travelling near Uranus (the transit will be more exact next year), earnings will tend to be high – unexpectedly high. The instability works in your favour. This is Aries heaven. You like the fast buck. You like quick wealth. This year you are likely to get it.

Uranus in your money house favours technology, the online world and companies that are involved with new inventions and innovations. It favours start-ups. If you're an investor these are good companies to look at (although always do your due diligence before investing). But even if you're not an investor, online activities and your technology skills are important in your finances, regardless of what you actually do.

Jupiter's position in your money house favours foreign companies, the travel business, airlines and for-profit colleges. Also, since Jupiter rules your 9th house of travel and education, there is likely to be business-related travel this year.

Fast-moving Venus is your financial planet, so there are many short-term trends in finance that depend on where she is and the kinds of aspects she receives at a particular time, which will be covered in the monthly reports. She will make one of her rare retrogrades (once every two years) in the year ahead, from July 23 to September 3. This will be a time to avoid major purchases, investments or other important financial decisions. Instead, it will be a time to achieve clarity about your finances and to resolve doubts.

A solar eclipse on April 20 occurs right on the cusp (the border) of your 1st and 2nd houses and is thus an influence in both houses. So, this will bring changes to your financial thinking and planning. I feel it will prepare you for the coming prosperity.

Your 10th house of career is still strong, but not as strong as in previous years. Pluto will move in and out of this house in the coming year. The past twenty-plus years have completely transformed your career and sense of mission, but this period is coming to its conclusion now. You should be in your ideal career path and life now. More importantly, your career planet, Saturn, changes signs this year. He moves into Pisces, your 12th house of spirituality, on March 8 and will stay there for the next two and a half years. So, as we said, you're more idealistic about your career. Many of you will want a more spiritual type of career. Others will opt for a worldly career but be involved in charities and non-profit organization. Being involved in these things not only brings personal satisfaction but boosts the career as well. Those of you who are managers might be more lax, more fluid in your management decisions. Less exacting. Less demanding.

Love and Social Life

As we mentioned earlier, 2023 is not an especially strong love and social year. Your 7th house is not a house of power. It will get a bit stronger later in the year, but only for short periods. So, those of you who are married will tend to stay married, and singles will tend to stay single. The year ahead is about getting your body, image and personal interests and goals in right order. The focus is on you.

Though marriage is not likely for singles, there will be love affairs. Venus, your love planet, spends an unusual amount of time in Leo, your 5th house of fun and creativity. Normally Venus spends approximately a month in any given sign or house. This year she will spend a bit more than four months in Leo. So, this indicates some love affairs happening. But such affairs are not likely to lead to marriage. They are more about entertainment – fun and games. And there's nothing wrong with this. It's just good to know what's what.

Venus being a fast-moving planet means that there are many short-term trends in love that depend on where she is and the kinds of aspects she receives. These are best dealt with in the monthly reports.

Parents or parent figures have a stable social year. Likewise, siblings and sibling figures. Singles can find love opportunities online or as they involve themselves with friends, groups and group activities. Siblings and sibling figures are very much love-at-first-sight people this year. Children and children figures have a much easier love life than last year: Saturn leaving their 7th house improves things. Venus in their sign from June 5 to October 9 makes them more romantic, more in the mood for relationship. Grandchildren (or those who play that role in your life) have a status quo love year. If they are married, they will tend to stay married. If single they will tend to stay single.

Self-improvement

Spirituality has been important for Aries for many years. Neptune, your spiritual planet, has been in your 12th house of spirituality for many years, and will be there for many more. Last year Jupiter moved through your 12th house, expanding and emphasizing spirituality even more. You had many spiritual breakthroughs last year. This year we see something new – stern Saturn will occupy the 12th house, from March 8 onwards. Where spirituality has been fun and freewheeling for the past few years, now it will be less so. Now it's time to pull in the horns a bit. Time to focus on the essence of your spiritual practice and let go of trivialities, such as are crop circles real? Who made them? Are UFOs real? Were Jesus and Mary Magdalene married? While these are interesting questions, they distract you from the essence of your practice. Ralph Waldo Emerson called these interests 'mumps of the soul'.

Saturn in your 12th house signals a need for steady, disciplined practice. Choose a path and follow it in a disciplined way. Spiritual practice has to yield practical, tangible results – and this comes from the daily discipline.

Since Saturn is your career planet, this transit indicates a shift to a spiritual type of career – something meaningful to you, as we've already said. Career can't just be about making money and achieving worldly success. It must have some spiritual import. It must benefit the planet as a whole. You've been feeling these urges for many years, but especially now. Some (as we said) will actually opt for some spiritual career. Some will opt for a position in a non-profit or charity. Others will pursue their worldly careers but be involved in charities and altruistic projects on the side.

Saturn in your 12th house favours the traditional mystical paths – the ones that have stood the test of time. You're more conservative in your spirituality these days.

There is also another way to read Saturn's transit: your spiritual practice, your spiritual growth, *is* your actual career, your actual mission this year, and for the next few years.

Pluto beginning to enter your 11th house (he hovers between the 10th and 11th houses for the next two years) indicates that friendships will now get the Pluto treatment. Old friendships will go. Some friends will have near-death kinds of experiences, and, over the next couple of decades, some could physically die. Your social circle is being transformed. The cosmos is giving birth to the social life of your dreams – your ideal of friendships. This won't happen overnight, but over the years as a process. In the short term it might not be pretty (no new birth ever is) but the result will be good.

Month-by-month Forecasts

January

Best Days Overall: 8, 9, 16, 17, 25, 26
Most Stressful Days Overall: 3, 4, 10, 11, 23, 24, 30, 31
Best Days for Love: 2, 3, 4, 12, 13, 21, 22, 30, 31
Best Days for Money: 2, 3, 8, 12, 13, 16, 18, 19, 21, 22, 23
Best Days for Career: 4, 10, 11, 12, 13, 22, 31

A happy month ahead, Aries. Enjoy! Jupiter in your own sign is bringing the good life – foreign travel, good food, good wine, and hosts of
sensual pleasures. There is great optimism in your life. But you do
need to be more careful health-wise, and especially with your weight.
There is nothing seriously wrong with the health, just short-term
stress caused by the short-term planets, and it will improve after the
20th. With your health planet Mercury retrograde until the 17th avoid
medical tests or procedures, if you can. Wait until after the 17th.

The pace of life will speed up this month. We begin the new year
with 30 per cent of the planets in retrograde motion; by the end of the
month *all* the planets are moving forward. Events move quickly, just as
you like it.

At least 90 per cent (and sometimes 100 per cent) of the planets are
in the independent Eastern sector of self at the moment, so, it's a
'me-oriented' month in a 'me-oriented' year. Personal independence
is strong now and will get even stronger in the coming months. With
Mars, the ruler of your Horoscope, going forward on the 12th you will
have more clarity about your personal goals. It is a good month to
make the changes that need to be made for your future happiness.

Though love doesn't seem like a big deal these days, love opportunities for singles happen as you involve yourself with friends, groups,
professional and trade organizations. Friends can play Cupid, or someone you thought of as a friend wants to be more than that. Social media
and online activities can also lead to romance.

Finance looks good. Your technological expertise seems important.
For investors the high-tech and online worlds seem like interesting
opportunities. You are spending more on technology, but you earn

from it as well. With Uranus moving forward on the 22nd high-tech purchases will go better after that.

Mars, your Horoscope's ruler, is 'out of bounds' all month, and will remain so until May 4. So, you're 'off the reservation', outside your normal orbit and seem to be enjoying it.

February

Best Days Overall: 4, 5, 6, 14, 15, 22, 23
Most Stressful Days Overall: 2, 3, 9, 10, 16, 17
Best Days for Love: 2, 3, 9, 10, 12, 13, 22
Best Days for Money: 2, 3, 4, 5, 12, 13, 14, 15, 22, 23, 24, 25
Best Days for Career: 1, 10, 16, 17, 19, 28

All the planets are moving forward this month and life moves swiftly. Goals are attained quickly – personally and in the world at large.

Venus, your love and financial planet, is having her solstice from the 21st to the 24th. She pauses in the heavens (in her latitudinal motion) and then changes direction. This is what happens in both love and finance. A pause – a stasis – then a change of direction. Don't be alarmed by this. It is healthy.

Planetary power is concentrated in your 11th house of friends this month, until the 18th. So, it is a social month. It is about being involved with groups, group activities and online activity. It is basically a happy month, as the 11th house is a beneficent house. It is also a good period for expanding your knowledge of high-tech, science, astronomy and astrology.

Children and children figures seem socially active this month. If they are of the appropriate age, there is romance. For you, love is spiritual and idealistic this month – until the 21st. Love and love opportunities occur in spiritual-type settings – at the yoga studio, the meditation class or lecture, the spiritual discourse or prayer meeting. And at charity events. The spouse, partner or current love seems hyper-sensitive this month (until the 21st). He or she seems easily hurt and is sensitive to voice tones and body language. In addition, he or she can't stand to see suffering – not in people and not in animals. Be more gentle with him or her. Things change after the 21st.

The financial intuition is very strong this month, especially from the 14th to the 16th. This is a good period for 'miracle money', money that comes in surprising ways. Prosperity will increase after the 21st as your money planet starts travelling with Jupiter – a classic signal of expanded earnings. Speculations are favourable, and there are nice paydays happening. After the 21st love blooms and there are happy romantic meetings for singles. Love will find you. There's nothing special that you need to do.

Health is excellent. And you can enhance it further in the ways mentioned in the yearly report.

March

Best Days Overall: 4, 5, 13, 14, 21, 22, 31
Most Stressful Days Overall: 1, 2, 8, 9, 10, 15, 16, 28, 29, 30
Best Days for Love: 4, 5, 8, 9, 10, 11, 12, 24, 25
Best Days for Money: 4, 5, 11, 12, 13, 14, 21, 22, 24, 25, 31
Best Days for Career: 11, 15, 16, 19, 28

An eventful and happy month ahead. You can feel the winds of long-term change happening. You probably don't know exactly what it is, but you can feel that things are going to be different from here on in.

On the 8th Saturn moves into your 12th house. On the 20th the Sun moves into your own sign and you begin a yearly personal pleasure peak. And on the 24th Pluto makes a major move into your 11th house. Personal independence is now at its maximum for the year. All the planets are moving forward. So by all means possible, make the changes that need to be made for your future happiness. There's no one you need to please but yourself. Of course, others should always be respected, but you're not a people pleaser now.

Your 12th house of spirituality has been powerful since February 18. And on the 8th it gets even stronger. This is definitely a spiritual kind of month. Those of you who work in the creative arts are especially inspired these days. Spiritual insights and breakthroughs come to you. There are supernatural kinds of experiences, and the dream life is more active.

The Sun's move into your sign on the 20th initiates a yearly personal pleasure period. Indeed, this one will be a lot stronger – more pleasurable – than those of the past twelve years or so. Your sign is filled with beneficent planets. There is travel, creativity, sensual delights, great self-esteem and self-confidence signalled. You're a happy camper. You have love and money on your own terms. Love and money seek you out. There will be windfalls and opportunities and there isn't much you need to do to get them. (The work will come later.) Women of childbearing age have been very fertile since the beginning of the year, and this month (from the 21st onwards), even more so. You're living the high life and the cosmos has a way of supporting this even if you don't have the money in your bank.

Mars has been 'out of bounds' since the beginning of the year, but this month he strays even further 'out of bounds' than before. So it is with you: you're really far outside your usual orbit. If you have a birthday this month, you're in a great period for staring new projects or launching new products, from the 20th onwards.

April

Best Days Overall: 1, 9, 10, 18, 27, 28, 29
Most Stressful Days Overall: 5, 6, 12, 13, 20, 25, 26
Best Days for Love: 3, 4, 5, 6, 14, 22, 23
Best Days for Money: 1, 3, 4, 10, 14, 19, 21, 22, 23, 28, 29
Best Days for Career: 7, 12, 13, 16, 25

This is basically a happy and prosperous month, and not even a solar eclipse in your sign on the 20th will do much to dampen things. It will just add some excitement and drama to the month.

You're still in a yearly personal pleasure peak until the 20th, so continue to enjoy the pleasures of the senses and get the body in the shape that you want. On the 20th, as the Sun moves into your money house, you begin a yearly financial peak. Earnings will be good and the focus will be on finance.

Mars, the ruler of your Horoscope, has been 'out of bounds' since the beginning of the year and is still 'out of bounds' this month. But now, from the 19th onwards, Venus also goes 'out of bounds'. So you're freewheeling and off the reservation personally, financially and in love. I'd say you're enjoying it. You're outside your normal orbit and so are your friends, love interests and the people involved in your finances.

The solar eclipse of the 20th will affect all of you to some degree but mostly those born very late in the sign – with birthdays from April 18–20. Those of you with these birthdays should reduce your schedule and take it nice and easy. Since this eclipse occurs on the cusp of your 1st and 2nd houses, it affects both houses. So, it brings a personal redefinition. You're changing your image and presentation to the world, and this will go on for a few months. Financial changes are also likely. I feel these financial dramas are preludes – stage setters – for the prosperity about to happen in your life in May. Every solar eclipse impacts children and children figures, because the eclipsed planet rules your 5th house of children. So they should be kept out of harm's way as much as possible during the eclipse period. And, since the eclipse impacts on Pluto, it brings financial dramas to the spouse, partner or current love too. He or she must make important changes. It can also signal encounters (normally psychological encounters) with death – near-death experiences, surgery, or dreams of death. Generally, it is not actual physical death.

May

Best Days Overall: 7, 8, 15, 16, 25, 26
Most Stressful Days Overall: 2, 3, 9, 10, 15, 16, 22, 23, 30, 31
Best Days for Love: 2, 3, 9, 10, 17, 18, 19, 30, 31
Best Days for Money: 2, 3, 8, 9, 10, 16, 17, 18, 19, 24, 25
Best Days for Career: 5, 9, 10, 13, 22

In spite of the lunar eclipse on the 5th this is still a happy and prosperous month. You're in the midst of a yearly financial peak and this peak will be stronger than you've had in many years. For Jupiter, the planet of wealth and abundance, also moves into your money house on the 17th. For many of you – depending on your age – this will be a lifetime financial peak. Prosperity will be strong for the rest of the year ahead.

The lunar eclipse of the 5th occurs in your 8th house of regeneration. So, just like last month, the spouse, partner or current love experiences financial dramas and needs to make important changes – course corrections in his or her finances are necessary. Again, like last month, there can be psychological encounters with death. This is not meant as punishment but, instead, as educational. You're supposed to think more deeply on this subject. It is meant to make you more serious about life. Life is fragile and can end at any time. You need to focus on the work you're supposed to accomplish for this incarnation.

Every lunar eclipse impacts the home and family, and this one is no different. There can be dramas at home and in the lives of family members. The dream life will be overactive but not reliable. Often repairs are needed in the home. Uranus, your planet of friends and technology, is sideswiped by this eclipse, affecting computers, high-tech equipment and gadgets. There can be dramas in the lives of friends. (Pluto is now in your 11th house of friends, adding to the drama.)

Mars, which has been 'out of bounds' all year, finally goes back in bounds on the 4th, and you return to your normal orbit. But Venus, which was 'out of bounds' last month, goes even further 'out of bounds' this month – way further than is usual. So in your finances you're in unexplored and unknown territory – perhaps you're bolder than usual. The same is true in love. Singles seek romance outside their usual circle, and the social life in general is outside your usual orbit.

June

Best Days Overall: 3, 4, 11, 12, 21, 22
Most Stressful Days Overall: 5, 6, 18, 19, 20, 26, 27
Best Days for Love: 2, 11, 21, 22, 26, 27
Best Days for Money: 2, 5, 6, 11, 14, 15, 21, 22, 23, 24
Best Days for Career: 1, 5, 6, 9, 18, 28

Retrograde activity among the planets will increase this month, but it's not a major increase. We begin the month with one planet retrograde and will end it with three planets moving backwards. You're still in a very prosperous period, though with the Sun now in your 3rd house the focus on finance is less than last month.

Venus, your money planet, is in your 4th house of home and family until the 5th. On the financial front this indicates spending on the home and family and earning from here as well. Family and family connections are important financially. On the 6th Venus moves into your 5th house and stays there for the rest of the month. This makes you more of a risk-taker than usual. You have speculative fever. Speculations are not limited to the casino or lottery. Often, we speculate on spending or investing. But it's a period for happy wealth – money that is earned in happy ways and spent on happy things. You're enjoying the wealth that you have. Jupiter in the money house signals that foreign investments, or foreigners in general, are playing an important role in finance. Beware of overspending on the 10th and 11th.

Venus is also your love planet, so her moves affect the love life too. Until the 5th you're entertaining more at home and with family members. Romantic opportunities are found close to home and come through family or family connections. After Venus moves into your 5th house on the 6th, love becomes about fun and games – another form of entertainment. Love is not very serious now. Venus remains in this house for the next four months. There are love affairs certainly, but marriage? Not likely.

Health needs watching from the 21st onwards. However, there's nothing serious afoot; this is just short-term stress caused by the movements of short-term planets. It passes. It would be good to rest when you feel tired, though.

Until the 20th the focus is on intellectual interests. It is a good period for students. The intellectual faculties are stronger than usual. Learning will go better if you make it fun. A video or movie on the subject you're studying will be better than just reading books about it.

Drive more carefully on the 4th and 5th.

July

Best Days Overall: 1, 2, 9, 10, 18, 19, 20, 28, 29
Most Stressful Days Overall: 3, 4, 16, 17, 23, 24, 30, 31
Best Days for Love: 2, 10, 19, 20, 23, 24, 29
Best Days for Money: 2, 3, 4, 10, 11, 12, 19, 20, 21, 22, 29, 30, 31
Best Days for Career: 3, 4, 7, 16, 26, 30, 31

Last month the planetary power was mostly in the bottom half of your chart, the night side, and this continues in the month ahead. This is a period for focusing on family rather than career. The two planets involved in your career – Saturn and Pluto – are both retrograde this month, so you may as well focus on the family.

Even more important than family is your emotional wellness. This is a great period for formal psychological therapies, for gaining insights into your feelings and emotional reactions. Even if you're not in any kind of formal therapy, the cosmos will fulfil this function for you – if you allow it. Old memories from the past will surface, and with greater frequency than usual. This happens so that you can re-interpret them from your present state of consciousness. This makes a big difference in your emotional life. It is a cosmic kind of healing. In general, you'll find yourself more nostalgic than usual. You'll be more interested in your personal history and in history in general. The past calls to you. Those of you on a spiritual path will have a greater interest in past incarnations and, perhaps, will recall some of them.

On the 22nd the Sun enters your 5th house and you begin a yearly personal pleasure peak (another one). This is a time to enjoy life and indulge in activities that bring happiness. Personal creativity will also be much stronger.

Health and energy will bounce back to normal levels after the 22nd.

Venus will make a rare retrograde on the 23rd. (This only happens every two years or so.) She will be travelling backwards until September 4. So, in love and finance, this is a time to take stock. A time to gain more facts and knowledge. Clarify your goals. Avoid making important decisions in love or finance until after September 4.

Retrograde activity increases again this month. After the 23rd 40 per cent of the planets are retrograde: a substantial percentage but still not at the maximum for the year. (The next two months will see the maximum levels.)

There are love and financial dramas on the 1st and 2nd. Drive more carefully on the 22nd and 23rd.

August

Best Days Overall: 5, 6, 14, 15, 16, 24, 25
Most Stressful Days Overall: 12, 13, 19, 20, 21, 26, 27
Best Days for Love: 5, 6, 14, 15, 19, 20, 21, 24, 25
Best Days for Money: 5, 6, 7, 8, 14, 15, 17, 18, 24, 25, 26, 27
Best Days for Career: 3, 12, 22, 26, 27, 30

Retrograde activity increases even further this month. From the 23rd to the 29th half the planets are retrograde, while on the 29th (and for the rest of the month) 60 per cent will be retrograde – the maximum for the year. So, Aries, patience is called for. And more patience. You won't be able to control or avoid all the delays that will be happening, but you can minimize their impact by being more of a perfectionist in all that you do. Handle the details of life perfectly.

You're still in the midst of a yearly personal pleasure peak, and, with all these retrogrades, not much is happening in the world right now so you may as well have fun. (The Sun, your planet of fun and friendship, never goes retrograde.)

Finances and romance are slower than usual. And no important decisions should be made about either. Of course, you shop for groceries and essentials, but big purchases are better off delayed. Mars will make a beautiful aspect to Jupiter on the 1st and this should bring a nice payday or financial opportunity.

Mars's good aspects to Uranus (on the 15th and 16th) bring harmony with friends and social invitations. You seem particularly good with computers and technology during this period.

Mars, the ruler of your Horoscope, will have his solstice from the 27th to September 2. He pauses in the heavens (in his latitudinal motion) and then changes direction. So, there is a personal pause in your affairs and then a change of direction next month.

There can be some love and financial dramas on the 8th and 9th. Be careful of overspending on the 21st and 22nd.

On the 23rd, the Sun enters your 6th house of health and work and you're ready to be more serious about life. This is a good transit for job-seekers – although job opportunities need close scrutiny during this period. This is a very good time to do those boring, detail-oriented tasks that you keep putting off. Health is good and you're focused here.

September

Best Days Overall: 2, 3, 11, 12, 21, 22, 29, 30
Most Stressful Days Overall: 8, 9, 10, 16, 17, 23, 24
Best Days for Love: 2, 3, 11, 12, 16, 17, 21, 22, 30
Best Days for Money: 2, 3, 4, 5, 11, 12, 14, 15, 21, 22, 23, 24, 30
Best Days for Career: 8, 18, 23, 24, 27

Venus finally starts to move forward on the 4th, bringing clarity to both the financial and love life. The Sun makes a nice aspect to Jupiter on the 7th and 8th, bringing increased earnings and financial opportunity – although there could be a delayed reaction here as Jupiter will be retrograde. Be careful of overspending on the 16th and 17th. There can be unexpected expenses on the 28th and 29th but you will be well able to handle them. The 28th and 29th can bring love dramas as well.

Until the 15th 60 per cent of the planets are in retrograde motion – the maximum extent for the year. After the 15th the figure drops to 50 per cent, which is still a substantial percentage. So, like last month, the keyword for you is patience. Patience, patience, patience.

Though the Western, social sector of your chart is far from dominant this year, right now – and especially from the 23rd onwards – it is the strongest it will be in 2023. So, although it's still a 'me first' period, you're cultivating more of the social graces. Others are more important than usual. Mars, the ruler of your Horoscope, will spend the month in your 7th house of love, while the Sun will enter this house on the 23rd. You're in a yearly love and social peak. You're reaching out to others. You're taking a more active role in the social life. And romantic opportunities will come.

With Mars in your 7th house you're less self-centred than usual, Aries. You try to go out of your way for others and you try to put them first – but trying does not always mean succeeding.

Health is good this month, though it is less good after the 23rd. There's nothing serious afoot; just short-term stress caused by the short-term planets.

Mercury, your health planet, is retrograde until the 15th, so this is not a good time for medical tests or procedures. The accuracy of these tests will be in doubt, and so if you can, avoid such things during this period. If you have to have medical tests and the results are not good, get a second opinion and perhaps even a second test.

The New Moon of the 15th occurs in your 6th house and will bring job opportunities for those of you who want them. More importantly, the New Moon will clarify health and job issues as the weeks progress – until the next New Moon.

October

Best Days Overall: 8, 9, 15, 16, 17, 26, 27
Most Stressful Days Overall: 6, 7, 13, 14, 20, 21
Best Days for Love: 9, 10, 11, 20, 21, 28, 29
Best Days for Money: 1, 2, 11, 12, 20, 21
Best Days for Career: 6, 15, 20, 21, 24

You're still in a yearly love and social peak, until the 23rd. This is perhaps the most active social month in your year. Your challenge is to balance your personal interests with those of others. You're trying, but it's not easy.

The main headline this month are the two eclipses that happen. There is a solar eclipse on the 14th and a lunar eclipse on the 28th.

The solar eclipse of the 14th has the stronger effect on you, so take it nice and easy. The cosmos will signal to you (it has its ways) when the eclipse is in effect (often a week before it actually happens and, with sensitive people, possibly even two weeks before). This is when you should start being more cautious. This eclipse happens in your 7th house of love and will test your current relationship. Good relation-ships tend to survive these things, but shaky ones – ones that are fundamentally flawed – can break apart. There are personal dramas in the lives of friends and with the current love. This is often the cause of the relationship crisis. Every solar eclipse affects children and children figures in your life, and this one is no different. They should be kept out of harm's way and avoid risky kinds of activities. Children figures can experience disruptions at school or college, changes to their educational plans and sometimes even a change of schools. They should drive more carefully, too.

The lunar eclipse of the 28th occurs in your 2nd money house and indicates a need for an important course correction in your finances. The events of the eclipse will show where your financial thinking and planning have been amiss and what changes need to take place. Every lunar eclipse brings dramas in the family, and especially with a parent or parent figure. Life-changing events tend to happen. The dream life can be hyperactive, but don't give it much weight. If you dream of terri-ble things, it would be good to discharge the energy though (through 'touch and let go' or some other kind of therapy) and to destroy the negative emotion surrounding them. Often repairs are needed in the home.

You're still in a prosperous period and the financial changes are likely to be good ones.

November

Best Days Overall: 4, 5, 6, 14, 15, 23, 24
Most Stressful Days Overall: 2, 3, 9, 10, 11, 16, 17, 29, 30
Best Days for Love: 8, 9, 10, 11, 18, 19, 27, 28
Best Days for Money: 7, 8, 9, 16, 18, 19, 25, 26, 27, 28
Best Days for Career: 2, 12, 16, 17, 29

The planetary power is now in the upper half of your Horoscope, the day side. So, it is time to focus on your outer life – your career and outer goals. At least 60 per cent (sometimes 70 per cent) of the planets are above the horizon now. So let go of family issues and serve the family by being successful.

Health is much better than last month. You have plenty of energy now and with energy the horizons are expanded. Formerly impossible things now become very possible. Mercury, your health planet, is 'out of bounds' from the 16th onwards. Thus, in health matters – and perhaps the job too – you're going outside your normal orbit. Perhaps you're exploring therapies that are outside the norm. Perhaps job responsibilities take you outside your comfort zone.

Venus moves into your 7th house on the 8th and stays there for the rest of the month. This is a good transit for love – it shows a love interest for singles – but again, balancing your personal desires with those of the beloved is the main challenge.

Since Venus is your financial planet, this transit also indicates that your social contacts are important in your finances. It is the kind of aspect of someone who socializes with the people he or she does business with and likes to do business with people he or she socializes with – with friends.

Venus has a solstice from the 9th to the 13th. She pauses in the heavens (in her latitudinal motion) and then changes direction. This is how it is in both love and finance – a pause and then a change of direction. This is a healthy pause. You can't change direction abruptly. A pause has to happen first.

Your 8th house of regeneration is powerful this month, especially until the 22nd. So this is a good month for projects involving personal transformation, for giving birth to the person that you want to be. This doesn't happen overnight, but you will make progress towards it.

December

Best Days Overall: 2, 3, 11, 12, 20, 21, 29, 30
Most Stressful Days Overall: 7, 8, 14, 15, 27, 28
Best Days for Love: 7, 8, 9, 18, 19, 28, 30
Best Days for Money: 4, 9, 14, 18, 19, 22, 23, 28, 30, 31
Best Days for Career: 9, 14, 15, 18, 26, 27

The day side of your Horoscope is even stronger than last month, and on the 22nd, as the Sun enters your 10th house of career, you begin a yearly career peak. It should be very successful. There's a lot of power behind you: 70 per cent (and sometimes 80 per cent) of the planets are above the horizon now. So continue to focus on your career and your mission for this life. Let family matters go for a while. (The Full Moon of the 27th will temporarily pull you to the home and family – but the focus should be on the career.)

Health is basically good this month, but after the 22nd it will need more attention. Again, there's nothing major afoot – just short-term stress caused by short-term planets. Overall, your energy is not as high as usual and if you let yourself get overtired you can become vulnerable to problems.

Mercury, your health planet, is still 'out of bounds' until the 14th. So, review our discussion of this last month.

This month Mars goes 'out of bounds' from the 22nd onwards. This happened early in the year as well, and, once again, on a personal level, you're outside your normal orbit. Personal desires take you outside. You're seen by others in this way too.

Venus will be in your 8th house from the 5th to the 30th, signalling an erotic kind of period. For singles, this shows that sexual magnetism is the most important attraction. In finance this is a good period to winnow the finances and the possessions. Expand by cutting back. Get rid of things that you don't need or use. Clear the decks. Sell things you don't need or give them to charity. Reduce redundant bank accounts. See where money is being wasted and remove the waste. Venus in the 8th house is a good period for tax and insurance planning, and for those of you of the appropriate age it is good for estate planning.

Taurus

THE BULL

Birthdays from
21st April to
20th May

Personality Profile

TAURUS AT A GLANCE

Element – Earth

Ruling Planet – Venus
   Career Planet – Uranus
   Love Planet – Pluto
   Money Planet – Mercury
   Planet of Health and Work – Venus
   Planet of Home and Family Life – Sun
   Planet of Spirituality – Mars
   Planet of Travel, Education, Religion and Philosophy – Saturn

Colours – earth tones, green, orange, yellow

Colours that promote love, romance and social harmony – red-violet, violet

Colours that promote earning power – yellow, yellow-orange

Gems – coral, emerald

Metal – copper

Scents – bitter almond, rose, vanilla, violet

Quality – fixed (= stability)

Quality most needed for balance – flexibility

Strongest virtues – endurance, loyalty, patience, stability,
   a harmonious disposition

Deepest needs – comfort, material ease, wealth

Characteristics to avoid – rigidity, stubbornness, tendency to be overly
   possessive and materialistic

Signs of greatest overall compatibility – Virgo, Capricorn

Signs of greatest overall incompatibility – Leo, Scorpio, Aquarius

Sign most helpful to career – Aquarius

Sign most helpful for emotional support – Leo

Sign most helpful financially – Gemini

Sign best for marriage and/or partnerships – Scorpio

Sign most helpful for creative projects – Virgo

Best Sign to have fun with – Virgo

Signs most helpful in spiritual matters – Aries, Capricorn

Best day of the week – Friday

Understanding a Taurus

Taurus is the most earthy of all the Earth signs. If you understand that Earth is more than just a physical element, that it is a psychological attitude as well, you will get a better understanding of the Taurus personality.

A Taurus has all the power of action that an Aries has. But Taurus is not satisfied with action for its own sake. Their actions must be productive, practical and wealth-producing. If Taurus cannot see a practical value in an action they will not bother taking it.

Taurus's forte lies in their power to make real their own or other people's ideas. They are generally not very inventive but they can take another's invention and perfect it, making it more practical and useful. The same is true for all projects. Taurus is not especially keen on starting new projects, but once they get involved they bring things to completion. Taurus carries everything through. They are finishers and will go the distance, so long as no unavoidable calamity intervenes.

Many people find Taurus too stubborn, conservative, fixed and immovable. This is understandable, because Taurus dislikes change – in the environment or in their routine. They even dislike changing their minds! On the other hand, this is their virtue. It is not good for a wheel's axle to waver. The axle must be fixed, stable and unmovable. Taurus is the axle of society and the heavens. Without their stability and so-called stubbornness, the wheels of the world (and especially the wheels of commerce) would not turn.

Taurus loves routine. A routine, if it is good, has many virtues. It is a fixed – and, ideally, perfect – way of taking care of things. Mistakes can happen when spontaneity comes into the equation, and mistakes cause discomfort and uneasiness – something almost unacceptable to a Taurus. Meddling with Taurus's comfort and security is a sure way to irritate and anger them.

While an Aries loves speed, a Taurus likes things slow. They are slow thinkers – but do not make the mistake of assuming they lack intelligence. On the contrary, Taurus people are very intelligent. It is just that they like to chew on ideas, to deliberate and weigh them up.

Only after due deliberation is an idea accepted or a decision taken. Taurus is slow to anger – but once aroused, take care!

Finance

Taurus is very money-conscious. Wealth is more important to them than to many other signs. Wealth to a Taurus means comfort and security. Wealth means stability. Where some zodiac signs feel that they are spiritually rich if they have ideas, talents or skills, Taurus only feels wealth when they can see and touch it. Taurus's way of thinking is, 'What good is a talent if it has not been translated into a home, furniture, car and holidays?'

These are all reasons why Taurus excels in estate agency and agricultural industries. Usually a Taurus will end up owning land. They love to feel their connection to the Earth. Material wealth began with agriculture, the tilling of the soil. Owning a piece of land was humanity's earliest form of wealth: Taurus still feels that primeval connection.

It is in the pursuit of wealth that Taurus develops intellectual and communication ability. Also, in this pursuit Taurus is forced to develop some flexibility. It is in the quest for wealth that they learn the practical value of the intellect and come to admire it. If it were not for the search for wealth and material things, Taurus people might not try to reach a higher intellect.

Some Taurus people are 'born lucky' – the type who win any gamble or speculation. This luck is due to other factors in their horoscope; it is not part of their essential nature. By nature they are not gamblers. They are hard workers and like to earn what they get. Taurus's innate conservatism makes them abhor unnecessary risks in finance and in other areas of their lives.

Career and Public Image

Being essentially down-to-earth people, simple and uncomplicated, Taurus tends to look up to those who are original, unconventional and inventive. Taurus people like their bosses to be creative and original – since they themselves are content to perfect their superiors' brainwaves. They admire people who have a wider social or political consciousness and they feel that someday (when they have all the comfort and security they need) they too would like to be involved in these big issues.

In business affairs Taurus can be very shrewd – and that makes them valuable to their employers. They are never lazy; they enjoy working and getting good results. Taurus does not like taking unnecessary risks and they do well in positions of authority, which makes them good managers and supervisors. Their managerial skills are reinforced by their natural talents for organization and handling details, their patience and thoroughness. As mentioned, through their connection with the earth, Taurus people also do well in farming and agriculture.

In general a Taurus will choose money and earning power over public esteem and prestige. A position that pays more – though it has less prestige – is preferred to a position with a lot of prestige but lower earnings. Many other signs do not feel this way, but a Taurus does, especially if there is nothing in his or her personal birth chart that modifies this. Taurus will pursue glory and prestige only if it can be shown that these things have a direct and immediate impact on their wallet.

Love and Relationships

In love, the Taurus-born likes to have and to hold. They are the marrying kind. They like commitment and they like the terms of a relationship to be clearly defined. More importantly, Taurus likes to be faithful to one lover, and they expect that lover to reciprocate this fidelity. When this doesn't happen, their whole world comes crashing down. When they are in love Taurus people are loyal, but they are also very possessive. They are capable of great fits of jealousy if they are hurt in love.

Taurus is satisfied with the simple things in a relationship. If you are involved romantically with a Taurus there is no need for lavish entertainments and constant courtship. Give them enough love, food and comfortable shelter and they will be quite content to stay home and enjoy your company. They will be loyal to you for life. Make a Taurus feel comfortable and – above all – secure in the relationship, and you will rarely have a problem.

In love, Taurus can sometimes make the mistake of trying to control their partners, which can cause great pain on both sides. The reasoning behind their actions is basically simple: Taurus people feel a sense of ownership over their partners and will want to make changes that will increase their own general comfort and security. This attitude is OK when it comes to inanimate, material things – but is dangerous when applied to people. Taurus needs to be careful and attentive to this possible trait within themselves.

Home and Domestic Life

Home and family are vitally important to Taurus. They like children. They also like a comfortable and perhaps glamorous home – something they can show off. They tend to buy heavy, ponderous furniture – usually of the best quality. This is because Taurus likes a feeling of substance in their environment. Their house is not only their home but their place of creativity and entertainment. The Taurus' home tends to be truly their castle. If they could choose, Taurus people would prefer living in the countryside to being city-dwellers. If they cannot do so during their working lives, many Taurus individuals like to holiday in or even retire to the country, away from the city and closer to the land.

At home a Taurus is like a country squire – lord (or lady) of the manor. They love to entertain lavishly, to make others feel secure in their home and to encourage others to derive the same sense of satisfaction as they do from it. If you are invited for dinner at the home of a Taurus you can expect the best food and best entertainment. Be prepared for a tour of the house and expect to see your Taurus friend exhibit a lot of pride and satisfaction in his or her possessions.

Taurus people like children but they are usually strict with them. The reason for this is they tend to treat their children – as they do most things in life – as their possessions. The positive side to this is that their children will be well cared for and well supervised. They will get every material thing they need to grow up properly. On the down side, Taurus can get too repressive with their children. If a child dares to upset the daily routine – which Taurus loves to follow – he or she will have a problem with a Taurus parent.

Horoscope for 2023

Major Trends

You've had a few years of strong career success, Taurus, and while career is good this year too, there is less focus here. You're not working as hard on it. Your previous efforts bear fruit. Saturn leaves your 10th house of career on March 8, while Pluto makes a short visit to your 10th house from March 24 to June 12. Your personal likeability and social grace become important career-wise. More on this later.

Pluto, your love planet, moving into your 10th house is also good for the love life. Pluto will be at or near the top of your chart for many years to come. This shows a focus on love and this focus tends to success. More details later.

With Jupiter moving through your 12th house of spirituality until May 17, you're in a very strong spiritual period. Important breakthroughs will happen. You will definitely know that wonderful spiritual beings care about you and guide you. More on this later.

On May 17 Jupiter enters your own sign and stays there for the rest of the year ahead. This is a very happy transit. It brings the good life – personal and physical delights. Many of you will travel more. You will live on a higher standard than usual (and the cosmos has its ways of supplying for this). There will be increased libido and more sex appeal to the image.

Uranus, your career planet, has been in your sign for many years now. This has brought career success but also many personal and sudden changes. Disruption of your routine is not your favourite kind of event. Yet it is happening and the spiritual message – as it has been for many years – is to learn to embrace change and make it your friend. All Taurus-born people are feeling this, but those of you who were born in the latter half of Taurus – from May 6-21 – will feel it most strongly.

Saturn's move into your 11th house of friends early in March indicates a winnowing of your friendships. You want quality rather than quantity. You'll probably socialize less, but there will be a higher quality to it.

Your most important interests this year are religion, philosophy, higher education and foreign travel (from January 1 to March 24 and from June 12 to the end of the year); career; friends, groups, group activities and the online world; spirituality (from January 1 to May 17); and the body, image and personal appearance (from May 17 onwards).

Your paths of greatest fulfilment are spirituality (from January 1 to May 17 and from July 19 onwards); and the body, image and personal appearance (all year).

Health

(Please note that this is an astrological perspective on health and not a medical one. In days of yore there was no difference, both these perspectives were identical. But these days there could be quite a difference. For a medical perspective, please consult your doctor or health practitioner.)

Now that Saturn is moving away from his stressful aspect to you on March 8, health will be much improved. Pluto will make a stressful aspect from March 24 to June 12, but only those of you born early in the sign (April 20–22) are likely to feel it. For most of you, health will be good this year. Of course, there will be periods in the year where your health and energy are less easy than usual, but these are short-term trends and not trends for the year. When these short-term stresses pass, your normally good health and energy will return.

Good though your health is, you can make it better. Give more attention to the following – the vulnerable areas of your Horoscope this year (the reflex points are shown in the chart opposite):

- The neck and throat. These are always important for Taurus as your sign rules these areas, so regular neck massage is always good for you. Tension tends to collect there and needs to be released. Craniosacral therapy and chiropractic massage are also good for the neck.
- The kidneys and hips. Regular hip massage is not only good for both the kidneys and hips but will strengthen the lower back as well.

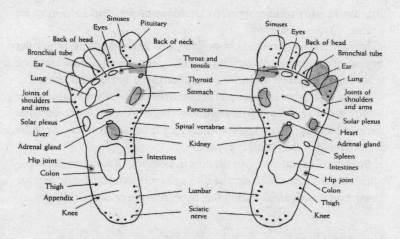

Important foot reflexology points for the year ahead

Try to massage all of the foot on a regular basis – the top of the foot as well as the bottom – but pay extra attention to the points highlighted on the chart. When you massage, be aware of 'sore spots' as these need special attention. It's also a good idea to massage the ankles and below them.

- The heart becomes important for you from June 5 to October 9. The important thing with the heart is to avoid worry and anxiety, as these emotions tend to stress it out. Replace worry with faith. Meditation is a big help here. Chest massage is also good for the heart.
- The stomach and breasts. These too only become important from June 5 to October 9, and the reflex points are shown above. Diet is important over this period.

Venus is your health planet (as well as ruling your Horoscope), so there is a vanity component to good health. The state of your health instantly reflects on your personal appearance. So good health will do more for your looks than hosts of lotions and potions. This tendency can also be used in healing. If you feel under the weather, buy a new outfit or accessory, or have your hair done – do things that improve your appearance. You'll feel better.

With Jupiter moving through your own sign, women of childbearing age will be more fertile this year. In addition, because Jupiter rules your

8th house, this transit signals that some of you will be opting for cosmetic types of surgery.

Jupiter in your sign tends to weight gain. But as he is also the ruler of your 8th house, that would tend to slimness. I read this as someone who binges and then diets, binges and diets – it goes on and on.

Venus is a fast-moving planet that moves through your entire chart in any given year. So, there are many short-term health trends that depend on where she is and the kind of aspects she receives. These are best covered in the monthly reports.

Venus will spend over four months in Leo, your 4th house, this year, which means that the heart, the diet and emotional harmony become important health areas during this time, from June 5 to October 9.

Home and Family

Your 4th house of home and family is not prominent this year – it is not a house of power. Thus, as our regular readers know, this tends to the status quo. It shows a basic contentment with things as they are, with no need to make dramatic changes.

Since the Sun is your family planet, the two solar eclipses this year – one on April 20 and the other on October 14 – indicate short-term disruptions at home. Perhaps repairs are needed in the home. Perhaps there are dramas – personal dramas – in the lives of family members. But a move is not likely this year.

Pluto will move into your 10th house briefly this year, from March 24 to June 12. This indicates some drama happening with a parent or parent figure – perhaps surgery or a near-death kind of experience.

As mentioned above, Venus will spend an unusual amount of time (four times longer, in fact) in your 4th house this year, from June 5 to October 9. This signals more personal involvement with the family and the home. Perhaps you'll be spending more time at home. Perhaps you'll be beautifying the home, redecorating and the like. This transit also indicates someone who works from home and someone who is making the home a healthier kind of place. Often people buy health or exercise equipment for the home. Sometimes they do things – such as asbestos, lead or mould removal – that has the effect of making the home healthier. This period will be exceptionally good too for your personal emotional healing. Those of you involved in formal therapies will make very good progress, because you focus on them.

If you're planning major house renovations, May 21 to July 11 looks a good period, while more cosmetic beautification of the home is good from June 5 to October 9. This is also a good time in which to buy art objects for the home.

A parent or parent figure is likely to move or renovate the house this year. Sometimes they acquire an additional home or gain access to an additional home. It looks happy. Siblings and sibling figures are having a status quo home and family year. Children and children figures in your life, however, are facing social tests. If they are married, the marriage is being tested. A move could happen later in the year – after May 17. Grandchildren – or those who play that role in your life – are likely to move, and it looks happy. (This move could have happened last year too.)

Finance and Career

The year ahead looks very prosperous, Taurus – and next year as well. Jupiter enters your own sign on May 17 and stays there for the rest of the year, bringing the good life – personal and sensual pleasures. One lives a higher lifestyle than usual. This is regardless of whether you have the actual money to cover this. The cosmos tends to provide for these things.

Jupiter is the financial planet of the spouse, partner or current love – whoever plays this role in your life. Thus, he or she is prospering and seems very generous with you. If you have good business ideas, this is a great period for attracting outside investors to your projects. It is a good time for paying down debt or obtaining finance – depending on your need. You have good access to outside capital.

Mercury is your financial planet. Aside from the Moon he is the fastest moving of all the planets, moving through your entire Horoscope in any given year. So, there are many short-term trends in finance that depend on where Mercury is and the kinds of aspects he receives. These are best dealt with in the monthly reports.

Saturn was in your 10th career house all last year. So, there was success, but it came through hard work – through merit. Perhaps bosses were more demanding than usual (though they felt they did it out of love). But this eases up in the year ahead. Your hard work over the past two years is starting to pay off. The year ahead seems a successful career year – and next year brings even more success.

Uranus, your career planet, has been in your sign for many years now, which means that you have had the image of a successful person. People see you this way – you dress the part. Now, Uranus is being joined in your sign by Jupiter, which will expand and enlarge your success. Jupiter and your career planet are travelling together in your sign. The aspect is not exact this year, but you're feeling the influence. There can be promotions and professional elevation. Your status, both professionally and socially, is increased. You have the devotion of bosses, parents and parent figures – the power people in your life. Career opportunities come to you – they seek you out – and there's not much you need to do.

Pluto's brief foray into your 10th house this year signals that it is beneficial to promote the career in social ways: by attending the right parties and gatherings and perhaps by hosting them. As we mentioned, your likeability is perhaps just as important as your actual professional skills.

Love and Social Life

Important changes are happening in the love life. This year you're feeling only the beginnings of it, but in the coming years you'll experience it much more strongly. Your love planet, Pluto, is changing signs. This year it is a brief flirtation; next year his visit will be longer; and in 2025 there will be a complete change as Pluto establishes himself in Aquarius.

For the past two decades or so, Pluto was in the sign of Capricorn. Thus, you were conservative and cautious in love. It took longer to fall in love. You needed to test your feelings constantly to see if they were real. Caution in love is a good thing. But, in some cases, it was fear – not a good thing.

Your love planet in Aquarius shows a more experimental attitude to love. You're ready to try new things, explore new people and new kinds of relationships. You're starting to throw out all the rule books about love and relationships – all the 'how to's – and learn what works for you. This transition doesn't happen overnight; it is more a process that happens over time.

Pluto's brief stay in your 10th house this year shows that love is high on your agenda and tends to success. Love is more freewheeling – less constricted – than it has been for many years. Pluto in Aquarius also shows an attraction to power and prestige. These are romantic allurements. You're attracted to people who can help you career-wise and perhaps to people who are involved in your career.

In the coming years, more of your socializing will be career related. In the meantime, romantic opportunities still happen at college or religious functions. Philosophical compatibility is still very important. Later career compatibility and worldly aspirations will become ever more important. There needs to be harmony here.

From March 24 to June 10, focus on the career and love opportunities will find you.

Self-improvement

The year ahead is very spiritual. For a start, Jupiter is moving through your 12th house of spirituality until May 17. In addition, on July 19, the north node of the Moon will enter your 12th house, which indicates great fulfilment in these activities.

Those of you not on a spiritual path should get on one. Those already on a path will make very good progress. There will be much spiritual growth. You will experience all the phenomena of spiritual growth. There will be synchronistic experiences – meaningful coincidences. Your latent ESP abilities will increase. You will become more idealistic and generous. There will be more charitable giving and more involvement with altruistic kinds of projects. The dream life will become more active and revelatory. The invisible world will make itself known to you – it will let you know that it is around, active and available to you. You have resources you do not know you have.

Jupiter moving through the 12th house favours the mystical paths of your native religion. Every religion has its mystical side, though few explore them. Underneath all the rules and regulations, the 'do's and don't's, is the mystical revelation and experience of the founders.

With Jupiter in the 12th house, spirituality is not about discarding religion but about going deeper into it. Penetrating it.

Jupiter is the ruler of your 8th house of regeneration. And so spirit is going to teach you about death – the true meaning of it. You will get the spiritual perspective on it. However, Jupiter's transit also shows other things. Spiritual progress is made by eliminating the obstructions to it – by purging the mind and emotions of the patterns that obstruct the flow of the Divine Power. It is about purging the doubts, the fears, the beliefs that inhibit your spiritual growth. It has been said that when one eliminates fear, worry, hate and anger, only the Divine is left in the consciousness.

Mars is your spiritual planet. He is relatively fast moving, and in any given year he will move though seven signs and houses of your chart. Thus, there are many short-term trends in the spiritual life that depend on where Mars is and the kinds of aspects he receives.

With Mars as your spiritual planet, you like to act on your spiritual ideals and knowledge. It is not enough for you that they be abstract. You tend to activism – and in some cases to militancy. Activism is good. We should put our beliefs into practice. Militancy often comes from a desire to force issues, however, and often defeats the purpose.

Month-by-month Forecasts

January

Best Days Overall: 1, 2, 10, 11, 18, 19, 28, 29
Most Stressful Days Overall: 6, 7, 12, 13, 25, 26
Best Days for Love: 2, 3, 6, 7, 11, 12, 13, 19, 20, 21, 22, 29
Best Days for Money: 1, 2, 8, 10, 11, 16, 18, 19, 21, 22, 23, 28, 29
Best Days for Career: 1, 2, 10, 11, 12, 13, 18, 19, 28, 29

Health is good as the year begins, but after the 20th it will need more attention. The important thing is to get enough rest. If you're overtired, you become vulnerable to all sorts of problems. Enhance the health with back and spine massage until the 3rd and with calf and ankle massage after then. Experimental kinds of therapies seem powerful

from the 3rd to the 27th. After the 27th foot massage will be beneficial. You will also respond well to spiritual-type therapies after the
27th.

Jupiter, a slow-moving planet, has his solstice almost the entire
month – from the 1st to the 27th. He pauses in his latitudinal motion
– almost like a stasis – and then changes direction. There is a long,
long pause and then a change of direction. This would impact the
finances of the spouse, partner or current love. It can also impact on
outside investors, if you're involved with business. A solstice this long
can be scary, but it will work out all right in the end.

The month ahead is a strong career period. Venus, the ruler of your
Horoscope, will be in your 10th house from the 3rd to the 27th. This
indicates personal success. Personal elevation. You're recognized not
just for your professional achievements but for who you are. Personal
appearance and overall demeanour seem big factors in your career
success. On the 20th the Sun, your family planet, enters your 10th
house, and you begin a yearly career peak. Family supports the career.
There is no conflict between family and career during this period. Your
success is a family project.

Finances are more complicated this month, as your financial planet,
Mercury, travels backwards until the 17th. So go slow here. Get the
facts. Avoid making overt moves (unless you have no choice). Mars in
your money house is also retrograde until the 12th, reinforcing what
we say.

Mars in the money house can make you more speculative and risk
taking than usual, but this should be avoided until after the 17th. Since
Mars is your spiritual planet, the financial intuition will be good, but
until the 12th it will need careful verification.

February

Best Days Overall: 7, 8, 16, 17, 24, 25
Most Stressful Days Overall: 4, 5, 6, 12, 13, 18, 19
Best Days for Love: 2, 3, 8, 12, 13, 17, 22, 25
Best Days for Money: 1, 4, 5, 8, 11, 14, 15, 18, 19, 22, 23, 27, 28
Best Days for Career: 7, 8, 16, 17, 18, 19, 24, 25

Health still needs watching until the 18th, but after that you should see a dramatic improvement in both your health and overall energy. Enhance the health with foot massage until the 21st and with scalp, face and head massage after that date. These kinds of massage not only strengthen those particular areas but the entire body as well. Spiritual-healing techniques are potent all month.

Finances are much improved over last month. Your financial planet is now moving forward, so there is forward motion in finance. There is more clarity. On the 10th and 11th Mercury travels with Pluto, your love planet, so social contacts or the beloved seem helpful financially. On the 11th Mercury moves into Aquarius, his most 'exalted' position. Here your financial planet is at his most powerful. Thus, earnings should increase. Your financial judgement will be sharp.

Mercury will spend the rest of the month here in your career house. This signals various things. Finance is your highest priority – almost your mission – this month. Your good career reputation increases earnings and brings opportunities for earnings. There can be pay rises – official or unofficial. Bosses, parents and parent figures – the authority figures in your life – seem favourably disposed to your financial goals. Mercury makes nice aspects to Mars from the 21st to the 23rd, which brings good financial intuition. There can be some financial drama on the 20th and 21st as well. Some change needs to be made.

Venus has her solstice from the 21st to the 24th. This brings a pause in your life, in your personal desires and perhaps in your work. Then there is a change of direction.

Mars, your spiritual planet, has been 'out of bounds' since the beginning of the year. This month he moves even further 'out of bounds'. Thus, in your spiritual life, and perhaps your charitable activities, you're operating way outside your normal orbit.

On the 18th the Sun moves into your 11th house and you begin a strong social period. This does not necessarily mean romance – it's more about friendships and being involved with groups. Platonic types of relationships.

March

Best Days Overall: 6, 7, 15, 16, 24, 25
Most Stressful Days Overall: 4, 5, 11, 12, 17, 18, 31
Best Days for Love: 4, 5, 7, 11, 12, 16, 24, 25, 26
Best Days for Money: 4, 5, 11, 12, 13, 14, 21, 22, 26, 27, 31
Best Days for Career: 6, 7, 15, 16, 17, 18, 24, 25

Get ready for a lot of change this month. Pluto makes a brief foray into Aquarius on March 24, a transit that will begin (over the years) to completely transform your career and your life work. This foray is merely an announcement of things to come. Saturn leaves your 10th house of career on the 8th and will spend the next two and a half years in your 11th house. Bosses should be less demanding now. You've passed your tests.

The past year you have had to earn your success through sheer merit, and by going the extra mile (in some cases an extra two miles). Now, you advance the career by social means. Your personal likeability is perhaps as important as your actual professional skills.

Pluto is your love planet, and his move into Aquarius shows changes in your love life. You become more experimental and less conservative. You find yourself attracted to people of power and prestige. Focus on the career and love will find you.

Your 11th house of friends is strong this month, indicating that it is a social month (although it's more about friendships than romance). On the 20th the Sun enters your 12th house and you begin a very strong spiritual period. This is stronger than usual, as the Sun joins Jupiter in this house. Much spiritual progress – insights, illuminations, peak experiences – happens now.

Finances will be good. Mercury, your money planet, spends the month in spiritual Pisces, from the 3rd to the 19th, and then spends the balance of the month in your 12th house. In addition, Mars, your spiritual planet, will be in your money house until the 25th. So, all roads lead to spirit – especially on the financial level. The financial intuition is sharp. There is financial guidance in dreams and hunches, through psychics, tarot readers, astrologers, ministers and other spiritual channels. Often intuition operates through a chance remark from a stranger or a chance headline in the paper. It hits you and you know this is a message. Your intuition is especially good on the 17th and 18th. The 27th and 28th are strong financial days.

Health is much improved this month, Taurus. Venus travels with Jupiter on the 1st and 2nd and if there have been problems there is good news. A happy career opportunity happens on the 30th and 31st.

April

Best Days Overall: 2, 3, 4, 12, 13, 30
Most Stressful Days Overall: 1, 7, 8, 14, 15, 20, 27, 28, 29
Best Days for Love: 3, 4, 5, 7, 8, 13, 14, 21, 22, 23
Best Days for Money: 1, 10, 12, 13, 19, 21, 22, 23, 24, 28, 29, 30
Best Days for Career: 3, 4, 12, 13, 14, 15, 21, 30

Though there is a solar eclipse right on the cusp of your sign this month, the month ahead still seems happy. The eclipse will only impact strongly on some of you – those born early in Taurus, April 20–22. If you fall into this category, take it nice and easy during the eclipse period. The eclipse happens on the 20th, but the effects can be felt up to a week beforehand and for a few days later. Sensitive people can feel an eclipse up to two weeks before it actually happens.

This solar eclipse occurs right on the border of your 12th and 1st houses, thus affecting both. So, there are spiritual changes happening. There are disruptions in a religious or charitable organization that you're involved with. Guru figures in your life experience personal dramas. The impact on your own 1st house indicates a need to redefine yourself, to redefine how you think of yourself and the kind of image you want to present to others. Over the next few months, you will be changing your wardrobe, hairstyle, your whole presentation to the world. An inner redefinition always leads to outer changes.

Pluto, your love planet, is also impacted – very directly – by the eclipse, leading to dramas in love. A current marriage or relationship gets tested. Sometimes it is the relationship itself that is tested; long-suppressed grievances – dirty laundry – surface and need to be dealt with. But sometimes the relationship gets tested because of some personal drama in the life of the beloved: it's not necessarily the fault of the relationship. Good relationships will weather the storm. But flawed ones are vulnerable.

Since the Sun is your family planet, every solar eclipse impacts on the home and family – especially a parent or parent figure. There are personal dramas in their lives. Often repairs are needed in the home. The eclipse will reveal hidden flaws and thus give you a chance to correct them.

Health is basically good this month. From the 20th onwards you're in a yearly personal pleasure peak. Finances are more complicated after the 21st, as Mercury starts to move backwards again. However, you experience this three, sometimes four times a year and by now you know how to deal with it.

May

Best Days Overall: 1, 9, 10, 17, 18, 19, 27, 28
Most Stressful Days Overall: 5, 6, 11, 12, 25, 26
Best Days for Love: 1, 2, 3, 6, 9, 10, 11, 17, 18, 19, 20, 29
Best Days for Money: 1, 8, 9, 10, 16, 17, 18, 19, 20, 21, 24, 25, 27, 28
Best Days for Career: 1, 9, 10, 11, 12, 17, 18, 19, 27, 28

This is another happy month, Taurus, in spite of a lunar eclipse on the 5th. The good things far outweigh the challenges.

You remain in a yearly personal pleasure period until the 21st. On the 17th benevolent Jupiter moves into your own sign and stays there for the rest of the year. So, there is optimism, the good life, sensual pleasure and more travel. On the 21st the Sun will enter your 2nd money house and you begin a yearly financial peak. Earnings improve even before the 21st as Mercury starts to move forward on the 15th. Mercury in your own sign signals windfalls and financial opportunities. Money seeks you rather than vice versa.

The lunar eclipse of the 5th occurs in your 7th house and again tests your current relationship. There are many issues to be resolved here. Friendships can also get tested and there can be dramas in the lives of friends. Since the Moon rules your 3rd house, this eclipse impacts strongly on siblings, sibling figures and neighbours. They have personal dramas, and there can be upheavals and disturbances in your neighbourhood. Students – especially those below college level – can experience disruptions at school, changes in educational plans and sometimes even a change of school. Cars and communication equipment can behave erratically (often repairs or replacements are necessary).

This eclipse grazes Uranus, your career planet. Happily, it is not a direct hit but there can be dramas in the career and in the lives of bosses, parents, parent figures and in your industry. The rules of the game can be changed.

Venus, the ruler of your Horoscope, went 'out of bounds' on April 19. This month she goes even further 'out of bounds', meaning that you're a long way from your normal orbit and comfort zone. This is true personally, at the job and in health matters.

The New Moon of the 19th is a happy day, the highlight of any month. It occurs in your sign, bringing extra energy, enhanced personal appearance and libido.

June

Best Days Overall: 5, 6, 14, 15, 23, 24, 25
Most Stressful Days Overall: 1, 2, 7, 8, 16, 21, 22, 28, 29
Best Days for Love: 1, 2, 6, 7, 11, 15, 21, 22, 25, 28, 29
Best Days for Money: 5, 6, 14, 15, 16, 17, 23, 24, 26, 27
Best Days for Career: 6, 7, 8, 4, 25

Personal pleasure and finance are the main headlines of the month. A happy month. You've experienced many personal changes – dramatic ones – over the past few years, but now, with Jupiter in your sign, the changes are happy ones. There is personal pleasure, good foods, good wines, travel and the pleasures of the five senses. Weight needs keeping an eye on though: this is the price we pay for the good life. Some of you might be contemplating some cosmetic surgery. The focus is on improving the appearance.

You've been in a yearly financial peak since May 21 and this continues until the 21st. There is good family support. Family and family connections are very helpful in finance, and you shine in the financial world. You're a financial star this month. On the 11th, Mercury moves into your money house – his own sign and house. This also bodes well for earnings as he is very strong in his own sign and house. The New Moon of the 18th also occurs in your money house and boosts the income. More importantly, the New Moon will clarify the financial life as the weeks progress (until the next New Moon). Thus, all the information that you need to make good financial decisions will come to you – and very naturally and normally. Your questions will be answered.

On the 21st the Sun enters your 3rd house of knowledge and communication. Your financial goals – the short-term ones at least – have been achieved and now your interest shifts to intellectual interests. You will read more, attend classes or seminars, and expand your knowledge. This transit is especially good for students as the mental faculties are very sharp and learning is much easier. Sales and marketing people should also do well as their skills are enhanced.

Health is good. The only long-term planet that was stressing you (and not all of you, only those born early in Taurus) moves away from his stressful aspect on the 12th. Your health planet Venus will be in Leo from the 5th onwards. Enhance the health further by giving more attention to the heart. Good emotional health is important after the 5th, and for many more months.

Your love planet Pluto went retrograde on May 1 and will remain so for many more months. This doesn't stop love from happening but does tend to slow things down. Your normal social confidence is not up to its usual standards, so caution in love is still advisable.

July

Best Days Overall: 3, 4, 11, 12, 21, 22, 30, 31
Most Stressful Days Overall: 5, 6, 18, 19, 20, 26, 27
Best Days for Love: 2, 4, 10, 12, 19, 20, 22, 26, 27, 29, 31
Best Days for Money: 3, 4, 8, 11, 12, 13, 14, 15, 18, 19, 21, 22, 30, 31
Best Days for Career: 4, 5, 6, 11, 12, 22, 31

Planetary retrograde activity increases this month, rising from 30 per cent at the beginning of July to 40 per cent after the 23rd. More importantly, the ruler of your Horoscope moves into retrograde motion from the 23rd onwards – so you're personally affected. (Keep in mind we're still not at the maximum level of retrograde activity for the year.)

With Venus retrograde, personal goals need more study. There is a feeling of being 'directionless'. The good news is that finances don't seem affected. Mercury moves speedily in the heavens. There is fast financial progress and good confidence. Until the 11th Mercury is in your 3rd house, so you spend on education, reading materials, etc. But you also earn from this. Buying, selling, trading, retailing, advertising and PR bring profits. From the 11th to the 29th Mercury is in Leo, your 4th house. You spend on the home and family but earn from there as well. You're probably more speculative and take more risks in this period. Family and family connections are important financially. Mercury enters your 5th house on the 29th. Thus, you still speculate, but are more careful about it. You spend on children and the children figures in your life, but they can also boost your income – depending on their age.

Health needs more attention after the 23rd. The important thing is to maintain high energy levels. If you're tired, rest. Health is enhanced in the ways mentioned in the yearly report, but also with good emotional health. Avoid depression and negative mindsets like the plague.

The good news is that you're in a good period for emotional health. Your 4th house is powerful all month but especially after the 23rd. Those of you in therapy will make great strides. And even if you're not in an orthodox therapy, healing will happen by cosmic means. Old memories will surface so that you can look at them from your present state of consciousness. This brings healing and resolution.

You're in a strong career year and it is important to you, but you can give more focus to the home and family now.

August

Best Days Overall: 7, 8, 17, 18, 26, 27
Most Stressful Days Overall: 1, 2, 14, 15, 16, 22, 23, 29
Best Days for Love: 5, 6, 8, 14, 15, 18, 22, 23, 24, 25, 27, 28
Best Days for Money: 7, 8, 10, 11, 17, 18, 26, 27
Best Days for Career: 1, 2, 8, 18, 27, 29

Health still needs watching, until the 23rd, but you will see dramatic improvement after then. There is no major problem, only short-term stress caused by the transits of short-term planets. Enhance the health with more rest and in the ways mentioned in the yearly report. With your health planet still retrograde, it is not advisable to have tests or procedures right now (especially if they're elective). Wait until Venus starts to move forward next month.

Uranus, your career planet, camps out in your sign this month. Those of you with birthdays from May 13–15 will feel the effect of this the strongest. The transit brings dramatic personal changes – disruptive kinds of changes. But it also brings career opportunities. These opportunities need careful study.

Retrograde activity increases still further this month and by the end of the month – from the 29th onwards – 60 per cent of the planets are retrograde, the maximum for the year. This month finances are affected: Mercury goes retrograde on the 23rd. So, try to wrap up important financial moves – investments or major purchases – before that date. You're in a speculative mood this month but avoid this after the 23rd.

Planetary power is still in your 4th house until the 23rd. So, focus on the family and your emotional wellness – career can take a back seat for a while. (With Uranus going retrograde on the 29th – and you'll feel the effect of this even before then – career issues will take time to resolve, so you may as well focus on the family.)

The New Moon of the 16th occurs in your 4th house, reinforcing the importance of home and family. Family and emotional issues will clarify themselves as the weeks go by. All the information you need on these issues will come to you in natural ways.

Your love planet Pluto is still retrograde, but he receives good aspects this month – especially after the 23rd. So, the love life is improving. It's not what it should be or will be, but it is improving.

September

Best Days Overall: 4, 5, 13, 14, 15, 23, 24
Most Stressful Days Overall: 11, 12, 18, 19, 25, 26
Best Days for Love: 2, 3, 5, 11, 12, 15, 18, 19, 21, 22, 24, 30
Best Days for Money: 4, 5, 6, 7, 13, 14, 15, 23, 24
Best Days for Career: 5, 14, 15, 24, 25, 26

Retrograde activity remains at its maximum extent (60 per cent) for the year until the 16th. After that the percentage reduces a little to 50 per cent, which is still very high! So, patience is required now. Time and time alone will resolve things. The good news for you is that we have a lot of Earth elements in the Horoscope this month. This is comfortable for you as this is your native element. Earth is patient.

Health is good this month. There are no major planets in stressful alignment with you. Only the Moon – and then only briefly – will make stressful aspects. This is negligible. Venus, your health planet, starts to move forward on the 4th and so it is safe to have diagnostic tests or procedures now. Mercury moves forward on the 15th.

Mercury's forward motion improves the financial judgement and clarifies the financial thinking. It is good for finances. Your money planet will be in your 5th house all month, indicating a more speculative attitude to finance (but not wildly speculative). It signals that you are spending more on the children or children figures in your life and perhaps earning from them as well. More importantly it shows happy money. Money is earned in fun ways and spent on fun things. You're in a yearly personal pleasure peak this month – it began on August 23 – and with so many planets retrograde you may as well enjoy life. Not much is happening in the world.

There are love opportunities happening, but your love planet is still retrograde, so go slow. Let love develop as it will. Avoid major love decisions just now.

Jupiter makes a station in your sign (at 16 degrees Taurus) this month. He camps out on that point. Those of you with birthdays from May 6–9 will feel this most strongly. It is very positive. It can bring an inheritance, or signal being named in someone's will or being appointed to some administrative position in an estate. For some it can bring cosmetic surgery or a connection with an investor. There is very good access to external finance over this period.

The New Moon of the 15th occurs in your 5th house and is a fun kind of day – it also seems a good financial day as well.

October

Best Days Overall: 1, 2, 11, 12, 20, 21
Most Stressful Days Overall: 8, 9, 15, 16, 17, 22, 23, 28, 29
Best Days for Love: 2, 9, 10, 11, 12, 15, 16, 17, 20, 21, 28, 29
Best Days for Money: 1, 2, 3, 4, 11, 12, 20, 21, 24, 28, 29
Best Days for Career: 2, 12, 21, 22, 23, 29

Retrograde activity is still strong but is diminishing. Until the 11th half the planets are retrograde; after then 40 per cent are retrograde.

Your financial planet Mercury has his solstice on the 7th and 8th. He pauses in the heavens and changes direction. So it is in your financial life.

The main headlines this month, however, are the two eclipses happening. The first is a solar eclipse on the 14th and the second a lunar eclipse on the 28th. The lunar eclipse seems to affect you more powerfully than the solar eclipse but still, it won't hurt to reduce your schedule around the solar eclipse period anyway.

The solar eclipse of the 14th occurs in your 6th house of health and work. Thus, there can be job changes – within your present company or with another one. If you employ others there can be high levels of employee turnover over the next few months. The eclipse's position also indicates important changes in your health regime (and now that

Venus is moving forward it is safer to make them). This eclipse, like every solar eclipse, impacts on the home and family and brings dramas there – personal dramas. Often repairs are needed in the home as the eclipse reveals hidden flaws.

The lunar eclipse of the 28th occurs in your own sign, which makes its effects more powerful for you. All of you will feel this in some degree, but especially those born on April 24–26. The eclipse signals a need to redefine yourself. In the coming months you will change the way you think about yourself and about how you want others to think of you. This will result in wardrobe changes, changes of hairstyle and the overall presentation of yourself to the world. If you haven't been careful in dietary matters, it can bring a detox of the body – this is not sickness though the symptoms seem the same. Every lunar eclipse affects the siblings, sibling figures in your life and neighbours. There are personal dramas in their lives. There can be disruptions in your neighbourhood. Cars and communication equipment can behave erratically and sometimes repairs or replacements are necessary. A good idea to drive more carefully over this period.

November

Best Days Overall: 7, 8, 16, 17, 25, 26
Most Stressful Days Overall: 4, 5, 6, 12, 13, 18, 19
Best Days for Love: 8, 9, 12, 13, 17, 18, 19, 26, 27, 28
Best Days for Money: 1, 2, 3, 7, 16, 23, 24, 25, 27, 28
Best Days for Career: 8, 17, 18, 19, 26

Retrograde activity diminishes this month. After the 4th only 30 per cent of the planets will be retrograde, so events are starting to move forward – both personally and in the world.

Your love planet Pluto started to move forward on October 11. On October 23 the Sun moved into your 7th house of love and will be there until the 22nd of this month. So, love is the main headline now. The love life is active and romantic opportunities for singles abound. Your social confidence and judgement are good. Mars spends almost all of the month in your 7th house (until the 29th). So, try to avoid power struggles in love. The beloved (or people you date) can be more belligerent and argumentative. Be more patient with them. Family members like to play Cupid. Love seems happy next month too. Your main challenge, though, is balancing your interests with the interests of others – especially the beloved. You're in a very 'me'-oriented year. Others are important this month, but you don't seem ready to put them first.

Health needs more attention this month, but after the 22nd you will see dramatic improvement. In the meantime, rest and relax more. Enhance the health with massage of the lower abdomen until the 8th and with hip massage afterwards. The good news is that health is important to you, and your focus is here.

Mercury, your financial planet, goes 'out of bounds' from the 16th onwards, showing that in your financial life you're going outside your normal orbit. Children and children figures also seem 'off the reservation'.

From the 22nd onwards your 8th house of regeneration becomes powerful. This will be a good period for weight loss and detox regimes. It will also be a good time to purge the mind and emotions of negative patterns and your life of possessions and things that you don't need or use. (Taurus tends to hoard.) Clear the decks of the irrelevant and make space for the new and better that wants to come in.

Be more mindful on the physical plane on the 10th and 11th.

December

Best Days Overall: 4, 5, 6, 14, 15, 22, 23, 31
Most Stressful Days Overall: 2, 3, 9, 10, 16, 17, 29, 30
Best Days for Love: 5, 6, 9, 10, 15, 18, 19, 23, 28, 30
Best Days for Money: 4, 14, 22, 24, 25, 30, 31
Best Days for Career: 5, 6, 15, 16, 17, 23

Health is good now and will get even better after the 22nd. Good social health seems as important as good physical health these days. Venus moves into your 7th house of love on the 5th and stays there until the 30th. So you are trying to put others first – a sincere attempt – but it's difficult. Your 1st house is still more powerful than the 7th house. But others notice the effort.

With Venus in Scorpio most of the month, this is a good time for losing weight and for detox regimes. Weight loss will be a challenge (Jupiter is still in your sign) but you can make progress.

Mercury behaves strangely this month. First he is 'out of bounds' until the 14th. So, like last month, you're going out of your normal orbit in financial matters. Then he goes retrograde on the 13th, meaning that you return to your normal financial orbit but are unsure of things! As always, avoid making important financial decisions, major purchases or investments after the 13th. Mercury's nice aspects to Jupiter on the 6th and 7th are especially good financial days. The financial intuition needs checking and extra verification on the 26th and 27th.

Your 8th house remains strong this month until the 22nd, so continue to focus on personal transformation and giving birth to the person that you want to be. They won't be accomplished this month (these are long-term projects) but progress will be made.

The New Moon of the 12th also occurs in your 8th house, which means that these activities go even better that day. More importantly, it will clarify many issues as the weeks progress – issues involving estates, inheritance, taxes and insurance. All the information you need will come to you – and very naturally too.

The spouse, partner or current love should have a good financial month until the 22nd, but there might be delayed reactions and glitches too.

Mars, your spiritual planet, was 'out of bounds' for over four months at the beginning of the year. He once more goes 'out of bounds' from the 22nd onwards. In spiritual matters, you're going outside your normal orbit again. This is probably so in your charitable activities as well.

Gemini

♊

THE TWINS

Birthdays from
21st May to
20th June

Personality Profile

GEMINI AT A GLANCE

Element – Air

Ruling Planet – Mercury
   Career Planet – Neptune
   Love Planet – Jupiter
   Money Planet – Moon
   Planet of Health and Work – Pluto
   Planet of Home and Family Life – Mercury

Colours – blue, yellow, yellow-orange

Colour that promotes love, romance and social harmony – sky blue

Colours that promote earning power – grey, silver

Gems – agate, aquamarine

Metal – quicksilver

Scents – lavender, lilac, lily of the valley, storax

Quality – mutable (= flexibility)

Quality most needed for balance – thought that is deep rather than superficial

Strongest virtues – great communication skills, quickness and agility of thought, ability to learn quickly

Deepest need – communication

Characteristics to avoid – gossiping, hurting others with harsh speech, superficiality, using words to mislead or misinform

Signs of greatest overall compatibility – Libra, Aquarius

Signs of greatest overall incompatibility – Virgo, Sagittarius, Pisces

Sign most helpful to career – Pisces

Sign most helpful for emotional support – Virgo

Sign most helpful financially – Cancer

Sign best for marriage and/or partnerships – Sagittarius

Sign most helpful for creative projects – Libra

Best Sign to have fun with – Libra

Signs most helpful in spiritual matters – Taurus, Aquarius

Best day of the week – Wednesday

Understanding a Gemini

Gemini is to society what the nervous system is to the body. It does not introduce any new information but is a vital transmitter of impulses from the senses to the brain and vice versa. The nervous system does not judge or weigh these impulses – it only conveys information. And it does so perfectly.

This analogy should give you an indication of a Gemini's role in society. Geminis are the communicators and conveyors of information. To Geminis the truth or falsehood of information is irrelevant, they only transmit what they see, hear or read about. Thus they are capable of spreading the most outrageous rumours as well as conveying truth and light. Geminis sometimes tend to be unscrupulous in their communications and can do both great good and great evil with their power. This is why the sign of Gemini is symbolized by twins: Geminis have a dual nature.

Their ability to convey a message – to communicate with such ease – makes Geminis ideal teachers, writers and media and marketing people. This is helped by the fact that Mercury, the ruling planet of Gemini, also rules these activities.

Geminis have the gift of the gab. And what a gift this is! They can make conversation about anything, anywhere, at any time. There is almost nothing that is more fun to Geminis than a good conversation – especially if they can learn something new as well. They love to learn and they love to teach. To deprive a Gemini of conversation, or of books and magazines, is cruel and unusual punishment.

Geminis are almost always excellent students and take well to education. Their minds are generally stocked with all kinds of information, trivia, anecdotes, stories, news items, rarities, facts and statistics. Thus they can support any intellectual position that they care to take. They are awesome debaters and, if involved in politics, make good orators. Geminis are so verbally smooth that even if they do not know what they are talking about, they can make you think that they do. They will always dazzle you with their brilliance.

Finance

Geminis tend to be more concerned with the wealth of learning and ideas than with actual material wealth. As mentioned, they excel in professions that involve writing, teaching, sales and journalism – and not all of these professions pay very well. But to sacrifice intellectual needs merely for money is unthinkable to a Gemini. Geminis strive to combine the two. Cancer is on Gemini's solar 2nd house of money cusp, which indicates that Geminis can earn extra income (in a harmonious and natural way) from investments in residential property, restaurants and hotels. Given their verbal skills, Geminis love to bargain and negotiate in any situation, and especially when it has to do with money.

The Moon rules Gemini's 2nd solar house. The Moon is not only the fastest-moving planet in the zodiac but actually moves through every sign and house every 28 days. No other heavenly body matches the Moon for swiftness or the ability to change quickly. An analysis of the Moon – and lunar phenomena in general – describes Gemini's financial attitudes very well. Geminis are financially versatile and flexible; they can earn money in many different ways. Their financial attitudes and needs seem to change daily. Their feelings about money change also: sometimes they are very enthusiastic about it, at other times they could not care less.

For a Gemini, financial goals and money are often seen only as means of supporting a family; these things have little meaning otherwise.

The Moon, as Gemini's money planet, has another important message for Gemini financially: in order for Geminis to realize their financial potential they need to develop more of an understanding of the emotional side of life. They need to combine their awesome powers of logic with an understanding of human psychology. Feelings have their own logic; Geminis need to learn this and apply it to financial matters.

Career and Public Image

Geminis know that they have been given the gift of communication for a reason, that it is a power that can achieve great good or cause unthinkable distress. They long to put this power at the service of the highest and most transcendental truths. This is their primary goal, to communicate the eternal verities and prove them logically. They look up to people who can transcend the intellect – to poets, artists, musicians and mystics. They may be awed by stories of religious saints and martyrs. A Gemini's highest achievement is to teach the truth, whether it is scientific, inspirational or historical. Those who can transcend the intellect are Gemini's natural superiors – and a Gemini realizes this.

The sign of Pisces is in Gemini's solar 10th house of career. Neptune, the planet of spirituality and altruism, is Gemini's career planet. If Geminis are to realize their highest career potential they need to develop their transcendental – their spiritual and altruistic – side. They need to understand the larger cosmic picture, the vast flow of human evolution – where it came from and where it is heading. Only then can a Gemini's intellectual powers take their true position and he or she can become the 'messenger of the gods'. Geminis need to cultivate a facility for 'inspiration', which is something that does not originate in the intellect but which comes through the intellect. This will further enrich and empower a Gemini's mind.

Love and Relationships

Geminis bring their natural garrulousness and brilliance into their love life and social life as well. A good talk or a verbal joust is an interesting prelude to romance. Their only problem in love is that their intellect is too cool and passionless to incite ardour in others. Emotions sometimes disturb them, and their partners tend to complain about this. If you are in love with a Gemini you must understand why this is so. Geminis avoid deep passions because these would interfere with their ability to think and communicate. If they are cool towards you, understand that this is their nature.

Nevertheless, Geminis must understand that it is one thing to talk about love and another actually to love – to feel it and radiate it. Talking about love glibly will get them nowhere. They need to feel it and act on it. Love is not of the intellect but of the heart. If you want to know how a Gemini feels about love you should not listen to what he or she says, but rather, observe what he or she does. Geminis can be quite generous to those they love.

Geminis like their partners to be refined, well educated and well travelled. If their partners are more wealthy than they, that is all the better. If you are in love with a Gemini you had better be a good listener as well.

The ideal relationship for the Gemini is a relationship of the mind. They enjoy the physical and emotional aspects, of course, but if the intellectual communion is not there they will suffer.

Home and Domestic Life

At home the Gemini can be uncharacteristically neat and meticulous. They tend to want their children and partner to live up to their idealistic standards. When these standards are not met they moan and criticize. However, Geminis are good family people and like to serve their families in practical and useful ways.

The Gemini home is comfortable and pleasant. They like to invite people over and they make great hosts. Geminis are also good at repairs and improvements around the house – all fuelled by their need to stay active and occupied with something they like to do. Geminis have many hobbies and interests that keep them busy when they are home alone.

Geminis understand and get along well with their children, mainly because they are very youthful people themselves. As great communicators, Geminis know how to explain things to children; in this way they gain their children's love and respect. Geminis also encourage children to be creative and talkative, just like they are.

Horoscope for 2023

Major Trends

The cosmic chess board gets rearranged this year. Many of you are already feeling the coming changes. Three major planets – long-term planets – will change signs this year, which is highly unusual. This signifies many changes in the world at large and for your personally, Gemini.

Pluto's flirtation with the sign of Aquarius this year – its first change in over twenty years – is basically happy for you. It will bring improvements in health and energy and, slowly but surely, as the years go by, completely transform your religious and theological beliefs. Your world view is about to be transformed. Thus, you will live your life in a different way.

Saturn moves into your 10th house of career on March 8. This puts stress on your health and energy (which we will discuss later) but, more importantly, impacts the career. Now success must be earned. You've just had two years of career expansion. You've been elevated professionally. Now you must earn your success. More on this later.

Jupiter, your love planet, will be in your 11th house of friendship until May 17. So the year ahead is both social and romantic. The lines between friendship and romance get blurred. One merges into the other. Your insights into astrology, astronomy, science and technology will grow. New (and significant) friends are coming into the picture. More details later.

On May 17 Jupiter will enter your spiritual 12th house, putting the focus for the year ahead on the spiritual. This is a year for making spiritual progress, Gemini – details below.

Your most important interests this year are occult studies, personal reinvention and sex (from January 1 to March 24 and from June 12 onwards); religion, theology, higher education and foreign travel (from March 24 to June 12); career; friends, groups and group activities (from January 1 to May 17); and spirituality (from May 17 onwards).

Your paths of greatest fulfilment will be friendships, groups activities, involvement with organizations and online activities (from January 1 to May 17 and from July 18 onwards); and spirituality.

Health

(Please note that this is an astrological perspective on health and not a medical one. In days of yore there was no difference, both these perspectives were identical. But these days there could be quite a difference. For a medical perspective, please consult your doctor or health practitioner.)

Health should be reasonable this year, albeit with a few caveats. Saturn's move on March 8 from Aquarius to Pisces will be stressful to you, and this stress will go on for the next two and a half years. So, your normal energy is not there. It is less than usual. This isn't anything serious, as the other long-term planets are either making nice aspects or are leaving you alone. But don't be alarmed if you can't jog or cycle your usual amount. Nor should this be forced.

The other change we see is Pluto's move from Capricorn into Aquarius from March 24 to June 12. This is the beginning of a major shift for Pluto. He will hover between Capricorn and Aquarius next year too and will finally enter Aquarius for the long term in 2025. There he will stay for at least twenty years (perhaps more). Since Pluto is your health planet, this major move has great ramifications for your health and the therapies that work for you. You're beginning now to change your health regime.

Though health is basically good, you can make it even better by giving more attention to the following – the vulnerable areas of your Horoscope this year (the reflex points are shown in the chart opposite):

- The lungs, arms, shoulders, and respiratory system. These are always important for Gemini, and regular arm and shoulder massage will be very beneficial. Tension tends to collect in the shoulders and needs to be released.
- The colon, bladder and sexual organs. These too are always important areas for Gemini, as Pluto is your health planet. Safe sex and sexual moderation are also very important.
- The heart only becomes an important area after March 8, but it will remain important for next two and a half years. The important thing with the heart is to avoid worry and anxiety, the two emotions that stress it out. Replace worry with faith.

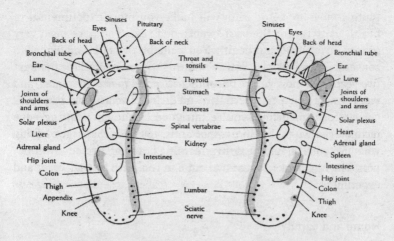

Important foot reflexology points for the year ahead

Try to massage all of the foot on a regular basis – the top of the foot as well as the bottom – but pay extra attention to the points highlighted on the chart. When you massage, be aware of 'sore spots' as these need special attention. It's also a good idea to massage the ankles and below them.

- The ankles and calves become important from March 24 until June 12, although over the coming years (especially from 2025 onwards) they will be important for the long term. So regular calf and ankle massage should become part of your regular health regime. If you're exercising, make sure you support the ankles. A weak ankle can knock the spine out of alignment, which can cause all kinds of other problems.
- The spine, knees, teeth, bones and overall skeletal alignment. These areas have been important for many years now, and remain so until March 24, and from June 12 onwards. Gradually, in the coming years – and especially from 2025 onwards – they will not be so much of an issue, but in the meantime continue with back and knee massage. Regular visits to a chiropractor or osteopath would be good. The vertebrae need to be kept in right alignment (the reflex points are shown in the chart above).

Pluto's move into Aquarius will make you more experimental in health matters. For the past twenty-odd years you have been very conservative about your health. You went 'by the book' and tended to conventional medicine. (You're still this way on and off for the next two years.) But now you're becoming attracted to new therapies, and you're more open to alternative medicine. Even if you stay with conventional medicine, you're intrigued by the new cutting-edge technologies within it. More importantly, you're on the verge of doing what everyone should be doing: learning how you, personally, function. The rule books get thrown out and you learn by trial, error and experiment.

Home and Family

Your 4th house of home and family is not prominent this year – it is not a house of power. Your 10th house of career is much more powerful. So, this would tend to the status quo. Home and domestic life will more or less continue as it has been. You seem basically content with the status quo, Gemini, and have no need to make major changes.

Home and family – and your emotional wellness – is always important to you. The ruler of your Horoscope, Mercury, is also your family planet, so it is an area close to your heart. But this year it is less important than usual. You will probably spend more time on the career than on the home. (And you should.)

A parent or parent figure seems less strict, softer, more spiritual this year. He or she could be having surgery or near-death kinds of experiences. However, he or she seems supportive of your career – perhaps even actively involved.

There are many short-term trends with the family. Mercury is a fast-moving planet, as our regular readers know, and will move through all the signs and houses of your chart in the coming year. So much depends on where Mercury is at any given time and the kinds of aspects he receives. This is best covered in the monthly reports.

Mars will be in your 4th house from July 11 to August 28. This can bring high passions in the family circle – perhaps conflicts. Do your best to minimize these things. However, this is a good period for undertaking renovations or major repairs in the home. October 9 to

November 8 will be a good time for redecorating, beautifying the home or buying objects of beauty for the home.

Siblings and sibling figures in your life will have their marriages tested in the coming years. However, love looks very happy this year – especially after May 17. They are probably contemplating a move, but it is more likely to happen in the coming years than now. Parents or parent figures might move after May 17, but it could happen next year too. Children and children figures are also contemplating a move, but this seems a complicated process and with many delays. If they are married the marriage is being tested. If they are single and of an appropriate age, marriage is not advisable this year. Their social life could be happier. Grandchildren, or those who play that role in your life, have been moving around a lot of late. Another move could happen after May 17. This seems happy.

Finance and Career

Though this is a strong career year, Gemini, finance seems less important. Your money house is not prominent and not a house of power. This can be seen as a good thing. You're basically satisfied with the status quo and have no need to make dramatic changes or give undue focus here. However, if problems arise, this lack of focus could be a root cause. You'll have to start paying more attention.

There will be times when finances are stronger or weaker than at other times. This comes from the transits of the short-term planets. When they are kind, earnings increase and come with greater ease. When they are unkind, there is more challenge involved. In addition, your financial planet is the Moon, the fastest moving of all the planets. She traverses your whole Horoscope in any given month, unlike the other fast-moving planets (such as the Sun, Mercury and Venus) that take a year to move through your chart. So, there are many short-term financial trends that depend on where the Moon is and the kinds of aspects she receives. These are best dealt with in the monthly reports.

In general, we can say that the times of the New Moon and Full Moon are always strong financial days. The period from the New Moon to the Full Moon, as the Moon waxes, will tend to be better financially than when she wanes and grows smaller, from the Full Moon to the

New Moon. You have more enthusiasm and energy for finance when the Moon is waxing.

When the Moon is growing it is good to spend on things that will increase your income. They are good periods for buying a house or making an investment. When the Moon is waning it is better to pay down debt or sell things – you're getting rid of things. The sale of a house or taking profits from an investment are better done under a waning Moon.

June 21 to July 23 will be an excellent financial period. There will be strong focus here and this is 90 per cent of success. You will be in a yearly financial peak then.

The real headline this year is the career. Saturn will move into your 10th house of career on March 8 and stays there for the next two and a half years, joining Neptune in this house. Neptune has been in your career house for many years now. Saturn and Neptune are opposite kinds of forces. Saturn is down to earth and practical. Neptune is otherworldly. Saturn likes order, right form, good management. Neptune likes the free-flowing intuitive approach. So, in career matters you're of two minds now. There is the idealistic, Neptune side of you and the down-to-earth, worldly, Saturn side of you. And somehow you must reconcile them. This is the main career challenge for the next couple of years. Do you opt for total idealism and ignore the world, or do you take a more worldly perspective? Probably you'll do a little bit of both. Your idealistic ventures – whether they are charities, non-profit organizations or spiritual ventures – will need more order and organization. Your worldly activities will need to be spiced with some idealism. Perhaps you will be involved in charities or altruistic ventures on the side as you pursue your worldly career.

Saturn in the 10th house signals a need to earn success through sheer merit. In the past year you caught many lucky career breaks. Now you have to demonstrate your worth. So, much work is involved in your career this year, and if you put in the work there is much success in store – long-lasting success. Often this work is manifested in demanding bosses who push you to your limits (and often beyond). My astrological advice is to give them even more than they ask for.

Love and Social Life

The love life is very interesting this year. Like last year, your love planet, Jupiter, spends approximately five months in one sign (Aries) and seven months (approximately) in another – Taurus. This indicates changes in the attitudes and needs in love. They are not fixed or static.

Until May 17 Jupiter is in Aries, your 11th house. The love planet in Aries shows an aggressiveness in love. You show your feelings immediately. You're a 'love at first sight' kind of person and have a tendency to jump into romantic relationships quickly – perhaps too quickly. You have a fearlessness in love (which is the whole point of this transit). Yes, your quickness to jump into relationships can lead to mistakes. There can be pain. But you get up, dust yourself down and jump back into the fray. Jupiter in the 11th house is very positive for love. It shows that fondest romantic hopes and wishes come to pass. The 11th house is a beneficent house. Love, overall, seems happy this period.

On May 17 Jupiter moves into your 12th house – the sign of Taurus – and the love needs change. Now, you become more conservative in love. You're slower to enter into relationships (perhaps because of the lessons learned over the previous five months!). The spiritual component becomes important. You need a partner with whom there is spiritual compatibility. You don't need to agree on every point but to at least support each other's spiritual practice and path. You find yourself attracted to spiritual types of people – yogis, spiritual channels, psychics, tarot readers, musicians, dancers, poets. Where previously love opportunities came from the online world, through friends or through involvement with groups, now they come at more spiritual-type venues – the yoga studio, the spiritual lecture or seminar, the prayer meeting, poetry reading or charity event.

Jupiter will be travelling near Uranus this year. The aspect won't be exact but you'll feel the influence. (The aspect becomes exact next year.) This adds much excitement to the love life. Romance can happen at any time or in any place. You never know when it will strike. But love becomes more unstable as well. It is the durability of these relationships that is in question. Instability is the price we pay for excitement. Marriage would not be advisable this year. (But next year it can certainly happen.) Enjoy love for what it is, but hold off on marriage.

Self-improvement

Spirituality has been important to you for many years. Uranus has been in your 12th spiritual house for a long time. Thus, you've been experimental in this area. You've been (figuratively speaking) like the ancient holy wanderer searching the world for wisdom, now visiting one holy man, now another. The eternal seeker. You've been going from one teaching to another, from one book to another, from one teacher to another. Perhaps you haven't literally wandered the world, but mentally you have done so. This is an important stage in the spiritual process, but it doesn't last for ever. This year you're likely to settle into a teaching and practice that suits you.

There are two interesting developments in your spiritual life this year, and both reinforce each other. Uranus is ruler of your 9th house of religion. Jupiter, the generic ruler of religion, moves into your 12th house on May 17 and stays there for the rest of the year.

The transit of these planets points to a need to go deeper – to explore – the mystical side of your native religion. It's not about exploring alien traditions, though you've probably been doing this. It's about penetrating the essence of your own religion. You've rejected it because you haven't delved deep enough. Underneath all the rules and regulations – the outer forms – lies a kernel of truth. This is what you must find.

There is more here. Jupiter is your love planet. His position in the 12th house shows that the path of love brings you closer to the Divine. You feel most 'connected' when you're in love. You will experience this in the year ahead. But there's still more here. You'll discover that the Divine is very interested in your love life. Guidance on love – whether you're single or married – will come. It can be in dreams, visions, or through psychics, mediums, astrologers or spiritual channels. There is a destiny here and the Divine wants to further it.

You have the kind of aspects where one surrenders the love life to the Divine. One 'casts the burden' of it and allows the Divine to handle things. This will straighten out love problems pretty quickly – provided that your surrender is sincere and from the heart, not just from the lips.

And, there's still more. In many cases (not all) the Divine is leading you to the Ultimate Love. Love between humans is always hedged with limitations. Some humans can love more than others. But even so, it can't be perfect. Only one power can love you perfectly – the Divine. When this is contacted, all the needs in love will be satisfied – whether you're in a relationship or not. That becomes irrelevant. You always feel as if you're on your honeymoon.

Month-by-month Forecasts

January

Best Days Overall: 3, 4, 12, 13, 21, 22, 30, 31
Most Stressful Days Overall: 1, 2, 8, 9, 14, 15, 28, 29
Best Days for Love: 2, 3, 8, 9, 12, 13, 16, 21, 22, 23
Best Days for Money: 2, 8, 10, 11, 16, 20, 21, 23, 24, 30, 31
Best Days for Career: 7, 14, 15, 24

Basically, it is a happy month ahead, Gemini, with a few glitches to keep things interesting. Health and overall energy are good, and there is only one long-term planet – Neptune – in stressful aspect to you. The short-term planets are either in harmony with you or leaving you alone. Health will improve even further after the 20th.

Mercury, the ruler of your Horoscope and a very important planet in your chart, is retrograde until the 17th. So personal desires are cloudy and uncertain. They need more thought. The same holds true with home and family issues.

Jupiter, your love planet, is in the sign of Aries and in your 11th house of friends. This suggests that the month ahead (and the next few months) are more about friendship than romance. You're attracted to relationships of equals. Friendship with the beloved is as important as being lovers. For singles, love opportunities happen as you get involved with friends, groups and group activities. The online world also seems a source of romance. Your love planet in Aries shows a 'love at first sight' kind of attitude. You know instantly who is for you, and you go after what you want aggressively. There is a tendency to jump into romantic relationships too quickly. You throw caution to the winds.

But there is more here. Your love planet will have his solstice this month. Because Jupiter is a slow-moving planet, his solstice lasts almost all month, from the 1st to the 27th. Jupiter is more or less stationary in the heavens – in his latitudinal motion – and at the end of the month he changes direction. So, there can be a pause in love and a change of direction.

Mercury makes nice aspects to Uranus from the 29th to the 31st. This can bring a foreign trip or good fortune in a legal matter. It is also a happy aspect for college-level students.

Finances are stable this month, although they will go more smoothly from the 11th to the 25th, the Moon's waxing phase.

February

Best Days Overall: 1, 9, 10, 18, 19, 27, 28
Most Stressful Days Overall: 7, 8, 14, 15, 20, 21
Best Days for Love: 2, 3, 4, 5, 12, 13, 14, 15, 22, 23
Best Days for Money: 1, 2, 3, 4, 5, 9, 10, 14, 15, 20, 22, 23
Best Days for Career: 3, 13, 20, 21

Mars has been in your own sign since the beginning of the year. This has good points and bad points. The good points are more energy, courage and a 'can do' spirit. You get things done quickly. The bad points are a tendency to be combative, argumentative and in a rush. This can lead to conflict and even accidents. So, make haste by all means, but in a mindful way.

Health needs more attention after the 18th, although there's nothing serious afoot. This is only short-term stress from short-term planets. It would be good to rest more, and to enhance the health in the ways mentioned in the yearly report.

The month ahead is a strong career month. Neptune, your career planet, has been in your 10th house for many years. Venus has been moving through here since January 27. And, on the 18th, the Sun moves in. Your career house is easily the strongest in the Horoscope this month, so the focus is on career and there is success happening. Home and family matters can take a back seat for a while. Your social and communication skills boost the career.

The New Moon of the 20th also occurs in your 10th house and just highlights this focus. It is a strong career day. Generally, the New Moon is a good financial day for you. But this one is less so than normal. Perhaps you're taking on extra financial responsibility. The good news is that you and the spouse, partner or current love are cooperating financially. The New Moon is a good financial day for him or her as well. More importantly, career issues and conundrums will clarify as the weeks progress – until the next New Moon.

Love seems happy and exciting this month. Venus starts to travel with your love planet after the 21st. Singles should continue to involve themselves in groups, group activities, with organizations and the online world.

Finance is still stable. The money house is still basically empty. But the 1st to the 5th and the 20th to the 28th are your strongest financial periods.

March

Best Days Overall: 8, 9, 10, 17, 18, 26, 27
Most Stressful Days Overall: 6, 7, 13, 14, 19, 20
Best Days for Love: 4, 5, 11, 12, 13, 14, 21, 22, 24, 25, 31
Best Days for Money: 1, 2, 4, 5, 12, 13, 14, 20, 21, 22, 28, 29, 30, 31
Best Days for Career: 2, 12, 19, 20, 29, 30

The whole landscape of your life (and the world at large) changes this month as two very long-term planets change signs. Pluto, your health planet, moves temporarily into Aquarius, your 9th house, on the 24th, and Saturn makes a major move into your 10th house on the 8th. Now, health needs more focus.

Pluto's move into Aquarius shows the importance of the ankles and calves in health. Also, it signals a more experimental approach. You're more likely to try alternative therapies now. Right now, this is a short-term trend, but over the coming years it will get ever stronger.

Career is still the major headline this month. You seem successful as Mercury crosses the top of your Horoscope from the 3rd to the 19th. The 17th and 18th seem particularly successful as Mercury travels with the Sun and your career planet, Neptune. But with Saturn in your 10th house now, success is earned the hard way – through sheer merit.

Venus travels with your love planet Jupiter on the 1st and 2nd – a classic signal for love and romance. The venue, as in the past few months, is the online world, social media, friends, groups and organizations. There are many scenarios here. A friend can want to be more than that. A friend can introduce you to someone. You can be involved in some group activity and meet someone there. There are many other scenarios as well.

Though the career is strong, finances still tend to the status quo. This can be considered a good thing. You're basically satisfied with things as they are and have no need to make major changes or pay undue attention. The 1st to the 7th and the 21st till the end of the month will tend to be your strongest financial periods. This is when the Moon waxes. From the 7th to the 21st it would be good to use any spare cash to pay down debt or to cut waste.

From the 20th onwards, as the Sun enters your 11th house, the focus is on the social life – friendships, groups and organizations. Your knowledge of technology, science, astronomy and astrology will increase. Many people have their Horoscopes done under these aspects.

April

Best Days Overall: 5, 6, 14, 15, 22, 23, 24
Most Stressful Days Overall: 2, 3, 4, 9, 10, 16, 17, 30
Best Days for Love: 1, 3, 4, 9, 10, 14, 19, 22, 23, 28, 29
Best Days for Money: 1, 10, 19, 25, 26, 28, 29, 30
Best Days for Career: 8, 16, 17, 26

Though Saturn is in stressful aspect with you, the other planets are either supporting you or leaving you alone. Health should be good – or at least reasonable. This Saturn transit will be felt most by those born from May 21–25, early in the sign of Gemini. All of you will feel it in some degree but not as much as those mentioned.

We have a solar eclipse on the 20th that occurs right on the cusp of your 11th and 12th houses. This means that it affects both houses. So, there are dramas in the lives of friends. Friendships can be tested. Computers and high-tech equipment can behave erratically and could need repairs or replacement. I've noticed that under these kinds of aspects software companies make upgrades that, though they mean well, disrupt all your settings. Make sure important files are backed up and that your anti-virus and anti-hacking software is up to date.

The eclipse's impact on your 12th house indicates important spiritual changes. These can take many forms. There can be changes in your practice, your teachers, teachings, etc. Your attitudes to spirituality get changed. There can be upheavals in charitable or altruistic organizations you're involved with. Guru figures in your life can experience personal dramas.

Because the Sun rules your 3rd house, every solar eclipse impacts the affairs of this house. So, students (especially those below college level) can experience disruptions at school, or change their educational plans, or sometimes even change schools. Cars and communication equipment can be erratic and might need replacing. It would be a good idea to drive more carefully over the eclipse period.

Siblings, sibling figures and neighbours are affected too. There are personal dramas in their lives and often there are disruptions in your neighbourhood.

Mars moved into your 2nd money house on March 26 and remains here over this month, indicating that friends and social connections are important in finance. You tend to be impulsive in love (this has been going on since the beginning of the year) and now you're impulsive in finances. Perhaps you are too much of a risk-taker.

May

Best Days Overall: 2,3,11,12,20,21,30,31
Most Stressful Days Overall: 1,7,8,13,14,27,28
Best Days for Love: 2,3,7,8,9,10,16,17,18,19,24,25
Best Days for Money: 1,8,9,10,16,17,18,19,22,23,24,25,30, 31
Best Days for Career: 6,13,14,23,24

We have two important headlines this month. Jupiter, your love planet, makes a major move from Aries into Taurus – from your 11th house into your 12th. This happens on May 17. This brings long-term changes to the love life. The needs in love change, and you're attracted to different kinds of people.

On the 5th we have a lunar eclipse that occurs in your 6th house of health and work. Thus, there could be job changes. These could be within your present situation or in a new position. If you employ others, there can be high levels of employee turnover and dramas in the lives of your employees. There will also be important changes in the health regime as well over the next few months.

With the Moon as your money planet, every lunar eclipse brings financial changes, usually through some disruption or unexpected event. You go through this twice a year (on average). So, course corrections are taking place in the financial thinking and planning. The events of the eclipse will show you where your thinking or planning has been amiss and where changes need to be made.

Since the Moon is the generic ruler of the home and family, there can be dramas here and in the lives of family members. Sometimes repairs are needed in the home.

Jupiter's move into your 12th house on the 17th signals an attraction to more spiritual people than before – idealists, musicians, poets, psychics, spiritual channels and ministers. Spiritual compatibility becomes very important in love. Your intuition will now be trained in love matters.

Though there is some financial turbulence caused by the eclipse, the month ahead seems prosperous as your money house has become prominent. Mars will be in your 2nd house until the 21st and Venus will enter there on the 8th. You still seem very speculative and risk-taking in finance.

June

Best Days Overall: 7, 8, 16, 17, 26, 27
Most Stressful Days Overall: 3, 4, 9, 10, 23, 24, 25
Best Days for Love: 2, 3, 4, 5, 6, 11, 14, 15, 21, 22, 23, 24
Best Days for Money: 5, 6, 7, 8, 14, 15, 17, 18, 19, 20, 23, 24, 28
Best Days for Career: 2, 9, 10, 19, 20, 29, 30

A happy and prosperous month ahead, Gemini. Enjoy. The Sun has been in your own sign since May 21 and will be there until the 21st. This is always a high point in any year. The Sun brings light and star quality to the image. Self-esteem and self-confidence are strong. Your normally good intellectual gifts are even further enhanced. Health will be good. Energy is high. If you want to enhance the health further, give more attention to the ankles and calves (massage them) until the 12th and then resume spine and knee massage again.

The New Moon of the 18th is particularly fortuitous as it occurs in your own sign. It brings financial windfalls and opportunities. More importantly, it will clarify issues involving personal appearance and image as the weeks progress (until the next New Moon). Prosperity grows stronger from the 21st onwards, as the Sun enters the money house and stays there for the rest of the month. You're in a yearly financial peak. There is focus on finance. The financial energy is strong. On the 27th Mercury, your ruling planet, moves into the money house, which further strengthens the finances. Personal appearance seems important in earnings. You are projecting an image of wealth. People see you this way. This brings all kinds of opportunities to you.

Mars is now in your 3rd house of intellectual interests and communication. You're a strong debater these days. You state your positions with great passion and vigour. And, perhaps, you can overdo it as well. Clear thinking requires coolness – a dispassionate approach; you could be too overheated.

Love, like last month, is very spiritual – very idealistic. The message of the Horoscope is: get right spiritually and love will take care of itself. This remains a month for an enhanced dream life, supernatural types of experiences and more involvement with charities. Last month was more so, but these things are still strong now.

The Full Moon of the 4th, which occurs in your 7th house, is good for both love and finance.

July

Best Days Overall: 5, 6, 13, 14, 15, 23, 24
Most Stressful Days Overall: 1, 2, 7, 8, 21, 22, 28, 29
Best Days for Love: 1, 2, 3, 4, 10, 11, 12, 19, 20, 21, 22, 29, 30, 31
Best Days for Money: 3, 4, 7, 8, 11, 12, 16, 17, 21, 22, 26, 30, 31
Best Days for Career: 7, 8, 17, 27

A prosperous month ahead. You're still in the midst of a yearly financial peak until the 23rd, and your natural gifts of communication, sales, marketing, advertising and PR enhance the earnings. Many Geminis are in these lines of work and they do well.

Health needs more attention from the 11th onwards. Mars joins Saturn and Neptune in stressful alignment with you. So, as always, make sure to get enough rest. Enhance the health with back and knee massage. Make sure your posture is good.

Mars moves into your 4th house of home and family on the 11th, which means that passions at home can run high. Be more patient with family members. This will be a good time for undertaking major renovations about the home. Friends – perhaps in a well-meaning way – could be obstructing the career.

The bottom half of your chart – the night side – is as strong this month as it will ever be in 2023. So, although career is the year's most dominant interest, it is good to shift some attention to the home and family now.

By the 23rd your financial goals (the short-term ones at least) have been more or less achieved, and now your focus can shift to your first love: intellectual interests and communication. Geminis are always good students, but now even more so. Your always strong mental and communication faculties are even stronger this month. Learning and teaching go easier.

After the 23rd the money people in your life get richer. They are having an outstanding financial period.

Love becomes more delicate after the 23rd. Your love planet, Jupiter, is receiving stressful aspects. You will need to work harder on your relationship. Most of the love trends that we discussed in past months are still in effect. Spiritual people and spiritual venues are important.

The New Moon of the 17th occurs in your money house, and this should be an outstanding financial day. But, more important than that, it will clarify – illuminate – your financial situation as the weeks progress. All the information you need to make the right decision will come to you – and rather naturally.

Mercury goes 'out of bounds' for a short period this month, from the 1st to the 6th. This shows that you and family members are outside your usual orbit.

Venus starts one of her rare retrograde moves on the 23rd. Thus, children and children figures in your life lack direction. They need to attain clarity on their personal goals.

There is a happy a career experience on the 19th and 20th. Be more mindful on the physical plane on the 22nd and 23rd.

August

Best Days Overall: 1, 2, 10, 11, 19, 20, 21, 29
Most Stressful Days Overall: 3, 4, 17, 18, 24, 25, 30, 31
Best Days for Love: 5, 6, 7, 8, 14, 15, 17, 18, 24, 25, 26, 27
Best Days for Money: 5, 6, 7, 8, 12, 13, 15, 16, 17, 18, 26, 27
Best Days for Career: 3, 4, 13, 23, 30, 31

Your 3rd house of communication and intellectual interests is still very powerful, making this a happy month. The cosmos urges you to do what you most love doing and what you're good at. You inhale information these days. It's like breathing. You're a fount of knowledge, even trivia.

On the 23rd, as the Sun enters your 4th house, health needs more attention. Make sure to rest more. Enhance the health in the ways mentioned in the yearly report.

This month, with your 4th house very strong, you face the classic conflict between home and career. You want a successful career *and* a successful domestic life, but it's not so easy to achieve both. I would say, though, that the career is more likely to win out.

However, since you're in the night-time – the midnight hour – of your year, you can work on your career by the methods of night: through meditation, visualization and entering the mood-feeling of where you want to be career-wise. Overt actions can be taken later. It's the inner work that seems more important now.

As you do this meditative work, old memories will surface and will indicate the obstructions hampering your career path. Looking at these memories without judgement will help you surmount them. Overall, you're in a more nostalgic kind of period. You're interested in your own past, and in history in general.

Finances tend to the status quo this month. Your money house is empty, with only the Moon moving through there on the 12th and 13th. This means that you're basically satisfied with the way things are and have no need to make major changes or pay undue attention.

The love life improves this month – especially after the 23rd. Your social grace is much stronger. The problem in love is you – you're not sure what you want: Mercury starts to go backwards on the 23rd.

Retrograde activity among the planets increases this month, bit by bit. Until the 23rd 40 per cent of the planets are retrograde. From the 25th to the 29th half are travelling backwards, and on the 29th the percentage rises to 60 per cent – the maximum for the year. The pace of life slows down.

September

Best Days Overall: 6, 7, 16, 17, 25, 26
Most Stressful Days Overall: 13, 14, 15, 21, 22, 27, 28
Best Days for Love: 2, 3, 4, 5, 11, 12, 14, 15, 21, 22, 23, 24, 30
Best Days for Money: 4, 5, 8, 9, 10, 13, 14, 15, 23, 24, 25
Best Days for Career: 1, 9, 10, 19, 27, 28

Like last month, the challenge is to balance the home and career. Both are important. Career seems more important, but you can't ignore the home, family and your emotional wellness. If you work on your career by the methods of night, it might be easier to balance things. Overt actions are not that important. Work on your career with your mind and feelings. Enter the mood of where you want to be. Visualize your goals. (It's good to do this before you go to sleep.) Overt action will happen later.

Keep in mind that a happy and harmonious family and domestic life – and harmonious feelings – are the foundation of career success. It is time to shore up your foundations.

The New Moon of the 15th occurs in your 4th house. It is a good financial day and shows good family support (it works both ways). More importantly, it will clarify family and emotional issues as the weeks progress. All the information you need to make the right decisions will come to you in a very natural way. The New Moon is basically a happy day, but this is not your best health day. Try to rest and relax more on the 15th.

Health still needs watching until the 23rd. So, make sure you get enough rest. High energy levels are the first defence against disease. If you can't run or jog your usual number of miles, it's no big deal. Respect the limits of the body. Energy will return after the 23rd.

We are still in the peak of retrograde activity, at least until the 16th; 60 per cent of the planets are retrograde. But retrograde activity is still strong after that date too, so patience is needed. On the 23rd the Sun enters your 5th house and you begin a yearly personal pleasure peak. With so many planets retrograde you may as well enjoy yourself as nothing much is happening in the world. Many Geminis are writers. This period, from the 23rd onwards, is excellent for creative kinds of writing.

Your financial planet, the Moon, never goes retrograde. So your finances continue to move forward. It is still a status quo kind of financial month, but earnings should be stronger from the 15th to the 28th – the waxing Moon phase.

October

Best Days Overall: 3, 4, 22, 23
Most Stressful Days Overall: 11, 12, 18, 19, 24, 25
Best Days for Love: 1, 2, 9, 10, 11, 12, 18, 19, 20, 21, 28, 29
Best Days for Money: 1, 2, 3, 4, 6, 7, 11, 12, 20, 21, 24
Best Days for Career: 7, 17, 24, 25

Health is much improved this month and you're still in the midst of a yearly personal pleasure peak. It should be a fun kind of month, but two eclipses will add some spice and challenge.

The two eclipses are the real headlines of the month. There is a solar eclipse on the 14th and a lunar eclipse on the 28th. Happily, both these eclipses are relatively mild in their effects on you, but it won't hurt to reduce your schedule anyway. (If either of the eclipses hits a sensitive point in your personal Horoscope – the one cast specifically for you – its effect can be strong indeed.)

The solar eclipse of the 14th occurs in your 5th house of children. So, children and children figures in your life are impacted. They should be kept out of harm's way over this period. They are having personal dramas. Some of these things can be normal – puberty, changing schools, going off to college, marriage, etc. – nevertheless it is disruptive. A parent or parent figure has some financial dramas and needs to make changes. Those of you in the creative arts are changing your creativity – taking a new approach. Cars and communication equipment can behave erratically and often repairs or replacements are necessary. Siblings, sibling figures and neighbours have personal dramas as well – often these are life-changing. It will be a good idea to drive more carefully over this time.

The lunar eclipse of the 28th occurs in your 12th house of spirituality. Thus, there are important changes happening here. Often one changes the spiritual practice and the teachings, sometimes the teacher. The whole approach to your spiritual life is altered. There are disruptions in charitable or spiritual organizations you're involved with. Guru figures have personal dramas. Since the Moon is your financial planet, you need to make course corrections in your financial thinking and planning. Friends are also making important financial changes.

Pluto, your health planet, starts to move forward on the 11th, so it is now safer to undertake medical tests or procedures; the results will be more reliable.

November

Best Days Overall: 1, 9, 10, 11, 18, 19, 27, 28
Most Stressful Days Overall: 7, 8, 14, 15, 21, 22
Best Days for Love: 7, 8, 9, 14, 15, 16, 18, 19, 25, 27, 28
Best Days for Money: 2, 3, 7, 12, 13, 16, 23, 25, 29, 30
Best Days for Career: 3, 13, 21, 22, 30

The Western, social sector of your chart is now as strong as it will ever be this year. It's not very dominant (except from the 8th to the 19th) but it is at its maximum for the year. So, this is a period for putting others first (and you are trying) and for attaining your goals through consensus rather than pure self-will. Charm, grace and social skills are more important than personal initiative and personal abilities at the moment. Let others have their way – so long as it isn't destructive – and your own good will come to you normally and naturally.

Love is complicated this month. On the one hand, you begin a yearly love and social peak on the 22nd. Your 7th house of love is very strong. On the other hand, your love planet, Jupiter, is moving backwards. So, there are romantic opportunities for singles – there is more dating and party going – but there are glitches and delays involved with love. Your social judgement is not up to its usual standards. Enjoy the opportunities that come, but don't rush anything.

Health becomes more problematic after the 23rd, too. As always, don't allow yourself to get overtired. Maintain high energy levels. Continue to enhance the health in the ways mentioned in the yearly report.

Until the 23rd your 6th house of health and work is strong. Thus, job opportunities happen for those who are looking for work. Those of you who employ others have good applicants.

Finances should be good this month. The Moon, your financial planet, will visit your money house twice this month – usually she only visits once. So there is an extra financial bounce. Finances go best from the 12th to the 27th as the Moon waxes. While the Moon waxes, spare cash should be used for savings and/or investments – things that you want to grow larger. From the 1st to the 12th and from the 28th to the 30th, as the Moon wanes, use any spare cash to pay off debts – things that you want to grow smaller.

Mercury, the ruler of your Horoscope, is 'out of bounds' from the 16th onwards. This signals that you're personally outside your natural orbit – especially in love matters. Family members also seem outside their usual orbit.

December

> Best Days Overall: 7, 8, 16, 17, 24, 25
> Most Stressful Days Overall: 4, 5, 6, 11, 12, 18, 19, 31
> Best Days for Love: 4, 9, 11, 12, 14, 18, 19, 22, 28, 30, 31
> Best Days for Money: 2, 3, 4, 11, 12, 14, 21, 22, 27, 28, 29, 31
> Best Days for Career: 10, 18, 19, 28

Mercury remains 'out of bounds' until the 14th. So, you and family members are still outside your normal orbits. You're pushing the boundaries of your orbit. Expanding them.

Health still needs keeping an eye on this month, but it will improve after the 22nd. Review our discussion of this last month.

Career is becoming more active and there are important changes happening. The two planets involved in your career – Saturn and Neptune – are starting to move forward. Saturn moved forward on November 4 and Neptune, your career planet, moves forward on the 6th. At last, career delays and log jams are resolving themselves. In addition, the planetary power is now in the upper half of your Horoscope – *all* the planets will be there from the 30th (only the Moon will be in the night side). It is time to start focusing on the career again. It's a successful year – but you're earning it.

Love is straightening out as well. You're still in a yearly love and social peak, until the 22nd, and your love planet Jupiter will start moving forward on the 31st. Love is still complicated, but it is on the verge of straightening out. Part of the problem is that both you and the beloved are not sure about things (Mercury is retrograde from the 13th onwards). But given time this will clarify itself into the New Year. The New Moon of the 12th occurs in your 7th house and this will further clarify the love situation as the weeks progress.

Finances are stable this month. Your money house is basically empty, with only the Moon moving through there on the 27th and 28th. The Full Moon of the 27th occurs in your money house and this should be an excellent day for finance. Mercury makes nice aspects to Jupiter on the 6th, 7th, 17th and 18th – these are excellent days for love and money (keep in mind the love complications we discussed above, though).

The Sun's move into your 8th house of regeneration on the 22nd improves the finances of the spouse, partner or current love. It is a good transit for weight loss and detox regimes. Good for getting rid of the extraneous in your life.

Cancer

THE CRAB

Birthdays from
21st June to
20th July

Personality Profile

CANCER AT A GLANCE

Element – Water

Ruling Planet – Moon
   Career Planet – Mars
   Love Planet – Saturn
   Money Planet – Sun
   Planet of Fun and Games – Pluto
   Planet of Good Fortune – Neptune
   Planet of Health and Work – Jupiter
   Planet of Home and Family Life – Venus
   Planet of Spirituality – Mercury

Colours – blue, puce, silver

Colours that promote love, romance and social harmony – black, indigo

Colours that promote earning power – gold, orange

Gems – moonstone, pearl

Metal – silver

Scents – jasmine, sandalwood

Quality – cardinal (= activity)

Quality most needed for balance – mood control

Strongest virtues – emotional sensitivity, tenacity, the urge to nurture

Deepest need – a harmonious home and family life

Characteristics to avoid – over-sensitivity, negative moods

Signs of greatest overall compatibility – Scorpio, Pisces

Signs of greatest overall incompatibility – Aries, Libra, Capricorn

Sign most helpful to career – Aries

Sign most helpful for emotional support – Libra

Sign most helpful financially – Leo

Sign best for marriage and/or partnerships – Capricorn

Sign most helpful for creative projects – Scorpio

Best Sign to have fun with – Scorpio

Signs most helpful in spiritual matters – Gemini, Pisces

Best day of the week – Monday

Understanding a Cancer

In the sign of Cancer the heavens are developing the feeling side of things. This is what a true Cancerian is all about – feelings. Where Aries will tend to err on the side of action, Taurus on the side of inaction and Gemini on the side of thought, Cancer will tend to err on the side of feeling.

Cancerians tend to mistrust logic. Perhaps rightfully so. For them it is not enough for an argument or a project to be logical – it must feel right as well. If it does not feel right a Cancerian will reject it or chafe against it. The phrase 'follow your heart' could have been coined by a Cancerian, because it describes exactly the Cancerian attitude to life.

The power to feel is a more direct – more immediate – method of knowing than thinking is. Thinking is indirect. Thinking about a thing never touches the thing itself. Feeling is a faculty that touches directly the thing or issue in question. We actually experience it. Emotional feeling is almost like another sense which humans possess – a psychic sense. Since the realities that we come in contact with during our lifetime are often painful and even destructive, it is not surprising that the Cancerian chooses to erect barriers – a shell – to protect his or her vulnerable, sensitive nature. To a Cancerian this is only common sense.

If Cancerians are in the presence of people they do not know, or find themselves in a hostile environment, up goes the shell and they feel protected. Other people often complain about this, but one must question these people's motives. Why does this shell disturb them? Is it perhaps because they would like to sting, and feel frustrated that they cannot? If your intentions are honourable and you are patient, have no fear. The shell will open up and you will be accepted as part of the Cancerian's circle of family and friends.

Thought-processes are generally analytic and dissociating. In order to think clearly we must make distinctions, comparisons and the like. But feeling is unifying and integrative.

To think clearly about something you have to distance yourself from it. To feel something you must get close to it. Once a Cancerian has accepted you as a friend he or she will hang on to you. You have to be really bad to lose the friendship of a Cancerian. If you are related to Cancerians they will never let you go no matter what you do. They will always try to maintain some kind of connection even in the most extreme circumstances.

Finance

The Cancer-born has a deep sense of what other people feel about things and why they feel as they do. This faculty is a great asset in the workplace and in the business world. Of course it is also indispensable in raising a family and building a home, but it has its uses in business. Cancerians often attain great wealth in a family business. Even if the business is not a family operation, they will treat it as one. If the Cancerian works for somebody else, then the boss is the parental figure and the co-workers are brothers and sisters. If a Cancerian is the boss, then all the workers are his or her children. Cancerians like the feeling of being providers for others. They enjoy knowing that others derive their sustenance because of what they do. It is another form of nurturing.

With Leo on their solar 2nd money house cusp, Cancerians are often lucky speculators, especially with residential property or hotels and restaurants. Resort hotels and nightclubs are also profitable for the Cancerian. Waterside properties attract them. Though they are basically conventional people, they sometimes like to earn their livelihood in glamorous ways.

The Sun, Cancer's money planet, represents an important financial message: in financial matters Cancerians need to be less moody, more stable and fixed. They cannot allow their moods – which are here today and gone tomorrow – to get in the way of their business lives. They need to develop their self-esteem and feelings of self-worth if they are to realize their greatest financial potential.

Career and Public Image

Aries rules the 10th solar career house cusp of Cancer, which indicates that Cancerians long to start their own business, to be more active publicly and politically and to be more independent. Family responsibilities and a fear of hurting other people's feelings – or getting hurt themselves – often inhibit them from attaining these goals. However, this is what they want and long to do.

Cancerians like their bosses and leaders to act freely and to be a bit self-willed. They can deal with that in a superior. They expect their leaders to be fierce on their behalf. When the Cancerian is in the position of boss or superior he or she behaves very much like a 'warlord'. Of course the wars they wage are not egocentric but in defence of those under their care. If they lack some of this fighting instinct – independence and pioneering spirit – Cancerians will have extreme difficulty in attaining their highest career goals. They will be hampered in their attempts to lead others.

Since they are so parental, Cancerians like to work with children and make great educators and teachers.

Love and Relationships

Like Taurus, Cancer likes committed relationships. Cancerians function best when the relationship is clearly defined and everyone knows his or her role. When they marry it is usually for life. They are extremely loyal to their beloved. But there is a deep little secret that most Cancerians will never admit to: commitment or partnership is really a chore and a duty to them. They enter into it because they know of no other way to create the family that they desire. Union is just a way – a means to an end – rather than an end in itself. The family is the ultimate end for them.

If you are in love with a Cancerian you must tread lightly on his or her feelings. It will take you a good deal of time to realize how deep and sensitive Cancerians can be. The smallest negativity upsets them. Your tone of voice, your irritation, a look in your eye or an expression on your face can cause great distress for the Cancerian. Your slightest gesture is registered by them and reacted to. This can be hard to get used to, but stick by your love – Cancerians make great partners once you learn how to deal with them. Your Cancerian lover will react not so much to what you say but to the way you are actually feeling at the moment.

Home and Domestic Life

This is where Cancerians really excel. The home environment and the family are their personal works of art. They strive to make things of beauty that will outlast them. Very often they succeed.

Cancerians feel very close to their family, their relatives and especially their mothers. These bonds last throughout their lives and mature as they grow older. They are very fond of those members of their family who become successful, and they are also quite attached to family heirlooms and mementos. Cancerians also love children and like to provide them with all the things they need and want. With their nurturing, feeling nature, Cancerians make very good parents – especially the Cancerian woman, who is the mother *par excellence* of the zodiac.

As a parent the Cancerian's attitude is 'my children right or wrong'. Unconditional devotion is the order of the day. No matter what a family member does, the Cancerian will eventually forgive him or her, because 'you are, after all, family'. The preservation of the institution – the tradition – of the family is one of the Cancerian's main reasons for living. They have many lessons to teach others about this.

Being so family-orientated, the Cancerian's home is always clean, orderly and comfortable. They like old-fashioned furnishings but they also like to have all the modern comforts. Cancerians love to have family and friends over, to organize parties and to entertain at home – they make great hosts.

Horoscope for 2023

Major Trends

For many years now (over twenty years in fact) the love and social life has been very stormy. Probably there have been divorces, break-ups and friendships that have ended. You've been in the process of giving birth to the love and social life of your dreams. This hasn't been pleasant, but the result will be good. And you're almost finished now. The two planets involved in your love and social life are changing signs this year. Pluto will move briefly into Aquarius from March 24 to June 12. He basically hovers between your 7th and 8th houses this year (and this will be the case next year too). More importantly, your actual love planet, Saturn, changes signs on March 8. He moves into your 9th house on that date and will stay there for the next two and a half years. This too improves the love life (and your overall health as well). More on this later.

Jupiter spends almost half the year – until May 17 – in your 10th house of career. This shows that, like last year, there is great success happening in your career. More details later.

Uranus has been in your 11th house for many years now and he will be there for some more years to come. Thus, your circle of friends is undergoing much change. Some friendships have been terminated. Some of this is not because of you but because of dramas in your erstwhile friends' personal lives. This trend continues in the year ahead. But this year Jupiter will move through this house – from May 17 onwards – so new friends are coming into the picture to supplant some of the ones that have been lost. These are significant kinds of friendships.

The year ahead should be prosperous, too, Cancer. Venus, your family planet, will spend a lot of time in your 2nd money house – over four months. Thus, earnings should be stronger than usual. More on this later.

Your major interests in the coming year are love and romance (from January 1 to March 24 and from June 12 onwards); sex, personal transformation and reinvention, and occult studies (from January 1 to March 8 and from March 24 to June 12); religion, theology, higher education and foreign travel; career (until May 17); and friends, groups and group activities, astrology, astronomy and science.

Your paths of greatest fulfilment will be career (until May 17 and from July 18 onwards); and friends, groups, group activities, astrology, astronomy and science.

Health

(Please note that this is an astrological perspective on health and not a medical one. In days of yore there was no difference, both these perspectives were identical. But these days there could be quite a difference. For a medical perspective, please consult your doctor or health practitioner.)

Health is good this year. Only two long-term planets are in stressful aspect with you – and those only part of the time. When Jupiter leaves Aries on May 17, health and energy will improve even further.

Good though your health is generally, there will be periods where it is less easy than usual – perhaps even stressful. However, this is not a trend for the year. These periods are caused by the short-term stresses of the short-term planets. When they pass, your normally good health and energy return.

Good though your health is, you can make it even better. Give more attention to the following – the vulnerable areas of your Horoscope this year (the reflex points are shown in the chart opposite):

- The stomach and breasts are always important areas for you, Cancer. As our regular readers know by now, what you eat is important – and should be checked with a professional. But *how* you eat is just as important. The act of eating needs to be elevated from mere animal appetite to an act of worship. The energy vibrations of the act need to be raised, so make a ritual out of the act. Say grace (in your own words) before and after meals. Bless your food (in your own words). Have nice soothing music playing as you eat. This will not only raise the energy vibrations of the food, but also of your digestive system. You will get the highest and best from the food and it will digest better. Women should have regular breast scans.
- The liver and thighs are also always important for you as Jupiter, which rules these areas, is your health planet. The liver reflex point is shown in the chart above, while regular thigh massage will not only strengthen the thighs and liver but the lower abdomen and lower back as well.
- The head and face are important until May 17. Regular scalp and face massage will not only strengthen these particular areas (the plates in the skull need to be in right alignment) but the whole body as well. Craniosacral therapy is also very good for this.
- The musculature in general (again, until May 17). You don't need to be a bodybuilder, just to have good muscle tone. Weak or flabby muscles can knock the spine and bones out of alignment, causing

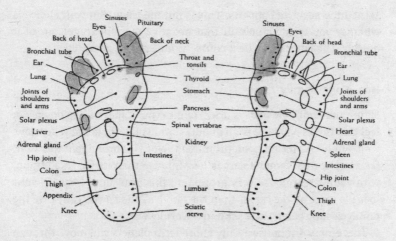

Important foot reflexology points for the year ahead

Try to massage all of the foot on a regular basis – the top of the foot as well as the bottom – but pay extra attention to the points highlighted on the chart. When you massage, be aware of 'sore spots' as these need special attention. It's also a good idea to massage the ankles and below them.

all kinds of other problems. So, regular physical exercise is important – each according to their age and stage in life. A visit to the gym could do you as much good as a visit to a doctor (in many cases).

- The adrenals are also important to you in the first half of the year, until May 17 (the reflex points are illustrated above). The important thing with the adrenals is to avoid anger and fear, the two emotions that stress them out. Meditation will be a big help here.

- The neck and throat become important after May 17, as your health planet moves into Taurus. Regular neck massage will be wonderfully good. Tension tends to collect there and needs to be released. Craniosacral therapy is good for this too.

In addition, good emotional health is always important for you. Avoid negative states of mind. Avoid depression like the plague. Meditation will be a big help for this. It is natural to react in a negative way when something negative happens. This is not the issue. But your choice is whether you want to stay in that negative state or to get out of it quickly. The latter is the best course from a health perspective.

Home and Family

Home and family are always important to you, Cancer. Deep down you feel that this is what life is all about – family. But for some years now, your 4th house hasn't been prominent. Nor is it prominent this year. So, your normal family focus is less intense than usual. In addition, with your career house very prominent this year (until May 17) your focus is more on the career than the family. You feel you can serve the family best by being successful in a worldly way.

This empty 4th house – only short-term planets will move through there this year, and then only briefly – can be read as a good thing. The family situation is more or less under control. You're basically satisfied with the status quo and have no need to pay special attention here. Thus, a move is not likely this year.

On October 14 there will be a solar eclipse in your 4th house. This will shake things up temporarily – we will cover this in the monthly report.

If you're planning major renovations or repairs around the home, August 28 to October 12 would be a good time. If you're redecorating in a cosmetic kind of way, November 8 to December 4 would be good. This period is also good for buying art objects or other objects of beauty for the home.

Your family planet, Venus, is a fast-moving planet. In any given year she moves through your entire Horoscope. Thus, there are many short-term trends in the home and family life that depend on where Venus is and the kinds of aspects she receives. These are best dealt with in the monthly reports.

A parent or parent figure is prospering this year and living the good life, but a move is not likely. He or she is travelling more this year. The other parent or parent figure is perhaps thinking of a move, but it probably won't happen this year. Siblings and sibling figures are having their relationships tested. Perhaps they are thinking of a move too, but it's unlikely to happen (there's nothing against it, however). Children and children figures in your life are more likely to move next year than this year. It can happen suddenly. The same is true for grandchildren or those who play that role in your life. A move is more likely next year than this.

Finance and Career

Though finances are good this year, 2023 is more of a career year than a financial one.

Venus, as we mentioned, will spend an unusual amount of time in your money house – from June 5 to October 9. This is quadruple the time of her usual transit in a sign, so it is significant. It indicates the financial support of friends, family and family connections. They can give actual material support or bring you financial opportunities. It also shows that you spend more on the home and family over that period. You could also earn money from the home, from residential real estate, online activities, the food and restaurant business, hotels, motels, and industries that cater to the homeowner.

The Sun is your financial planet. As our regular readers know, he is a fast-moving planet, moving through your entire Horoscope during the year. So, there are many short-term financial trends that depend on where the Sun is and the kinds of aspects he receives. These are best dealt with in the monthly reports.

Twice a year (usually) the Sun gets eclipsed. This year this happens on April 20 and on October 14. Though these things tend not to be pleasant, in your case they are good: twice a year you get a chance to make course corrections in your financial thinking and planning. The events of the eclipses will show what changes are necessary. We will cover this more fully in the monthly reports.

As we said above, the career is the main headline this year. Jupiter entered your 10th career house last year on May 11 and stayed there until October 28, five months approximately. Then he moved back into Pisces until December 21. So major career developments happened last year – which are continued this year.

There are promotions and career elevation happening. Both your professional and social status are elevated. In many cases there are honours and awards, recognition of your work and abilities. The career horizons are broadened. You see vistas and possibilities that were heretofore hidden.

With the Moon's North Node moving into your 10th house on July 18, there is much satisfaction in your career. It brings happiness.

Your career planet Mars is 'out of bounds' this year until May 4 (almost the whole of Jupiter's 2023 transit through your 10th house). This signals that in career matters you're outside your normal orbit. In fact, this contributes to your success. You're willing to think outside the box, to venture into the unknown, to take some risks.

Love and Social Life

As we have already mentioned, the love life is beginning to improve. It is becoming less stormy. You are, more or less, in the love and social life of your dreams – your personal ideal. But it didn't happen easily (it rarely does).

The main headline here is your love planet Saturn's move into Pisces on March 8. This changes the love attitudes and needs. For the past two years it was sexual magnetism that was the most important thing (especially for singles), but this changes after March 8. You see now that while sex is important, there is more to a relationship and to love than just that. Your love planet in Pisces makes you more idealistic about love. You search for the ultimate love – the ideal.

Spiritual and philosophical compatibility become important in a possible partner from March 8 onwards. Saturn in your 9th house shows someone who can fall in love with their minister, priest, rabbi, imam, or professor. You're attracted to people you can learn from – mentor types. So, love and social opportunities can happen at religious or university functions.

Sex can be great, but if philosophical compatibility is not there the relationship will not last. Philosophical compatibility doesn't mean that you agree on every point, but that you have the same view of life and the same values.

The love planet in Pisces introduces a spiritual element in love. You find spiritual-type people – gurus, psychics, tarot readers, spiritual channels, actors, musicians, poets – alluring. You'll be meeting these inspired kinds of people in the year ahead. Love and social opportunities will also happen in spiritual venues – at spiritual seminars or lectures, prayer meetings, meditation sessions and charitable functions.

In essence, you're interested in a deeper kind of love – carnal plus.

With Jupiter moving into your 11th house on May 17, the social life in general increases. However, this is not so much about romance but more about friendships and group activities. New and significant friends are coming into the picture this year, as was mentioned. You make friends at work, or as you involve yourself in professional or trade organizations related to your job.

Self-improvement

Love, as we've just said, is more spiritual and idealistic this year. You search for the 'perfect', 'ideal' love. There's nothing wrong with this, but you could be searching in the wrong places – outside yourself. Perfect love is rarely given to us on a platter. It is a journey that is travelled. It's something to strive for. Here on planet Earth, among humans, love is seldom perfect. Some humans can love more than others, but always there are limitations to it. This is the human condition. With your love planet in spiritual Pisces, you know what real love is, and everything else – even good relationships – inevitably falls short. So, there is a subtle feeling of dissatisfaction. However, if you continually improve your relationship, you're on the road to perfection though still far from the goal. The important thing is to keep improving it.

With the love planet in spiritual Pisces, you will receive guidance in love matters from the spirit – through dreams, intuition and the advice of psychics, tarot readers, astrologers and spiritual channels. You will find that spirit is very interested in your happiness in love and will be actively involved.

The position of Saturn in Pisces suggests a need to surrender the love life – or a given relationship – to the Divine and let it handle things. If this is done sincerely, you will see many problems straighten out. Try saying: 'I surrender the burden of this relationship (or you can name the person), and I go free in perfect love and romance.' Repeat this regularly until you feel a change in the energy.

Neptune has been in your 9th house for many years and will be there for many more to come. He is the most mystical of the planets. Thus, you've been exploring the mystical – supernatural – side of your native religion. Every religion has this mystical side to it. When you begin to understand this (and it's been happening) you will find that you need not depart your native religion. It has everything you need. It only needed to be understood better.

Mercury is your spiritual planet. He is, as our regular readers know, the fastest-moving (aside from the Moon) of all the planets. His movements also tend to be erratic. Sometimes he speeds through the heavens, sometimes he moves slowly. Three times a year (this year four times) he goes backwards. So, this reflects in your spiritual life. Sometimes progress is rapid, sometimes it is slow, sometimes you feel you're going backwards. Thus, there are many short-term trends in your spiritual life that depend on Mercury's position, his speed and the aspects he receives, which are best dealt with in the monthly reports.

Month-by-month Forecasts

January

Best Days Overall: 6, 7, 14, 15, 23, 24
Most Stressful Days Overall: 3, 4, 10, 11, 16, 17, 30, 31
Best Days for Love: 2, 3, 10, 11, 12, 13, 21, 22
Best Days for Money: 2, 8, 10, 11, 16, 20, 21, 23, 25, 26, 30, 31
Best Days for Career: 3, 4, 12, 13, 16, 17, 21, 22, 30, 31

Health is basically good – on an overall level – this year. But this month short-term planets are creating some stress. So, make sure to get enough rest. Enhance the health with exercise and face and scalp massage.

You begin your year in the midst of a yearly love and social peak, so the love life should be going well. Singles have many romantic opportunities with many kinds of people. Your problem can be too much of a good thing. Too many choices can be confusing – still, it is a good problem to have. The New Moon of the 11th occurs in your 7th house, making it an especially good love and social day. More importantly, the love situation will clarify dramatically as the weeks progress (until the next New Moon).

Finances will also be good this month. The Sun, your financial planet, will be in your 7th house until the 20th. Thus, your social contacts (and perhaps the current love) are important financially. On the 20th your financial planet enters your 8th house of regeneration, signalling a good time for a purge of your possessions and financial life. Good to get rid of possessions that you don't use or need. Sell them or give them to charity. Good to cut financial waste (not things that you need). This is a good period for tax and insurance planning. And, if you're of the appropriate age, for estate planning. These things go especially well on the 4th and 5th. The 17th and 18th are good for speculations – though these should be well hedged and calculated. A pay rise, official or unofficial, can happen on the 20th and/or 31st. The Full Moon of the 25th occurs in your money house and this will be another excellent financial day.

Career is super right now – red hot. All the planets are above the horizon (with the exception of the Moon, and that only from the 23rd to the 31st). Jupiter is in your 10th house – a classic signal of success. Career will grow even stronger in the coming months. Jupiter is having his solstice from the 1st to the 27th – he pauses in the heavens (in his latitudinal motion) and then changes direction. So it is with your career. There is a pause and a change of direction. Don't be alarmed by the pause, it will only make things better. The pause doesn't negate the success.

February

Best Days Overall: 2, 3, 12, 13, 20, 21
Most Stressful Days Overall: 9, 10, 16, 17, 22, 23
Best Days for Love: 1, 2, 3, 10, 12, 13, 16, 17, 19, 22, 28
Best Days for Money: 1, 4, 5, 6, 9, 10, 14, 15, 20, 22, 23
Best Days for Career: 1, 9, 10, 18, 19, 22, 23, 27, 28

Health is much improved this month. It is only those of you born late in the sign (July 21–23) that are feeling some stress from the short-term planets. Most of you are OK. Head, face and scalp massage,

massage of the adrenal reflexes and exercise will enhance the health. Health will improve even further after the 18th.

Career is still going great guns this month, and is headed in a new and positive direction. On the 21st Venus joins Jupiter in your 10th house, enhancing the career even further. Your career planet, Mars, spends the month in your spiritual 12th house. This suggests that being involved in charities and altruistic kinds of activity will further boost the career. You have a great work ethic and your superiors are impressed.

Your 8th house remains powerful until the 18th. This a good period for giving birth to the person you want to be – your ideal self. This will probably not happen in its fullness this month, but progress will be made and this is what counts. It is also a very erotic kind of month. Libido is high; regardless of your age or stage in life it is greater than usual.

Finances are good, but will become even better after the 18th. Until the 18th the focus is on prospering others – seeing to their financial best interest. As you do this your own prosperity will happen very naturally (you don't always see it right away but it's like putting money into your spiritual bank account – you can draw upon it when you need it).

On the 18th your financial planet moves into your 9th house – a wonderful financial transit! The 9th house is always beneficent, so earnings increase. Your financial intuition is good. The Full Moon of the 5th occurs in your 2nd money house and is another excellent financial day. There are some bumps on the road though. From the 3rd to the 5th there can be some sudden financial drama, and perhaps some disagreement with the beloved on finance. On the 15th and 16th there is some extra financial responsibility.

The New Moon of the 20th occurs in your 9th house and brings religious and philosophical insights. And, because it happens right on your love planet, Saturn, it is an excellent romantic day.

March

Best Days Overall: 1, 2, 11, 12, 19, 20, 28, 29, 30
Most Stressful Days Overall: 8, 9, 10, 15, 16, 21, 22
Best Days for Love: 4, 5, 11, 12, 15, 16, 19, 24, 25, 28
Best Days for Money: 1, 2, 4, 5, 12, 13, 14, 20, 21, 22, 31
Best Days for Career: 9, 10, 17, 18, 21, 22, 28

An eventful month both for you personally and in the world. Pluto makes a monumental but brief foray out of your 7th house and into your 8th on the 24th. He will hover between these two houses this year and the next. This means that much of the social and love stress you've been experiencing is being reduced. Along with this, Saturn, your actual love planet, moves into Pisces, your 9th house, on the 8th. Love is much happier now. You're more idealistic about it. You're searching for perfect love – ideal love. And it will happen – although perhaps not in ways that you expect – in the coming years.

Your 9th house is powerful all month, especially until the 20th, which means that this is a month for religious and philosophical studies. Many of you will be travelling to foreign lands – either physically or mentally (through education and reading). Finances are still good this month. The financial intuition is super now, especially on the 15th and 16th. (These look like nice paydays.)

On the 20th the Sun crosses your Mid-heaven and enters your 10th house of career. You begin a yearly career peak. A career crescendo. There could be promotions (they could have happened in the past few months as well), pay rises (official or unofficial) and perhaps honours and recognition from your peers. The New Moon of the 21st occurs in your 10th house and just increases the career success even more. This New Moon will have effects even after it actually happens, as it will clarify career issues until the next New Moon.

Health is excellent until the 20th but needs watching after then. The career demands are strong and this can tax your energy. So by all means focus on the career, but schedule in rest times too. Focus on the things that are really important and let lesser things go. Enhance the health in the ways mentioned in previous months. Perhaps it would be good to schedule more massages or to spend time at a health spa as well.

Mars, your career planet, moves into your own sign on the 26th. This also signals career success. You look and dress the part and people see you as successful. But avoid arguments and confrontations. You could be more combative than usual.

April

Best Days Overall: 7, 8, 16, 17, 25, 26
Most Stressful Days Overall: 5, 6, 12, 13, 18, 19
Best Days for Love: 3, 4, 7, 12, 13, 14, 16, 22, 23, 25
Best Days for Money: 1, 10, 27, 28, 29, 30
Best Days for Career: 7, 8, 16, 17, 18, 19, 25, 26

A solar eclipse on the 20th occurs right on the border between your 10th and 11th houses and is thus an influence on both. All of you will feel this eclipse to some degree, but those of you born late in the sign of Cancer – July 21–23 – will feel it most powerfully. If you're in this category, take it nice and easy over this period.

The eclipse brings career changes – probably good ones, but it will be disruptive. It can bring personal dramas in the lives of bosses, parents and parent figures. The government can change the rules for your industry. The rules of the game change and you need to change your approach. In rare cases people change their career path. The impact on your 11th house shows that friendships are affected. There will probably be life-changing events in the lives of friends. There are disruptions and shake-ups in professional or trade organizations you're involved with. Computer and high-tech gadgetry can develop glitches and play up, and sometimes repairs or replacements become necessary. Every solar eclipse affects your finances, because the Sun is your money planet, and this one is no different. A financial course correction is necessary. Your financial thinking and planning haven't been realistic – as the events of the eclipse will show – and so changes are necessary. You go through these course corrections twice a year usually, and by now you know how to handle these things. Parents or parent figures are also making financial changes.

This eclipse is a direct hit on Pluto. So, children and children figures in your life are affected. They should reduce their schedules and avoid risky activities. They are having personal dramas, although some of these things can be quite normal depending on their age. They can be having a sexual awakening, or going off to school, or getting their own place to live, etc. But still, it is disruptive. If the children or children figures are married or in a relationship, the relationship gets tested.

In spite of the eclipse, the career is still going well. Mars, your career planet, remains in your sign all month. So, the powers that be in your life seem devoted to you and on your side.

May

Best Days Overall: 13, 14, 22, 23
Most Stressful Days Overall: 2, 3, 5, 9, 10, 15, 16, 30, 31
Best Days for Love: 2, 3, 5, 9, 10, 13, 17, 18, 19, 22
Best Days for Money: 1, 8, 9, 10, 16, 17, 18, 19, 24, 25, 26, 30, 31
Best Days for Career: 14, 15, 16, 24, 25

There's a lot going on this month, Cancer. Jupiter will move into your 11th house on the 17th and stay there for the rest of the year ahead. Career goals have been more or less achieved and now the focus is on friends, groups and organizations – the social life.

A lunar eclipse on the 5th affects you strongly, so make sure you've a nice easy schedule over that period. The things that need to be done should be done, but electives are better off being rearranged. Every lunar eclipse is powerful on you because your sign is ruled by the Moon; you're particularly affected by her movement and aspects – and by her eclipses. So, once again (you have this twice a year) you're forced to redefine yourself – to refine and tweak how you think of yourself and how you want others to see you. So, in the coming months there will be a new you presented to the world – a new look, new kinds of accessories, hairstyles, etc. This is the natural consequence of this redefinition. Inner changes become outer changes by the spiritual law. Sometimes this kind of eclipse brings a detox – a purge of the body –

especially if you haven't been careful in dietary matters. Though the symptoms are real this is not really sickness. Just cleansing.

This eclipse occurs in your 5th house and children and children figures in your life are impacted again. There are more dramas in their lives. Again, keep them out of harm's way. Those of you involved in the creative arts will be making important changes to your creativity. Once again, a parent or parent figure is making important financial changes. Avoid speculations at this time, though you will be sorely tempted.

Uranus, the ruler of your 8th house of regeneration, gets sideswiped by this eclipse. Happily, it is not a direct hit, merely a glancing blow. There can be psychological encounters with death or kinds of near-death experiences. Most assuredly not an actual physical death, but there can be dreams of death or deaths happen among people you know – things of that nature.

On the 21st the Sun enters your 12th house of spirituality and you begin a strong spiritual period. With your financial planet in your spiritual house, financial intuition is spot on. You'll get financial guidance in dreams and through hunches, psychics, tarot readers, spiritual channels and ministers. The invisible universe, the Divine, is very interested in your prosperity.

June

Best Days Overall: 1, 2, 9, 10, 18, 19, 20, 28, 29
Most Stressful Days Overall: 5, 6, 11, 12, 26, 27
Best Days for Love: 1, 2, 5, 6, 9, 11, 18, 21, 22, 28
Best Days for Money: 5, 6, 7, 8, 14, 15, 17, 18, 21, 22, 23, 24, 28
Best Days for Career: 3, 4, 11, 12, 21, 22

Retrograde activity creeps up this month. We begin the month with only 10 per cent of the planets retrograde and will end it with 30 per cent of them travelling backwards. A reasonable amount.

The month ahead is happy. Health and energy are good. There is only one planet (Pluto) in stressful alignment with you and most of you won't feel it. (Only those born late in your sign – July 21–22 – will feel it strongly.) The rest of the planets are either in harmonious aspect or leaving you alone.

Finances will be good – but more so after the 21st than before. Until the 21st your financial planet is in your 12th house of spirituality. Thus, you're more generous and charitable. The financial intuition will be good. Financial guidance will come from the spirit world. This is a good period to work on the spiritual laws of affluence. On the 21st, though, the Sun moves into your own sign, which brings financial windfalls, opportunities and the image of wealth. You spend on yourself and dress like a prosperous person. Money chases you rather than the other way around. The money people in your life seem very devoted to you. Your career planet, Mars, will be in your money house all month. This indicates that bosses, parents, parent figures – the authority figures in your life – are supportive of your financial goals. Your good career reputation brings new financial opportunities.

Though your love planet Saturn is retrograde, love seems happy after the 21st. Singles need not rush into anything, but love is there.

This is also a month for spiritual insights and breakthroughs. Your 12th house is very strong until the 21st. The New Moon of the 18th also occurs in this house, bringing more spiritual insights – and increasing your already strong financial intuition. Spiritual issues will clarify as the weeks go by. Spiritual questions (and we all have them) get answered in natural and normal ways.

Drive more carefully on the 4th and 5th.

July

Best Days Overall: 7, 8, 16, 17, 26, 27
Most Stressful Days Overall: 3, 4, 9, 10, 23, 24, 30, 31
Best Days for Love: 2, 3, 4, 7, 10, 16, 19, 20, 26, 29, 30, 31
Best Days for Money: 3, 4, 7, 8, 11, 12, 17, 21, 22, 26, 30, 31
Best Days for Career: 2, 9, 10, 11, 21, 30, 31

A happy and prosperous month, Cancer. Enjoy. You've been in a yearly personal pleasure peak since June 21 and this goes on until the 23rd of this month. Health is good. The personal appearance shines and the opposite sex takes notice. You have a star quality about you. Like last month there are financial windfalls and opportunities that come to you. People see you as prosperous. The prosperity continues – and perhaps increases – from the 23rd onwards. Your financial planet, the Sun, enters the money house then – his own sign and house – and you begin a yearly financial peak. The focus is on finances, as it should be. The financial planet in his own sign and house – where he is powerful and comfortable – signals increased earning power. You could be more speculative than usual, and most likely these speculations will work out. But keep in mind that the cosmos has many ways to prosper you; it doesn't have to come from speculations.

Family and family support is strong this month. Family connections are important financially. However, Venus, your family planet, makes one of her rare, once-every-two-year retrogrades from the 23rd, so these opportunities need more study. Things are not as they seem.

Love still seems happy this month, but the beloved seems to lack direction and isn't sure of what he or she wants. Your social judgement is not up to its usual standard – so go slow in love.

With your 1st house very powerful until the 23rd, and with the Eastern, independent sector of your chart very strong, you're in a period of maximum independence. Take responsibility for your own happiness. Make any changes that need to be made. The cosmos supports you. Later in the year, this will be more difficult to do.

With Venus retrograde from the 23rd, family issues need time to resolve. There are no 'quickie' solutions. Avoid major family decisions after this date.

Mars moves into your 3rd house of communication on the 11th. This can make siblings and sibling figures in your life more argumentative and belligerent. Be patient with them. And try not to speed when you drive.

August

Best Days Overall: 3, 4, 12, 13, 22, 23, 30, 31
Most Stressful Days Overall: 5, 6, 19, 20, 21, 26, 27
Best Days for Love: 3, 5, 6, 12, 14, 15, 22, 24, 25, 26, 27, 30
Best Days for Money: 5, 6, 7, 8, 14, 15, 16, 17, 18, 26, 27
Best Days for Career: 5, 6, 7, 8, 17, 18, 27, 28

Retrograde activity is strong all month, and on the 29th it reaches its maximum extent for the year with 60 per cent of the planets travelling backwards. Events in your life and in the world at large are slowed down. Nothing much seems to be happening. (Behind the scenes, though, there is much going on.) The good news is that finances don't seem affected. Your financial planet, the Sun, moves through the heavens at his normal pace, and you remain in a yearly financial peak until the 23rd. The New Moon of the 16th occurs in your money house and it is an excellent financial day. More importantly, it will have an effect for the next few weeks (until the next New Moon). Financial issues will be clarified. All the information that you need to make a good decision will come to you. Your questions will be answered – normally and naturally.

Your career planet, Mars, has been in your 3rd house since July 11, and he will remain there almost all this month too, until the 28th. This indicates that career is enhanced through good communication, good sales, marketing and PR. Your knowledge and intellectual keenness enhance the career. Neighbours, siblings and sibling figures can help you career-wise too.

Your 3rd house becomes a house of power after the 23rd when your financial planet moves in there. So, you can earn through good sales, marketing, advertising and PR. Good use of the media is important in finances. Whatever you're doing, good sales and marketing are important. People have to know about your product or service. This is also an excellent month for students as the mind is sharp and the intellectual faculties are enhanced. Students seem very serious about their studies – it is their mission in life at this time – and this tends to success.

Health is still excellent. If you want to enhance it further do more neck massage.

Mars, your career planet, has his solstice from the 27th to the 2nd of next month. He pauses in the heavens – in his latitudinal motion – and then changes direction. So it is with your career. A pause and then a change of direction.

September

Best Days Overall: 8, 9, 10, 18, 19, 27, 28
Most Stressful Days Overall: 2, 3, 16, 17, 23, 24, 29, 30
Best Days for Love: 2, 3, 8, 11, 12, 18, 21, 22, 23, 24, 27, 30
Best Days for Money: 4, 5, 11, 12, 13, 14, 15, 23, 24, 25
Best Days for Career: 2, 3, 6, 16, 17, 25, 26, 29, 30

Planetary retrograde activity is still at its maximum extent for the year – an astounding 60 per cent retrograde – until the 16th. (After which, 50 per cent of the planets will be retrograde, still a very high number.) So, just relax and do what is possible. Time and time alone will unblock things. The good news is that Venus, your family planet, starts to move forward on the 4th and family issues become clearer. It is safe now to make important family decisions. A financial opportunity from a family member or family connection moves forward on the 4th.

Health is still excellent, but needs some attention paid to it after the 23rd. There is nothing serious afoot, just short-term stress caused by the short-term planets. Jupiter, your health planet, goes retrograde on the 4th so it's not advisable to rely on medical tests or to book procedures now (and for the next few months). This is especially so if they are elective tests or procedures. If they can't be put off, and the results are not to your liking, make sure to get a second, even a third opinion. When the health planet is retrograde the results are more likely to be flawed.

Your 3rd house is still very strong this month. So many of the trends we discussed last month are still in effect, at least until the 23rd. This is an excellent time for reading, studying or teaching. Gaining knowledge will help your bottom line. Students seem successful in school. Money can be earned through trading – buying and selling – and, as we mentioned last month, through good sales, marketing, advertising and PR. The New Moon of the 15th is a great financial day, and it occurs in your 3rd house. This will bring clarity to educational issues and issues involving neighbours, siblings and sibling figures over the next few weeks.

On the 23rd your financial planet moves into your 4th house of home and family. So, you spend more on these things (you're in a good period for doing renovations and repairs to the home) but you can also earn from the family or from family connections. This is a great transit for those of you who are builders, contractors, or who deal with real estate.

October

Best Days Overall: 6, 7, 15, 16, 17, 24, 25
Most Stressful Days Overall: 13, 14, 20, 21, 26, 27
Best Days for Love: 6, 9, 10, 11, 15, 20, 21, 24, 28, 29
Best Days for Money: 1, 2, 3, 4, 9, 11, 12, 20, 21, 24, 28, 29
Best Days for Career: 3, 4, 15, 24, 25, 26, 27

Two powerful eclipses dominate the month ahead. The first is a solar eclipse on the 14th and the second is a lunar eclipse on the 28th. Both have a strong effect on you. You should be reducing your schedule anyway until the 23rd, but especially during these eclipse periods.

The solar eclipse of the 14th occurs in your 4th house of home and family, bringing family dramas, disturbances and perhaps some upheavals. Repairs could be needed in the home. Passions in the family run high. The dream life is probably active and unpleasant, although you shouldn't put too much stock in these dreams: it's just psychic debris stirred up by the eclipse. Every solar eclipse forces financial changes on you, as we've mentioned, and this one is no different. It is time for a course correction in your financial life. You will see where your assumptions and planning have been unrealistic. This is something you go through twice a year (usually) and you know how to handle it. Siblings and sibling figures have to make financial changes too. They are undergoing spiritual changes as well – dramatic changes.

The lunar eclipse of the 28th occurs in your 11th house and tests friendships. Often there are dramas in the lives of friends, and this is the cause of the testing. Computer and high-tech equipment can

behave erratically and sometimes repairs or replacements are necessary. Make sure your anti-virus, anti-hacking software is up to date,
and that important files are backed up. Avoid opening emails from
people you don't know – and even if you know the people, be careful of
following their links.

Every lunar eclipse affects you powerfully, regardless of where it
occurs. The Moon, the eclipsed planet, is the ruler of your Horoscope
and you're especially sensitive to all lunar phenomena, not just
eclipses. So once again (you went through this on May 5) you need to
redefine yourself – the way that you think of yourself and the way you
want other people to think of you. This is a healthy thing. We're always
growing and evolving, and our self-concept should reflect this. So, in
the coming months you'll change your mode of dress, hairstyle and
overall presentation to the world.

November

Best Days Overall: 2, 3, 12, 13, 21, 22, 29, 30
Most Stressful Days Overall: 9, 10, 11, 16, 17, 23, 24
Best Days for Love: 2, 8, 9, 12, 16, 17, 18, 19, 27, 28, 29
Best Days for Money: 2, 3, 4, 5, 6, 7, 12, 13, 16, 23, 25
Best Days for Career: 2, 3, 12, 13, 22, 23, 24

Health is much improved this month. Last month on the 23rd you
began a yearly personal pleasure peak, which goes on until the 22nd of
this month. It's time to enjoy life – to do things that bring joy and happiness. Very often problems are solved by merely not thinking about them
and doing something enjoyable instead. When you focus on the problem again, often you find that there are all kinds of solutions available.
Having fun and indulging in leisure activities helps the bottom line as
well. You're in a period for happy money – money that is earned in
happy ways and spent on happy things. On the 22nd, as the financial
planet moves into Sagittarius, your 6th house, money is earned the
old-fashioned way again, through work and productive service. Still, the
financial planet in Sagittarius tends to increased income.

The New Moon of the 12th occurs in your 5th house. This is another
good financial day – and brings luck in speculations. It is a fun kind of

day. Issues involving your personal creativity and children will clarify themselves in the coming weeks (until the next New Moon). The cosmos is going to answer your questions in normal and natural ways.

The power in your 6th house from the 22nd onwards is wonderful for job-seekers. There are many good job opportunities coming to you. Even if you're employed, there are opportunities for overtime or second jobs.

A powerful 6th house shows a focus on health as well, although keep in mind that your health planet Jupiter is still retrograde; dramatic changes to your health regime need more study and research.

Mercury goes 'out of bounds' from the 16th onwards. Thus, in your spiritual life and in your tastes in reading, you're outside your usual orbit. You seem to be exploring this period.

Venus, now moving forward, enters your 4th house of home and family on the 8th. This is an excellent transit for bringing harmony to the family circle and for redecorating or buying objects of beauty for the home.

December

Best Days Overall: 9, 10, 18, 19, 27, 28
Most Stressful Days Overall: 7, 8, 14, 15, 20, 21
Best Days for Love: 9, 14, 15, 18, 19, 26, 27, 28, 30
Best Days for Money: 2, 3, 4, 11, 12, 14, 21, 22, 29, 30, 31
Best Days for Career: 2, 3, 11, 12, 20, 21, 29, 30

The planetary power is now mostly in the Western, social sector of your Horoscope – the sector of others. On the 22nd it will be at almost its maximum Western position for the year (only January was stronger). So, the focus is on others and the cultivation of your social graces. Personal initiative, though important, takes a back seat to social skills. Your good comes through others, and your likeability is very important. So let others have their way, so long as it isn't destructive.

The love life is much improved these days. Saturn, your love planet, went forward last month on the 4th and is forward the entire month ahead. On the 22nd, you begin a yearly love and social peak. There is more clarity in love now. We get a sense that it is moving forward.

Progress is happening. Singles can find romance on a foreign trip or with foreigners in general. There are romantic opportunities at college and college functions and at your place of worship or religious functions. Philosophical compatibility in a partner is important this month, and next year as well.

Mars, your career planet, has been 'out of bounds' for a long time this past year. He was 'out of bounds' from the beginning of the year until early May, and this month he goes 'out of bounds' again from the 22nd to the end of the year. So, the pursuit of career success requires you to go outside your normal orbit again this month. This aspect can also show that a parent or parent figure in your life is also outside of his or her natural orbit.

Mercury remains 'out of bounds' until the 14th. Refer to our discussion of this last month.

Health is good this month and you're very focused on it. The New Moon of the 12th occurs in your 6th house, making this an especially good health and financial day. It is fortunate both for job-seekers and those who employ others. More importantly, your health and job situation will become clear as the weeks progress. Doubts will be resolved and questions answered. Your health planet Jupiter will start to move forward on the 31st and this too will bring more clarity to these areas.

Health needs some attention after the 22nd, although it seems to be nothing serious. Just the usual short-term stresses caused by short-term planets. Make sure to get enough rest though.

Leo

♌

THE LION

Birthdays from
21st July to
21st August

Personality Profile

LEO AT A GLANCE

Element – Fire

Ruling Planet – Sun
  Career Planet – Venus
  Love Planet – Uranus
  Money Planet – Mercury
  Planet of Health and Work – Saturn
  Planet of Home and Family Life – Pluto

Colours – gold, orange, red

Colours that promote love, romance and social harmony – black, indigo, ultramarine blue

Colours that promote earning power – yellow, yellow-orange

Gems – amber, chrysolite, yellow diamond

Metal – gold

Scents – bergamot, frankincense, musk, neroli

Quality – fixed (= stability)

Quality most needed for balance – humility

Strongest virtues – leadership ability, self-esteem and confidence, generosity, creativity, love of joy

Deepest needs – fun, elation, the need to shine

Characteristics to avoid – arrogance, vanity, bossiness

Signs of greatest overall compatibility – Aries, Sagittarius

Signs of greatest overall incompatibility – Taurus, Scorpio, Aquarius

Sign most helpful to career – Taurus

Sign most helpful for emotional support – Scorpio

Sign most helpful financially – Virgo

Sign best for marriage and/or partnerships – Aquarius

Sign most helpful for creative projects – Sagittarius

Best Sign to have fun with – Sagittarius

Signs most helpful in spiritual matters – Aries, Cancer

Best day of the week – Sunday

Understanding a Leo

When you think of Leo, think of royalty – then you'll get the idea of what the Leo character is all about and why Leos are the way they are. It is true that, for various reasons, some Leo-born do not always express this quality – but even if not they should like to do so.

A monarch rules not by example (as does Aries) nor by consensus (as do Capricorn and Aquarius) but by personal will. Will is law. Personal taste becomes the style that is imitated by all subjects. A monarch is somehow larger than life. This is how a Leo desires to be.

When you dispute the personal will of a Leo it is serious business. He or she takes it as a personal affront, an insult. Leos will let you know that their will carries authority and that to disobey is demeaning and disrespectful.

A Leo is king (or queen) of his or her personal domain. Subordinates, friends and family are the loyal and trusted subjects. Leos rule with benevolent grace and in the best interests of others. They have a powerful presence; indeed, they are powerful people. They seem to attract attention in any social gathering. They stand out because they are stars in their domain. Leos feel that, like the Sun, they are made to shine and rule. Leos feel that they were born to special privilege and royal prerogatives – and most of them attain this status, at least to some degree.

The Sun is the ruler of this sign, and when you think of sunshine it is very difficult to feel unhealthy or depressed. Somehow the light of the Sun is the very antithesis of illness and apathy. Leos love life. They also love to have fun; they love drama, music, the theatre and amusements of all sorts. These are the things that give joy to life. If – even in their best interests – you try to deprive Leos of their pleasures, good food, drink and entertainment, you run the serious risk of depriving them of the will to live. To them life without joy is no life at all.

Leos epitomize humanity's will to power. But power in and of itself – regardless of what some people say – is neither good nor evil. Only when power is abused does it become evil. Without power even good things cannot come to pass. Leos realize this and are uniquely qualified to wield power. Of all the signs, they do it most naturally. Capricorn,

the other power sign of the zodiac, is a better manager and administrator than Leo – much better. But Leo outshines Capricorn in personal
grace and presence. Leo loves power, whereas Capricorn assumes
power out of a sense of duty.

Finance

Leos are great leaders but not necessarily good managers. They are
better at handling the overall picture than the nitty-gritty details of
business. If they have good managers working for them they can
become exceptional executives. They have vision and a lot of
creativity.

Leos love wealth for the pleasures it can bring. They love an opulent
lifestyle, pomp and glamour. Even when they are not wealthy they live
as if they are. This is why many fall into debt, from which it is sometimes difficult to emerge.

Leos, like Pisceans, are generous to a fault. Very often they want to
acquire wealth solely so that they can help others economically. Wealth
to Leo buys services and managerial ability. It creates jobs for others
and improves the general well-being of those around them. Therefore
– to a Leo – wealth is good. Wealth is to be enjoyed to the fullest.
Money is not to be left to gather dust in a mouldy bank vault but to be
enjoyed, spread around, used. So Leos can be quite reckless in their
spending.

With the sign of Virgo on Leo's 2nd money house cusp, Leo needs
to develop some of Virgo's traits of analysis, discrimination and purity
when it comes to money matters. They must learn to be more careful
with the details of finance (or to hire people to do this for them). They
have to be more cost-conscious in their spending habits. Generally,
they need to manage their money better. Leos tend to chafe under
financial constraints, yet these constraints can help Leos to reach their
highest financial potential.

Leos like it when their friends and family know that they can depend
on them for financial support. They do not mind – and even enjoy –
lending money, but they are careful that they are not taken advantage
of. From their 'regal throne' Leos like to bestow gifts upon their family
and friends and then enjoy the good feelings these gifts bring to every-

body. Leos love financial speculations and – when the celestial influences are right – are often lucky.

Career and Public Image

Leos like to be perceived as wealthy, for in today's world wealth often equals power. When they attain wealth they love having a large house with lots of land and animals.

At their jobs Leos excel in positions of authority and power. They are good at making decisions – on a grand level – but they prefer to leave the details to others. Leos are well respected by their colleagues and subordinates, mainly because they have a knack for understanding and relating to those around them. Leos usually strive for the top positions even if they have to start at the bottom and work hard to get there. As might be expected of such a charismatic sign, Leos are always trying to improve their work situation. They do so in order to have a better chance of advancing to the top.

On the other hand, Leos do not like to be bossed around or told what to do. Perhaps this is why they aspire so for the top – where they can be the decision-makers and need not take orders from others.

Leos never doubt their success and focus all their attention and efforts on achieving it. Another great Leo characteristic is that – just like good monarchs – they do not attempt to abuse the power or success they achieve. If they do so this is not wilful or intentional. Usually they like to share their wealth and try to make everyone around them join in their success.

Leos are – and like to be perceived as – hard-working, well-established individuals. It is definitely true that they are capable of hard work and often manage great things. But do not forget that, deep down inside, Leos really are fun-lovers.

Love and Relationships

Generally, Leos are not the marrying kind. To them relationships are good while they are pleasurable. When the relationship ceases to be pleasurable a true Leo will want out. They always want to have the freedom to leave. That is why Leos excel at love affairs rather than commitment. Once married, however, Leo is faithful – even if some Leos have a tendency to marry more than once in their lifetime. If you are in love with a Leo, just show him or her a good time – travel, go to casinos and clubs, the theatre and discos. Wine and dine your Leo love – it is expensive but worth it and you will have fun.

Leos generally have an active love life and are demonstrative in their affections. They love to be with other optimistic and fun-loving types like themselves, but wind up settling with someone more serious, intellectual and unconventional. The partner of a Leo tends to be more political and socially conscious than he or she is, and more libertarian. When you marry a Leo, mastering the freedom-loving tendencies of your partner will definitely become a life-long challenge – and be careful that Leo does not master you.

Aquarius sits on Leo's 7th house of love cusp. Thus if Leos want to realize their highest love and social potential they need to develop a more egalitarian, Aquarian perspective on others. This is not easy for Leo, for 'the king' finds his equals only among other 'kings'. But perhaps this is the solution to Leo's social challenge – to be 'a king among kings'. It is all right to be regal, but recognize the nobility in others.

Home and Domestic Life

Although Leos are great entertainers and love having people over, sometimes this is all show. Only very few close friends will get to see the real side of a Leo's day-to-day life. To a Leo the home is a place of comfort, recreation and transformation; a secret, private retreat – a castle. Leos like to spend money, show off a bit, entertain and have fun. They enjoy the latest furnishings, clothes and gadgets – all things fit for kings.

Leos are fiercely loyal to their family and, of course, expect the same from them. They love their children almost to a fault; they have to be careful not to spoil them too much. They also must try to avoid attempting to make individual family members over in their own image. Leos should keep in mind that others also have the need to be their own people. That is why Leos have to be extra careful about being over-bossy or over-domineering in the home.

Horoscope for 2023

Major Trends

Basically a happy and successful year ahead, Leo. Enjoy.

Important, long-term planets are changing signs this year. This signals new long-term trends in your life. Pluto is beginning a two-year process of moving from Capricorn into Aquarius. This year and next year you will see the start of this, but in 2025 he will move into Aquarius for the long term. Now, he hovers between your 6th and 7th houses – impacting on both the love life and health needs. More on this later.

Saturn's major move from Aquarius to Pisces on March 8 improves the overall health and energy. More importantly, the love life is improved. Again, there's more on this later.

With Saturn in your 8th house of regeneration for the next two and a half years, Leo, you will have to be more careful in sexual matters. There is a need to focus more on quality rather than quantity. Less but better-quality sex is preferred over more sex of lesser quality. You need to be more choosy, more discerning. Saturn is your health planet, so this discernment is important in health matters. More details later.

Jupiter will be in your 9th house until May 17. This shows more fun in life. There will be more foreign travel. It is a wonderful transit for college-level students and for those applying to colleges. There is good fortune here. It is also a period that brings religious and theological insights and breakthroughs, changing the way that you live your life – very important.

On May 17 Jupiter will cross your Mid-heaven and enter your 10th house of career. You enter a major period of career success, which goes on until the end of the year. There is good fortune here. This transit will also be great for love. More on this later.

Venus spends over four months in your own sign this year, which is highly unusual – her usual transit is a month. So, she is hanging out with you and this increases your physical beauty and appearance. You become more gracious and charming. It also shows happy career opportunities coming to you.

Solar eclipses are always unusually strong on you since the Sun rules your Horoscope. This year we have two – the usual number. These will bring redefinitions of the image and personality. It would be a good thing to reduce your schedule over those periods. These solar eclipses happen on April 20 and October 14, and we will discuss them more fully in the monthly reports.

Your most important interests this year are health and work (up until March 24 and from June 12 to the end of the year); love and romance (until March 8 and from March 24 to June 12); sex, occult studies, personal reinvention and transformation; religion, theology, foreign travel and higher education (until May 17); and career.

Your paths of greatest fulfilment are religion, theology, foreign travel and higher education (from January 1 to May 17) and career.

Health

(Please note that this is an astrological perspective on health and not a medical one. In days of yore there was no difference, both these perspectives were identical. But these days there could be quite a difference. For a medical perspective, please consult your doctor or health practitioner.)

As we mentioned above, health and energy are much improved this year. Saturn, your health planet, will move away from his stressful aspect to you on March 8. Pluto will put some slight stress on you from March 24 to June 12 – but this will only impact those of you born early in Leo (July 22–24). Most of you won't feel it this year.

The big news is that your health planet Saturn changes signs. This will change your health needs and attitudes. Your health regime will change.

Good though your health is, you can make it better. Give more attention to the following – the vulnerable areas of your Horoscope this year (the reflex points are shown in the chart opposite). This way many problems can be either avoided or softened:

- The heart is always an important area for Leo as this sign rules the heart. The important thing with the heart, as our regular readers know, is to avoid worry and anxiety. Worry can be defined as 'lack of faith'. Cultivate more faith.

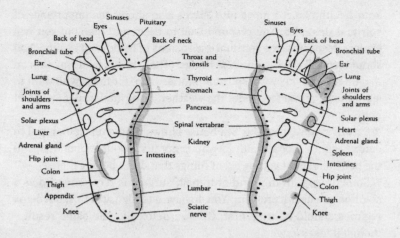

Important foot reflexology points for the year ahead

Try to massage all of the foot on a regular basis – the top of the foot as well as the bottom – but pay extra attention to the points highlighted on the chart. When you massage, be aware of 'sore spots' as these need special attention. It's also a good idea to massage the ankles and below them.

- The spine, knees, teeth, bones and overall skeletal alignment. These areas are also always important for Leo as Saturn, the planet that rules them, is your health planet. The reflex points are shown above.
- The colon, bladder and sexual organs. These have been important for the past twenty years as Pluto was in your 6th house of health. And they will remain significant this year and next. Safe sex and sexual moderation are important health-wise.
- The ankles and calves have only been important for the past two and a half years as your health planet has been in Aquarius. But they will still be important until March 8, so regular ankle and calf massage will be beneficial. It would also be a good idea to give the ankles more support when you exercise.
- The feet become important on March 8 as Saturn, your health planet, moves into Pisces: Pisces rules the feet. They will remain an important area for the next two and a half years. Regular foot massage should be part of your daily health regime. You not only strengthen the feet themselves but also the whole body.

Your health planet's move into Pisces also shows the importance of spiritual therapies. You respond well to them and many of you will explore deeper into the spiritual dimensions of health and healing. You should read all you can on these things. (There is much information on this on my website, www.spiritual-stories.com, for those who want to learn more.) If you feel under the weather, a spiritual healer can be of help.

Saturn's move into your 8th house shows that you respond well to detox regimes. Good health for you is not just about adding things to the body but about getting rid of things that don't belong there.

Sometimes with this kind of transit, surgery is recommended as a solution to a health problem. You do have a tendency to this, but detox regimes should be tried first. Often a detox has the same result – though it takes longer.

Your health planet's move into a Water sign on March 8 indicates a strong connection to the healing powers of the Water element. It would be a good idea to spend more time near water – near oceans, rivers, lakes, etc. Swimming, sailing and water sports are good health-wise. Good to soak in the tub for an hour or so if you feel under the weather.

Home and Family

There are changes brewing here as your family planet, Pluto, is in the process of changing signs. This, as we mentioned, will be a two-year process (Pluto is the slowest moving of all the planets). So, some of you are planning moves, although they are not likely to happen this year. Much more likely next year.

For many years, with your family planet in your 6th house, you've been making the home more like a health spa and/or office. You've been installing gym equipment, home offices and perhaps even running a home-based business. This process is almost over with. This year Pluto will briefly occupy your 7th house of love, from March 24 to June 12. This signals more socializing at home and with the family and family members. It also tends to show a desire to beautify the home. This beautification will not happen overnight but as a process. The physical appearance of the home will become ever more important. In the coming years the home will be a social centre as much as a home.

The home will also become more 'high tech' in coming years. I can see a tendency to install smart appliances and lights and other high-tech innovations.

If you're planning renovations or major repairs to the home, October 12 to November 24 would be good. Beautifying the home, or buying objects of beauty for the home, will go well from March 24 to June 12 and from December 4–29.

A parent or parent figure is likely to move this year, and it looks happy. The other parent or parent figure also seems ready to move but this can happen next year. Siblings and sibling figures in your life are probably planning changes in the home, but a move is not likely this year. Children and children figures probably moved last year. The year tends to the status quo for them, although they are having a fun kind of year. If the children are female, they are very fertile. Grandchildren, or those who play that role in your life, seem happy and successful. They prosper this year. A move is not likely, although there is nothing against it.

Finance and Career

The year ahead is a very strong career and love year, Leo, but finances seem quiet. Your money house is basically empty this year. Only short-term planets will move through there – and their effects are also short term.

'Quiet' can be read as a good thing. You're more or less satisfied with earnings as they are and have no need to make dramatic changes. You don't need to pay too much attention here. However, if financial problems do occur, this could be the root cause – a lack of attention. If a problem does happen you may have to force yourself to pay more attention.

Mercury is your financial planet. He is the fastest moving (except for the Moon) of the planets and in any given year he will move through all the signs and houses of your horoscope. Thus, there are many short-term trends in finance that depend on where Mercury is and the kinds of aspects that he receives. These trends are best dealt with in the monthly reports.

Keep in mind, too, that Mercury's movements tend to be erratic. Sometimes he moves very fast (and thus you make quick financial progress). Sometimes he moves slowly (and earnings happen slowly). Sometimes he stands still and sometimes he moves backwards. All these movements impact on your finances.

Mercury will have his solstice twice this year. Once from March 20-21 and again from October 7-8. These indicate pauses in your financial affairs and a change of direction.

Generally, Mercury goes retrograde three times a year. This year it happens four times – from January 1-17; April 21 to May 14; August 23 to September 14; and December 13-31. These are times to avoid major purchases or important investments. Instead, they are times to gain mental clarity on your finances.

The real headline this year is the career. Career has been prominent for many years now as Uranus has been in your 10th house. (He will be there for many more years, too.) Thus, you're experimental in career matters. You like change and excitement. You favour the freelance lifestyle over the corporate one. You need a lot of freedom and variety in the career. This year, on May 17 benevolent Jupiter moves into your 10th house and stays there for the remainder of the year. This is a classic indicator of success – of promotion and elevation. Very happy (and prestigious) career opportunities open up to you. This transit favours the entertainment and music industries – Leo's natural love. You can be more involved in these industries or people from these industries can be important in your career. Children and children figures seem very successful too and they are helping the career. (Sometimes, especially if they are young, they motivate you to succeed.) Next year will also be very successful.

Jupiter is your planet of fun and creativity. Thus, you seem to be enjoying your career path now. Your personal creativity is important in your success. Leos are very creative types of people, and this year your creativity gets more respect.

Usually, career success translates to financial success. But this year it will not happen right away. This is a year where you will choose prestige over money. If you have the prestige and elevation, the money will come eventually.

Love and Social Life

The love life is definitely improving this year. Saturn is leaving your 7th house on March 8. This has been the sore spot for two years now. Not only was he in your 7th house but he was making stressful aspects to your love planet, Uranus. Now, after March 8, he will be making good aspects to your love planet (and next year the aspects will be even better).

Jupiter's move into Taurus on May 17 is also excellent for love. He begins to travel with your love planet. The aspect isn't exact this year (that will happen next year), but you're feeling the influence. The social circle is expanding. New friends are coming into the picture and they seem like powerful and prestigious kinds of people. You have been attracted to these sorts of people for many years now – and now there are more of them.

With your love planet sitting in your career house for many years, a good deal of your socializing has been career related or with people involved in your career. This tendency is even stronger this year. You have been attracted to people of power – people above you in status – for some years now, and this year the tendency is even stronger. There are romantic opportunities with these kinds of people. The problem here is that you could be tempted to a relationship of convenience rather than true love.

Jupiter travelling with the love planet often indicates a marriage. However, this is more likely to happen next year. This year it is more probably a love affair.

Pluto's brief move into your 7th house of love from March 24 to June 12 is really more a flirtation – an announcement of things to come in the future. In the years to come you will be giving birth to your ideal love and social life. Your ideal relationship. This will be a long-term process that will go on for more than twenty years.

His flirtation does signal more socializing at home and with the family members, however. Family and family connections can be important in love. Sometimes an old flame comes back into the picture. There is a re-kindling of the passion.

Self-improvement

Spiritual Neptune has been in your 8th house of regeneration for many years now. Thus, as we have noted in previous years, the sex life is being raised in vibration. It is becoming spiritualized. It is being raised from pure animal lust into an act of worship. This trend continues in the year ahead (and for many more years to come). It is doubtful that sex just for the sake of sex is satisfying to you these days. There has to be more to it. As in past years (this is a long-term trend) there is a need to study the spiritual teachings on sex – karezza, kundalini, tantra and hermetic science. Done correctly the sexual act can bring healing, the manifestation of desires (not just physical desires) and even illumination. There's a lot more to it than the 'how to' books say.

Saturn's move into the 8th house on March 8 will reinforce this. Saturn will have the effect of limiting sexual activity – of making you focus more on quality rather than quantity. Also, since Saturn is your health planet, you will explore more deeply the use of sex for healing (again this is dealt with in the spiritual teachings mentioned above).

The Moon is your spiritual planet. Where the other fast-moving planets take a year to move through your chart, the Moon does so every month. So, there are many short-term spiritual trends that depend on where the Moon is and the kinds of aspects she receives at any given time. In general, the New and Full Moons – regardless of where they occur – will be strong spiritual days for you. These are great days for meditation and spiritual practice. Your ESP abilities are always stronger on the New or Full Moon. The dream life will tend to be more active and revelatory as well. So be alert for spiritual insights on those days.

The Moon will be eclipsed twice this year. Once on May 5 and again on October 28. The eclipses will bring spiritual changes – changes in practice, teachings and attitudes. Often these changes are quite normal, the result of spiritual growth. A practice that was good at one time needs changing when new revelation comes. The dream life and intuition that happen over these periods are not to be taken too seriously, though. Most of it will be psychic debris stirred up by the eclipses.

Month-by-month Forecasts

January

Best Days Overall: 8, 9, 16, 17, 25, 26
Most Stressful Days Overall: 6, 7, 12, 13, 18, 19
Best Days for Love: 1, 2, 3, 10, 11, 12, 13, 18, 19, 21, 22, 28, 29
Best Days for Money: 1, 2, 8, 10, 11, 16, 18, 19, 23, 28, 29
Best Days for Career: 2, 3, 12, 13, 18, 19, 21, 22

The planetary power is overwhelmingly in the Western, social sector of your chart: 80 per cent, sometimes 90 per cent of the planets are there – a huge percentage. So, this is a month for focusing on others and their needs. Their way is probably the best way nowadays. Go along with this so long as it isn't destructive. Social grace is more important than personal initiative or personal skills at this time, and it seems that you're really trying to do this – especially after the 20th.

Health needs watching this month – but especially after the 20th. The important thing is to maintain high energy levels. Never allow yourself to get overtired. Enhance the health in the ways mentioned in the yearly report.

Your financial planet, Mercury, is retrograde until the 17th, so avoid major purchases, investments or important decisions until after then. Until the 17th the focus should be on fact finding – gaining clarity.

Your 6th house of health and work is strong until the 20th and job-seekers will have good prospects. This period is also good for those who employ others. The focus on health will stand you in good stead for later in the month when health becomes more stressed.

The New Moon of the 11th occurs in your 6th house, making it especially good for job-seekers. But it also brings spiritual insights and enhanced ESP. Health and job issues will clarify as the weeks progress until the next New Moon.

On the 20th the Sun, the ruler of your Horoscope, enters your 7th house of love and you begin a yearly love and social peak. You seem proactive in love. You seem in control of the social life. The 4th and 5th are excellent love and social days.

You're into foreign travel these days, with Jupiter in your 9th house (and this will go on until May 17), but with Mars retrograde until the 12th it would be best to delay foreign travel until after this date. Mars is 'out of bounds' until May 4. Thus, you're attracted to exotic destinations – destinations that are off the beaten path – outside your normal orbit.

February

Best Days Overall: 4, 5, 6, 14, 15, 22, 23
Most Stressful Days Overall: 12, 13, 18, 19, 24, 25
Best Days for Love: 2, 3, 7, 8, 12, 13, 16, 17, 18, 19, 22, 24, 25
Best Days for Money: 4, 5, 7, 8, 11, 14, 15, 18, 19, 22, 23, 27, 28
Best Days for Career: 2, 3, 12, 13, 22, 24, 25

Health still needs keeping an eye on until the 18th. So, again, make sure to get enough rest. Enhance the health in the ways mentioned in the yearly report. There is a dramatic improvement after the 18th, however.

All the planets are moving forward this month, so the pace of life quickens – both personally and in the world. This is how you like things, Leo. There is fast progress towards your goals.

You're still in the midst of a yearly love and social peak, so love should be going well – albeit with a few dramas (also how you like things). There is some love drama from the 3rd to the 5th – but it does resolve itself quickly.

The Sun, the ruler of your Horoscope, travels with Saturn on the 15th and 16th and you are probably called on to take on more work responsibility. Also, a job offer could be made. The New Moon of the 20th occurs very near Saturn as well, bringing more of the same.

The New Moon of the 20th occurs in your 8th house, and so libido is greatly increased. It is a good financial day for the spouse, partner or current love. And, as with every New Moon, there are spiritual insights and enhanced ESP abilities. New Moons tend to bring supernatural kinds of experiences – things that can't be explained scientifically or logically. This New Moon is even stronger in that regard as it occurs in the spiritual sign of Pisces.

Now that Mercury, your financial planet, is moving forward again, finances also move forward. Until the 11th money comes from work - from productive service. After the 11th, as your financial planet moves into your 7th house, the social contacts (and your social grace) become more important for your finances. Putting others first is good for the bottom line.

Foreign travel is much easier and safer now. Mars, your travel planet, is even more 'out of bounds' this month than last month. You really like 'out of the way' places.

March

Best Days Overall: 4, 5, 13, 14, 21, 22, 31
Most Stressful Days Overall: 11, 12, 17, 18, 24, 25
Best Days for Love: 4, 5, 6, 7, 11, 12, 15, 16, 17, 18, 24, 25
Best Days for Money: 4, 5, 6, 7, 11, 12, 13, 14, 21, 22, 31
Best Days for Career: 4, 5, 11, 12, 24, 25

Your 8th house became very powerful on February 18 and remains so this month until the 20th. Libido is high, but Saturn's move into your 8th house on the 8th tamps it down a bit. The focus should be on quality rather than quantity. You seem focused - and active - in the finances of the spouse, partner or current love. Even your financial planet is in the 8th house from the 3rd to the 19th. So, prosper others - focus on their financial interests - and your own prosperity will happen very naturally. You might not see it right away, but you've made deposits in your spiritual bank account. You'll be able to draw on it in due course.

Intuition is important in finances this period, from the 3rd to the 19th and especially on the 17th and 18th. If you have good business ideas this is an excellent month to attract outside investors or to otherwise access outside money. This is also a good month (especially from the 3rd to the 19th) to pay down debt as well. It is good for creative financing, tax and insurance planning and, for those of you of an appropriate age, for estate planning.

On the 19th Mercury, your financial planet, enters your 9th house. The Sun follows on the 20th. This is a wonderful aspect for earnings as the 9th house is a beneficent one. The Sun travelling with Mercury on the 17th and 18th brings wonderful financial days. On the 27th and 28th Mercury travels with Jupiter, bringing more financial largesse.

Health improved last month and is further improved this month now that Saturn has moved away from his stressful aspect with you. Now your health needs change. Foot massage and spiritual techniques are very potent now.

Mercury has his solstice on the 20th and 21st. He pauses in the heavens (in his latitudinal motion) and then changes direction. So it is with your finances. A new direction is happening.

Pluto's move into your 7th house on the 24th will only impact those of you born early in the sign of Leo – from July 22–24 – at the moment. But eventually, as the years go by, it will completely transform your social circle.

April

Best Days Overall: 1, 9, 10, 18, 27, 28, 29
Most Stressful Days Overall: 7, 8, 14, 15, 20, 21
Best Days for Love: 3, 4, 12, 13, 14, 15, 21, 22, 23, 30
Best Days for Money: 1, 2, 3, 4, 10, 12, 13, 19, 21, 28, 29, 30
Best Days for Career: 3, 4, 14, 20, 21, 22, 23

The main headline of the month is the total solar eclipse on the 20th. All of you feel it in some degree, but those born late in Leo, August 21–23, will feel it most strongly. All of you should reduce your schedule from the 20th onwards, around the eclipse period, and especially those of you with birthdays from August 21–23.

This eclipse occurs right on the cusp of your 9th and 10th houses. Thus, it has an influence in both these houses. The influence in the 9th house affects foreign travel; this has been active over the past few months but it is best to avoid it during the eclipse period – a few days before and after. (Sensitive people will feel the effects of an eclipse as many as two weeks before it actually happens.) It also impacts on college-level students. There can be disruptions at school and changes in educational plans. Sometimes people even change schools. Your religious beliefs get tested too. Some will have to be modified, some will get discarded as the events of the eclipse will show their fallacy. There are upheavals in your place of worship and in the lives of worship leaders.

The eclipse's impact on your 10th house affects the career. There are changes going on there. Sometimes it signals shifts in the hierarchy of your company, or changes in government regulations in your industry. The rules of the game change. Parents, parent figures and bosses have personal dramas.

Pluto, your family planet, receives a direct hit from this eclipse, causing dramas in the family – dramas in family members' personal lives. A family member who has been chronically ill for a long time can pass from the scene as the eclipse pushes him or her over the edge. Often repairs are needed in the home.

Every solar eclipse impacts very strongly on you. With the Sun as your ruling planet, you're hypersensitive to solar phenomena – all solar phenomena, including eclipses. So, the eclipse provokes a need to redefine yourself – to revise your opinion of yourself. This is basically a good thing, as we are evolving, growing beings, and you get this opportunity twice a year. This redefinition will lead to wardrobe and image changes in the coming months. You will present a new and updated image of yourself to the world.

This eclipse disrupts the career, but in a good way. Blockages and career obstructions get blasted away. You're in a yearly career peak from the 20th onwards and much success is happening.

May

Best Days Overall: 7, 8, 15, 16, 25, 26
Most Stressful Days Overall: 5, 6, 11, 12, 17, 18, 19
Best Days for Love: 1, 2, 3, 9, 10, 11, 12, 17, 18, 19, 27, 28
Best Days for Money: 1, 8, 9, 10, 16, 17, 18, 19, 24, 25, 27, 28
Best Days for Career: 2, 3, 9, 10, 17, 18, 19

A lunar eclipse on the 5th again brings turmoil to the home and family as it occurs in your 4th house. This area was impacted by the solar eclipse last month too. Be more patient with family members as passions run high. The dream life is probably overactive and unpleasant. Pay it no heed. You're only seeing psychic debris stirred up by the eclipse.

Because the Moon is your spiritual planet, every lunar eclipse brings spiritual changes – changes in practice, attitudes, teachings and teachers. Some of this is quite normal as you understand things more and thus old ways of working are no longer valid. A lunar eclipse often brings upheavals in spiritual or charitable organizations that you're involved with. Guru figures have personal dramas.

You're still in a yearly career peak. And this one is stronger than any you've had in recent years. Jupiter moves into your 10th house of career on the 17th, which further boosts the career. In addition, the New Moon of the 17th also occurs in your 10th house – a double career boost! You're successful both personally and professionally. Career issues will clarify themselves as the weeks after the New Moon progress.

Your career planet, Venus, has been 'out of bounds' since April 19, but this month she strays even further from her natural orbit all month. So, in your career, you're in uncharted territory. You're thinking 'outside the box'. You have to be willing to go 'outside the box' in order to achieve your goals.

The Sun travels with Mercury on the 1st, making it an excellent financial day. On the 8th and 9th, the Sun travels with Uranus, your love planet, and brings happy social and romantic experiences. Those already in a relationship are close to the beloved. Singles will meet someone special.

Health still needs watching until the 21st. Make sure, as always, to get enough rest. You should see dramatic improvement in health after the 21st.

June

Best Days Overall: 3, 4, 11, 12, 21, 22
Most Stressful Days Overall: 1, 2, 7, 8, 14, 15, 16, 28, 29
Best Days for Love: 2, 6, 7, 8, 11, 15, 21, 22, 24, 25
Best Days for Money: 5, 6, 14, 15, 16, 23, 24, 25, 26, 27
Best Days for Career: 2, 11, 14, 15, 21, 22

Career is still successful this month, and because your financial planet is also in your career house (until the 11th) there can be pay rises, official or unofficial. The financial planet in the 10th house signals that your good career reputation brings earnings opportunities to you. It also indicates the financial favour of bosses, parents or parent figures. There could be financial disruption – a need for dramatic change – on the 4th and 5th. This could also happen because money suddenly comes to you in ways that you didn't plan for.

Mercury moves into his own sign and house on the 11th. He is strong in that position and this bodes well for earnings. Mercury in your 11th house (until the 27th) favours investments in technology and electronic media, and trading, buying and selling, marketing, sales and PR. The Sun moved into your 11th house on May 21 and stays there until the 21st of this month, presaging a strong social period. It's not so much about romance, more about friendships, groups and group activities. You have an especially good grasp of technology, science, astronomy and astrology. This is a good period for buying any high-tech equipment you need. Many people have their Horoscopes done under this kind of transit.

Mercury will be 'out of bounds' from the 25th to July 6. In financial matters and in friendships you're venturing outside your normal orbit. On the 27th Mercury enters your 12th house of spirituality. The financial intuition becomes important, and it is likely that this intuition is taking you outside your normal comfort zone.

Though the Sun has now moved out of your 10th house, career is still super. It is expanding. Honours and recognition most likely happened last month, but they could still happen now.

Jupiter is moving ever closer to your love planet Uranus. The aspect won't be exact this year, but you're feeling the influence. Romance is going well.

Health is basically good this month. Pluto's move out of Aquarius and back into Capricorn on the 12th is a positive for health.

Mars is in your own sign all month, which means that foreign countries and foreign travel still call to you. But be careful of rush and haste as this can lead to accident and injury. And mind the temper.

July

Best Days Overall: 1, 2, 9, 10, 18, 19, 20, 28, 29
Most Stressful Days Overall: 5, 6, 11, 12, 26, 27
Best Days for Love: 2, 4, 5, 6, 10, 11, 12, 19, 20, 22, 29, 31
Best Days for Money: 3, 4, 8, 11, 12, 18, 19, 21, 22, 30, 31
Best Days for Career: 2, 10, 11, 12, 19, 20, 29

Retrograde activity is gradually increasing. Last month began with 10 per cent of the planets retrograde but ended with 30 per cent of them travelling backwards. This month the percentage increases to 40 per cent after the 23rd. This is a substantial percentage.

Venus, your career planet, has been in your own sign since June 5. Jupiter has been in your 10th house since May 17. So, the career has been red hot. Happy career opportunities have been coming to you. You have the favour of bosses, parents, parent figures and even the government. You look successful and people see you this way. You dress the part. Now, on the 23rd, Venus starts to go backwards, and things slow down a bit. This is probably a good thing – it's difficult to handle this kind of pace for too long. A breather is welcome. Career opportunities that come need more study. Things might not be as they seem.

Health is good this month and gets even better on the 23rd as the Sun enters your own sign. This is a happy period. You begin one of your yearly personal pleasure peaks. Time to enjoy all the pleasures of the body and the five senses. Time to appreciate the body – to reward it – for all the years of selfless service it has given you. A very good period to get the body into the shape that you want.

On the 11th Mercury enters your sign, bringing financial windfalls and opportunities. There's nothing much that you need to do to prosper; just go about your business. Money will find you.

Every New Moon brings spiritual insights and gifts. However, this one on the 17th brings more than is normal. It occurs in your 12th house of spirituality and, in the coming weeks, it will clarify and illuminate doubts and questions on spiritual issues.

Mars moves into your money house on the 11th. This too is good for finance as the ruler of the 9th house is a beneficent planet. The only problem here is that you can take even more risks than usual – and Leo is a legendary risk-taker.

August

Best Days Overall: 5, 6, 14, 15, 16, 24, 25
Most Stressful Days Overall: 1, 2, 7, 8, 22, 23, 29
Best Days for Love: 1, 2, 5, 6, 8, 14, 15, 18, 24, 25, 27, 29
Best Days for Money: 7, 8, 17, 18, 26, 27
Best Days for Career: 5, 6, 7, 8, 14, 15, 24, 25

Leo likes everything to move quickly, but it's not going to happen this month. Retrograde activity will reach its maximum extent for the year from the 29th – 60 per cent of the planets are retrograde. But even before that, from the 23rd, half the planets are going backwards. The spiritual lesson for the month therefore is patience, patience, patience and more patience. Trying to push things on will probably not work; however, you can minimize delays (though you won't put a stop to them entirely) by doing everything as perfectly as you can. Handle the details of life perfectly.

You're still in a yearly personal pleasure peak until the 23rd. So, though many planets are retrograde, you can still work on your body and image – bring it up to scratch. The Sun, the ruler of your Horoscope, never goes retrograde.

Normally, with your money house as powerful as it is from the 23rd onwards, this would be a very prosperous month. You're in a yearly financial peak and Mercury, your financial planet, is in his own sign and house. But Mercury starts to retrograde on the 23rd and, as was mentioned, many other planets are also retrograde. So, I would say that prosperity is happening, but behind the scenes and perhaps with a delayed reaction.

Your love planet, Uranus, makes a halt before reversing direction, which will impact very strongly on those of you with birthdays from August 13–16. It can bring dramatic personal changes. Surprising happenings. Problems with the beloved – perhaps major disagreements. Love will require more work. However, after the 23rd a lot of these problems ease up and harmony will be restored.

Mars is still in your money house until the 28th, so there is a tendency to take risks and to make snap financial decisions. This is not advisable right now, especially after the 23rd. If you can't act overtly in your financial life, you can review things and see where improvements can be made. Then when the planets move forward again, you can move forward with them.

Health is good this month.

September

Best Days Overall: 2, 3, 11, 12, 21, 22, 29, 30
Most Stressful Days Overall: 4, 5, 18, 19, 25, 26
Best Days for Love: 2, 3, 5, 11, 12, 14, 15, 21, 22, 24, 25, 26, 30
Best Days for Money: 4, 5, 13, 14, 15, 23, 24
Best Days for Career: 2, 3, 4, 5, 11, 12, 21, 22, 30

Retrograde activity is still at its maximum extent for the year until the 16th, with 60 per cent of the planets retrograde. And even after the 16th half of them will still not be moving forward. So, keep in mind our discussion of this last month.

You remain in a yearly financial peak until the 23rd, but there are delays and glitches involved. Things should go more smoothly after the 15th as Mercury, your financial planet, starts to move forward. There is more good news on the financial front. The New Moon of the 15th occurs in your money house, and this should be a strong financial day. More importantly, the Moon (your spiritual planet) will bring financial clarity as the weeks progress – long after the actual New Moon happens. There could be good reasons for all these delays – not to punish you, but to make finance even better.

Venus, your career planet, starts to move forward on the 4th after a few months of retrograde motion. So, issues around the career are starting to be clarified. There are still happy career opportunities for you, and it's safer now to accept them. Your discernment is better. You look successful, you dress the part, and others see you that way.

There is much power in your 3rd house of intellectual interests and communication from the 23rd. A good period (and next month too) to read and study more, to take courses in subjects that interest you, to catch up on the letters, emails and texts that you owe. With so many planets still retrograde you might as well take time to study and educate yourself. It is something constructive you can do amid the worldly stasis.

Health is good this month. However, your health planet Saturn is still retrograde so avoid making dramatic changes to the health regime now. Study things more. Also, this is not an especially good time for taking medical tests or undergoing procedures. If you have the choice, best to reschedule them.

Love is much improved over August. There is more harmony with the beloved this month – especially on the 14th and 15th. But your love planet is retrograde (and will be so for almost the whole year ahead). So go slow. Enjoy love for what it is. As the line goes, 'You can't hurry love.'

October

Best Days Overall: 8, 9, 15, 16, 17, 26, 27
Most Stressful Days Overall: 1, 2, 13, 14, 15, 16, 17, 22, 23, 28, 29
Best Days for Love: 2, 9, 10, 11, 12, 20, 21, 22, 23, 28, 29
Best Days for Money: 1, 2, 11, 12, 20, 21, 24, 28, 29
Best Days for Career: 1, 2, 9, 10, 11, 20, 21

There's a lot happening this month. Mercury, your financial planet, has his solstice on the 7th and 8th. He pauses in the heavens and then changes direction (in latitude). So, there is a pause in your financial life and then a change of direction.

Venus, your career planet, moves into Virgo, your money house. This transit can bring pay rises, official or unofficial, and the financial favour of the authority figures in your life – even the government.

But the main headline is the two eclipses that happen this month. There is a solar eclipse on the 14th and a lunar eclipse on the 28th. Both eclipses have a strong effect on you, but for different reasons. So, reduce your schedule over these periods and avoid high-stress activities.

The solar eclipse of the 14th occurs in your 3rd house, which means that siblings, sibling figures and neighbours experience dramas in their lives. There can be disruptions in your neighbourhood (construction work, car accidents, weird kinds of crimes, etc.). Cars and communication equipment can behave erratically. Sometimes repairs or even replacements are necessary. It will be a good idea to drive more carefully at this time.

Every solar eclipse impacts your image and self-concept. As has been mentioned, you're extremely sensitive to solar phenomena as the Sun rules your Horoscope. So once again (just like in April) you get a chance to redefine yourself and to upgrade your image and presentation to the world. This is a healthy thing. If you haven't been careful in dietary matters, there could be a physical detox. (This is not sickness, though the symptoms are often the same.)

The lunar eclipse of the 28th occurs in your 10th house and brings career changes and disruptions – the result of this will be positive in the end. The career is still very strong. Parents, parent figures and bosses can have personal, life-changing dramas. There are spiritual changes happening as well, and often shake-ups in spiritual or charitable organizations that you're involved with. Guru figures experience personal dramas.

November

Best Days Overall: 4, 5, 6, 14, 15, 23, 24
Most Stressful Days Overall: 12, 13, 18, 19, 25, 26
Best Days for Love: 8, 9, 17, 18, 19, 26, 27, 28
Best Days for Money: 2, 3, 7, 8, 16, 23, 24, 25
Best Days for Career: 8, 9, 18, 19, 25, 26, 27, 28

Health needs some attention this month – especially until the 22nd. Now that Saturn, your health planet, is moving forward it is safer to make changes to the health regime and to undergo tests and procedures. Make sure to get enough rest, and if you feel under the weather a spiritual healer could be very helpful.

The focus this month is on home and family – but the career is still important. Your challenge is to balance both areas of life. You'll tend to switch from one to the other and back again. A good way to handle both is to work on your career from home, by the methods of night. You can be devoted to the family while working on your career through meditation, visualization and getting into the frame of mind – the mood – of where you want to be career-wise. Overt actions can happen later. Your career planet Venus is moving forward, but the two other planets involved with the career – Jupiter and Uranus – are still retrograde. So there's a lot of behind-the-scenes activity going on in this area.

This is a month for emotional healing. You have great opportunities to heal the traumas of the past. As a famous writer once said, 'The past is still with us and it's not even past.' So when these memories surface – and many will – look at them and reinterpret the events from your present state of consciousness. What was a trauma to a four-year-old provokes only smiles to an adult. Emotional healing doesn't happen overnight, but progress will be made.

Mercury is 'out of bounds' from the 16th onwards, so financial goals can only be achieved outside your normal orbit. Your financial planet will be in your 4th house until the 10th. Thus, family support should be good for finances – and it works both ways; you're financially supportive of the family and they are supportive of you. Family connections can be important financially. On the 10th Mercury moves into your 5th house and earnings should increase. The only possible issues are too much speculation and overspending. There is a happy-go-lucky attitude to money from the 10th onwards, but you rather like this.

December

Best Days Overall: 2, 3, 11, 12, 20, 21, 29, 30
Most Stressful Days Overall: 9, 10, 16, 17, 22, 23
Best Days for Love: 5, 6, 9, 15, 16, 17, 18, 19, 23, 28, 30
Best Days for Money: 4, 5, 6, 14, 22, 30, 31
Best Days for Career: 9, 18, 19, 22, 23, 28, 30

Health and energy dramatically improved on November 22 and are still excellent in the month ahead. On that date you began a yearly personal pleasure peak, a fun period, which continues until the 22nd. It's party time – and no one knows how to party better than you, Leo! Leos are also very creative and this period even more so than usual.

Your financial planet Mercury is still 'out of bounds' until the 14th. He is also shuttling between two signs – Sagittarius and Capricorn. He starts off in Sagittarius, moves into Capricorn on the 2nd, retrogrades on the 13th and moves back into Sagittarius on the 24th. So, finances are more erratic than usual this month. The good news is that from the 2nd to the 13th the financial judgement is sound and conservative. You're not likely to overspend. But Mercury's retrograde after the 13th signals a need to slow down financially and to avoid major purchases or investments. Holiday shopping is best done before the 13th. The 6th, 7th, 17th and 18th are excellent financial days. The 17th and 18th will bring increases in earnings but with a delayed reaction. Financial intuition needs to be verified on the 26th and 27th – also, be careful of overspending on those days.

Mars, the ruler of your 9th house, once again goes 'out of bounds' from the 22nd onwards. He has spent a good part of the year 'out of bounds'. So, your travel interests are again outside your normal sphere. The same is true in your religious and philosophical studies. There are probably no philosophical answers to be found in your normal orbit and you must seek them outside elsewhere.

Love improves after the 22nd, but Uranus is still retrograde all month, so go slow. The partner, spouse or current love is not sure of what he or she wants.

The New Moon of the 12th occurs in your 5th house and is an unusually fun and creative kind of day. It brings spiritual illumination and inspiration to your creativity and, in general, spiritual insights. Issues involving children, creativity and leisure activities will be clarified as the weeks go on.

Virgo

♍

THE VIRGIN

Birthdays from
22nd August to
22nd September

Personality Profile

VIRGO AT A GLANCE

Element – Earth

Ruling Planet – Mercury
  Career Planet – Mercury
  Love Planet – Neptune
  Money Planet – Venus
  Planet of Home and Family Life – Jupiter
  Planet of Health and Work – Uranus
  Planet of Pleasure – Saturn
  Planet of Sexuality – Mars

Colours – earth tones, ochre, orange, yellow

Colour that promotes love, romance and social harmony – aqua blue

Colour that promotes earning power – jade green

Gems – agate, hyacinth

Metal – quicksilver

Scents – lavender, lilac, lily of the valley, storax

Quality – mutable (= flexibility)

Quality most needed for balance – a broader perspective

Strongest virtues – mental agility, analytical skills, ability to pay attention to detail, healing powers

Deepest needs – to be useful and productive

Characteristic to avoid – destructive criticism

Signs of greatest overall compatibility – Taurus, Capricorn

Signs of greatest overall incompatibility – Gemini, Sagittarius, Pisces

Sign most helpful to career – Gemini

Sign most helpful for emotional support – Sagittarius

Sign most helpful financially – Libra

Sign best for marriage and/or partnerships – Pisces

Sign most helpful for creative projects – Capricorn

Best Sign to have fun with – Capricorn

Signs most helpful in spiritual matters – Taurus, Leo

Best day of the week – Wednesday

Understanding a Virgo

The virgin is a particularly fitting symbol for those born under the sign of Virgo. If you meditate on the image of the virgin you will get a good understanding of the essence of the Virgo type. The virgin is, of course, a symbol of purity and innocence – not naïve, but pure. A virginal object has not been touched. A virgin field is land that is true to itself, the way it has always been. The same is true of virgin forest: it is pristine, unaltered.

Apply the idea of purity to the thought processes, emotional life, physical body and activities and projects of the everyday world, and you can see how Virgos approach life. Virgos desire the pure expression of the ideal in their mind, body and affairs. If they find impurities they will attempt to clear them away.

Impurities are the beginning of disorder, unhappiness and uneasiness. The job of the Virgo is to eject all impurities and keep only that which the body and mind can use and assimilate.

The secrets of good health are here revealed: 90 per cent of the art of staying well is maintaining a pure mind, a pure body and pure emotions. When you introduce more impurities than your mind and body can deal with, you will have what is known as 'dis-ease'. It is no wonder that Virgos make great doctors, nurses, healers and dieticians. They have an innate understanding of good health and they realize that good health is more than just physical. In all aspects of life, if you want a project to be successful it must be kept as pure as possible. It must be protected against the adverse elements that will try to undermine it. This is the secret behind Virgo's awesome technical proficiency.

One could talk about Virgo's analytical powers – which are formidable. One could talk about their perfectionism and their almost superhuman attention to detail. But this would be to miss the point. All of these virtues are manifestations of a Virgo's desire for purity and perfection – a world without Virgos would have ruined itself long ago.

A vice is nothing more than a virtue turned inside out, misapplied or used in the wrong context. Virgos' apparent vices come from their inherent virtue. Their analytical powers, which should be used for healing, helping or perfecting a project in the world, sometimes get misapplied and turned against people. Their critical faculties, which should be used constructively to perfect a strategy or proposal, can sometimes be used destructively to harm or wound. Their urge to perfection can turn into worry and lack of confidence; their natural humility can become self-denial and self-abasement. When Virgos turn negative they are apt to turn their devastating criticism on themselves, sowing the seeds of self-destruction.

Finance

Virgos have all the attitudes that create wealth. They are hard-working, industrious, efficient, organized, thrifty, productive and eager to serve. A developed Virgo is every employer's dream. But until Virgos master some of the social graces of Libra they will not even come close to fulfilling their financial potential. Purity and perfectionism, if not handled correctly or gracefully, can be very trying to others. Friction in human relationships can be devastating not only to your pet projects but – indirectly – to your wallet as well.

Virgos are quite interested in their financial security. Being hard-working, they know the true value of money. They do not like to take risks with their money, preferring to save for their retirement or for a rainy day. Virgos usually make prudent, calculated investments that involve a minimum of risk. These investments and savings usually work out well, helping Virgos to achieve the financial security they seek. The rich or even not-so-rich Virgo also likes to help his or her friends in need.

Career and Public Image

Virgos reach their full potential when they can communicate their knowledge in such a way that others can understand it. In order to get their ideas across better, Virgos need to develop greater verbal skills and fewer judgemental ways of expressing themselves. Virgos look up to teachers and communicators; they like their bosses to be good communicators. Virgos will probably not respect a superior who is not their intellectual equal – no matter how much money or power that superior has. Virgos themselves like to be perceived by others as being educated and intellectual.

The natural humility of Virgos often inhibits them from fulfilling their great ambitions, from acquiring name and fame. Virgos should indulge in a little more self-promotion if they are going to reach their career goals. They need to push themselves with the same ardour that they would use to foster others.

At work Virgos like to stay active. They are willing to learn any type of job as long as it serves their ultimate goal of financial security. Virgos may change occupations several times during their professional lives, until they find the one they really enjoy. Virgos work well with other people, are not afraid to work hard and always fulfil their responsibilities.

Love and Relationships

If you are an analyst or a critic you must, out of necessity, narrow your scope. You have to focus on a part and not the whole; this can create a temporary narrow-mindedness. Virgos do not like this kind of person. They like their partners to be broad-minded, with depth and vision. Virgos seek to get this broad-minded quality from their partners, since they sometimes lack it themselves.

Virgos are perfectionists in love just as they are in other areas of life. They need partners who are tolerant, open-minded and easy-going. If you are in love with a Virgo do not waste time on impractical romantic gestures. Do practical and useful things for him or her – this is what will be appreciated and what will be done for you.

Virgos express their love through pragmatic and useful gestures, so do not be put off because your Virgo partner does not say 'I love you' day-in and day-out. Virgos are not that type. If they love you, they will demonstrate it in practical ways. They will always be there for you; they will show an interest in your health and finances; they will fix your sink or repair your video recorder. Virgos deem these actions to be superior to sending flowers, chocolates or Valentine cards.

In love affairs Virgos are not particularly passionate or spontaneous. If you are in love with a Virgo, do not take this personally. It does not mean that you are not alluring enough or that your Virgo partner does not love or like you. It is just the way Virgos are. What they lack in passion they make up for in dedication and loyalty.

Home and Domestic Life

It goes without saying that the home of a Virgo will be spotless, sanitized and orderly. Everything will be in its proper place – and don't you dare move anything about! For Virgos to find domestic bliss they need to ease up a bit in the home, to allow their partner and children more freedom and to be more generous and open-minded. Family members are not to be analysed under a microscope, they are individuals with their own virtues to express.

With these small difficulties resolved, Virgos like to stay in and entertain at home. They make good hosts and they like to keep their friends and families happy and entertained at family and social gatherings. Virgos love children, but they are strict with them – at times – since they want to make sure their children are brought up with the correct sense of family and values.

Horoscope for 2023

Major Trends

Last year was a fabulous love year, Virgo. Many of you married or got involved in serious relationships – relationships that were like a marriage. Many of you met your ideal love. Where 2022 signalled an expansion of the social life – you socialized more, met all kinds of new people, expanded your social horizons – 2023 is more about pulling in your horns, socially. The focus (especially from March 8 onwards) is about socializing less, but more effectively. It's about selecting the best quality and weeding out the mediocre. Less socializing, but of higher quality, is better than a lot of poor-quality socializing. You're becoming more choosy, more discerning about these things. More on this later.

Pluto has been in your 5th house for over twenty years now. This year (and next year) he is starting to change signs. This is a major celestial event. Briefly this year he will move into your 6th house, from March 24 to June 12. This indicates the beginnings of major changes in your health regime and perhaps at the job too. More details later.

Saturn has been in your 6th house for the past two and a half years, but on March 8 he leaves and enters your 7th house. This also signals changes in the health regime.

Jupiter will be in your 8th house until May 17. This indicates an erotic kind of year. In many cases it signals an inheritance or profiting from an estate. The spouse, partner or current love has a super financial year. More on this later.

On May 17 Jupiter will enter your 9th house and stay there for the rest of the year. This is a happy transit. Jupiter is very comfortable in the 9th house. This indicates good fortune for college-level students – or those applying to college. There will be foreign travel – happy travel – this year. There will be religious and theological insights as well.

Your major interests this year will be fun, creativity and children (from January 1 to March 24 and from June 12 to the end of the year); health and work (until March 8 and from March 24 to June 12); love and romance; sex, occult studies, death, personal transformation and reinvention (until May 17); religion, theology, higher education and foreign travel; and spirituality (from June 5 to October 9).

Your paths of greatest fulfilment will be sex, death, occult studies, personal transformation and reinvention (from January 1 to May 17 and from July 18 onwards); and religion, theology, foreign travel and higher education.

Health

(Please note that this is an astrological perspective on health and not a medical one. In days of yore there was no difference, both these perspectives were identical. But these days there could be quite a difference. For a medical perspective, please consult your doctor or health practitioner.)

Health needs more attention this year, especially when Saturn starts to make an inharmonious aspect to you from March 8 onwards. The good news is that Virgo is always focused on health, and you should be on top of things. You will have it under control.

Pluto's flirtation with your 6th house of health from March 24 to June 12 indicates a tendency to surgery. But it also shows that you respond well to detox regimes. Unless the situation is life threatening, there's no rush to have surgery: try detox first.

There are many things you can do to enhance the health and prevent problems from developing. And even if you can't totally prevent them, you can soften their impact. They need not be devastating. Give more attention to the following – the vulnerable areas of your Horoscope this year (the reflex points are shown in the chart below):

- The small intestine is always an important area for Virgo.
- The ankles and calves are also always important for you. Regular ankle and calf massage would be excellent. A weak ankle can knock the spine out of alignment, and this can cause all kinds of other problems. Give the ankles more support when you exercise.
- The neck and throat. This has only become an important area in recent years as your health planet has been in Taurus. Regular neck massage will be wonderful, as tension tends to collect there and needs to be released. Craniosacral therapy is also good for this.

Important foot reflexology points for the year ahead

Try to massage all of the foot on a regular basis – the top of the foot as well as the bottom – but pay extra attention to the points highlighted on the chart. When you massage, be aware of 'sore spots' as these need special attention. It's also a very good idea to massage the ankles and below them.

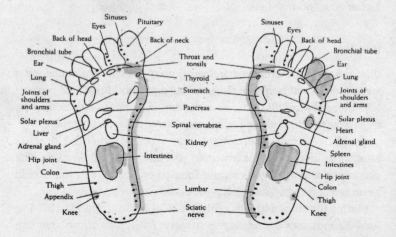

- The spine, knees, teeth, bones, skin and overall skeletal alignment became important since 2021, and will remain so this year until March 8. Regular back and knee massage will be very beneficial, as would regular visits to a chiropractor or osteopath. The vertebrae need to be kept in right alignment. Yoga and Pilates are wonderful exercises for the spine, and therapies such as Feldenkrais, Rolfing and Alexander Technique are also good. If you're out in the Sun, use a good sunscreen. Make sure to get enough calcium for the bones. Good dental hygiene is important.
- The heart gains in importance after March 8. The important thing with the heart is to avoid worry and anxiety (Virgo is prone to these things) and to develop more faith. Worry and anxiety are the main root causes of heart problems, according to many spiritual healers.
- The colon, bladder and sexual organs. These are important this year from March 24 to June 12, but over the coming years will become increasingly so. Safe sex and sexual moderation are called for.

Saturn in stressful aspect is not enough by himself to cause serious health problems, and the other long-term planets are either in harmonious aspect or leaving you alone. However, don't be alarmed if you can't jog or run your usual distance. Or if you can't perform your normal amounts of exercise. There's nothing wrong. It is only that energy is not up to its usual standards.

Jupiter's move into Taurus on May 17 will improve the health. He will make harmonious aspects to you. Also, since he travels near to Uranus, your health planet, over that period, you will get best-case scenarios to any health problems that arise.

Home and Family

Your 4th house of home and family is not a house of power this year. Not prominent. Normally this tends to the status quo. This year, I'm not so sure about this. Jupiter, your family planet, will change signs on May 17, moving from Aries, your 8th house, into Taurus, your 9th. So, changes are brewing here.

Your family planet in the 8th house of regeneration until May 17 suggests that family members, perhaps a parent or parent figure, are undergoing surgery or having near-death kinds of experiences. It would also suggest that major renovations are going on to enlarge the home. It doesn't show a move per se, but more like an extension of the home. Jupiter's move into your 9th house also suggests an enlargement of the home and an expansion of the family circle.

Your family planet in Aries indicates that you're buying exercise equipment for the home. The home is as much a gym as a home. Jupiter in your 9th house in the second half of the year suggests that you might be interested in living in foreign countries. Perhaps you acquire a home abroad. Perhaps you have access to a home abroad. Perhaps you stay in a foreign country for a long time.

Family members in general seem interested in religion, theology and higher education. And this interest further intensifies after May 17. Often with this position we see the home being used as a place of worship. Perhaps prayer meetings or religious talks are happening in the home.

Renovations of the home can happen any time this year. But if you have the choice, January 1 to May 17 and November 24 to the end of the year are good times. If you're merely redecorating – repainting or rearranging the furniture, or buying objects of beauty for the home – May 17 to the end of the year is good.

A parent or parent figure might be thinking of moving. Perhaps there is a need for a change – perhaps he or she feels cramped in the home – but this is not a year for that. He or she is better off making better use of the existing space. Siblings and sibling figures have perhaps had multiple moves in recent years. More could happen this year, and they seem happy. Children and children figures in your life are likely to move. If they are women of childbearing age, they are more fertile than usual. Grandchildren, if you have them, or those who play that role in your life, are having an exciting and happy year. They can be living in different places for long periods of time, but a formal move isn't likely.

Finance and Career

Your money house is not prominent this year. Of course, there will be periods – but short ones – where finance is more important and better than at other times. But these come from the transits of the short-term planets. They are temporary and not trends for the year.

This, as our regular readers know, tends to the status quo. Finances will pretty much be as they were last year. You seem satisfied with earnings as they are and have no need to make major changes or pay undue attention here. A solar eclipse on October 14 occurs in your money house, which will shake things up temporarily and force some important changes.

Venus, your financial planet, will spend over four months (four times the length of her usual transit) in your 12th house this year. She will also make one of her rare (once every two years) retrogrades, from July 23 to September 3. This indicates a need to avoid major financial decisions – major purchases or investments – during that period. Earnings will come but with more delays and glitches. This is a period for gaining financial clarity rather than for making overt moves.

Your financial planet's long stay in Leo, from June 5 to October 9, favours investments in entertainment, music, electric utilities, power companies and gold. You will tend to spend more on the children or children figures in your life. It favours investments in companies that cater to the youth market. It also makes you much more speculative than usual. Money will tend to come easily and be spent freely. Though you're more speculative, avoid this when Venus is retrograde. Venus in your 12th house of spirituality signals good financial intuition (although, when she is retrograde, the intuition needs verification). It also shows greater generosity and charitableness. Most importantly, it shows explorations into the spiritual laws of wealth.

Venus is a very fast-moving planet, as our regular readers know. She moves through your entire chart in the course of a year, and so there are many short-term trends in finance depending on where Venus is and the kinds of aspects she receives. These trends will be covered in the monthly reports.

As with finance, career is not prominent this year. Your 10th house is basically empty. Only short-term planets will move through there, with short-term effects. However, because Jupiter will move into your 10th house next year, I feel that this year is a kind of preparation period. You're getting prepared, mentally and emotionally, for the major career successes that will happen next year.

An empty 10th house shows a stable career year. You seem satisfied with things as they are and have no need to make major changes.

Mercury is your career planet. Like Venus, he is fast moving. And, in any given year, he will move through your entire Horoscope. So, there are many short-term career trends that depend on where Mercury is and the kinds of aspects he receives. These are best dealt with in the monthly reports.

The lack of focus on money and career should not alarm you. The Horoscope aims at a balanced development. It urges focus on different areas in different years.

Love and Social Life

Your 7th house of love has been prominent for many, many years. It was especially prominent last year. And it is prominent again this year as well, but in a different way. Last year was a banner love and social year. As we mentioned, serious romance happened. Marriages or relationships that were 'like' marriage happened. It was social bliss. Your love ideals were pretty much realized. Now, with Saturn moving into your house of love on March 8, your relationship and friendships get tested.

When things are going well, we don't know if love is real. We only find out during the tough times. The testing reveals this to us, and this is what is going on this year. Your relationship is getting 'road tested' much in the way that a car manufacturer road tests a vehicle. The manufacturer will put the car through gruelling tests to see how well it stands up and to learn where improvements can be made. So it is in love. If the relationship endures through Saturn's 'road tests' you'll know you have something good.

You will see the same sort of thing in friendships as well. You made many new friends last year. Your social circle expanded tremendously. Now these friendships get tested so that you can see who's who and what's what.

As we mentioned earlier, social activity will be less this year, but of higher quality. This is as it should be.

If there are any Virgos who are still single or unattached, this is not a year for marriage. Sure, you will date and meet people – there are two love interests this year – but marriage isn't in the cards. There's no need to rush into things. Enjoy love for what it is.

Romantic opportunities occur in spiritual settings – as has been the case for many years. Parties given by spiritual or charitable organizations can lead to romance. You're attracted to spiritual-type people in general, and spiritual compatibility is very important.

Self-improvement

Neptune, as we mentioned, has been in your 7th house of love for many years. So, the love and social life is being elevated and refined. It is being spiritualized. This process will go on for some more years to come but will result – in some cases – in the discovery of the Love Divine; the only perfect love there is. Not everyone will attain this, but all of you will make progress towards it. This is the spiritual agenda for you.

Your intuition is being trained, as has been the case for many years now, in love and social matters. The love life is your spiritual training ground. Having the right friends is part and parcel of your spiritual development and practice. Good spiritual friends will enable your progress and assist in your growth.

Saturn, as we've seen, will be testing your relationship and friendships. There will be challenges and difficulties. One of the best ways – especially given your Horoscope – to deal with these challenges is to surrender the love life, the relationship, to the Divine and let that handle things. If you do this sincerely, you'll see amazing results. The knottiest problems straighten right out. But sincerity is essential. If nothing happens right away, keep at it.

The Sun is your spiritual planet and he moves through every sign and house in your chart in any given year. Thus, there are many short-term trends in your spiritual life that depend on where the Sun is and the kinds of aspects he receives. These are best dealt with in the monthly reports.

Two solar eclipses this year – on April 20 and on October 14 – will bring changes to the spiritual life and practice. Sometimes one changes teachers or teachings. Often these changes are very normal. A practice that was good for a time, has served its purpose, brought you to the desired realization. Now a new practice is called for. Sometimes though, it is not that harmonious, especially if there have been errors in attitude or practice. So, things need to be shaken up.

The Sun as the spiritual planet favours the solar religions – Christianity, Surya and Krishna Yoga and the paths of creativity. By being creative one learns the laws of the Great Creator, for the same laws apply (though in different magnitude) in creating a song, painting or dance as are involved in the creation of a cosmos.

For more information on these subjects see my website, www.spiritual-stories.com.

Month-by-month Forecasts

January

Best Days Overall: 1, 2, 10, 11, 18, 19, 28, 29
Most Stressful Days Overall: 8, 9, 14, 15, 21, 22
Best Days for Love: 2, 3, 7, 12, 13, 14, 15, 21, 22, 24
Best Days for Money: 2, 3, 4, 8, 12, 13, 16, 21, 22, 23, 30, 31
Best Days for Career: 1, 2, 10, 11, 18, 19, 21, 22, 28, 29

Basically a happy month ahead, Virgo. Enjoy. You begin the year in the midst of a yearly personal pleasure peak. A time to enjoy life. Personal creativity is also very strong. (Being in the midst of a good creative flow is one of the great pleasures in life.)

With Mercury, the ruler of your Horoscope, retrograde until the 17th, you start the year off slowly. There is a lack of direction both in your personal desires and in your career: Mars, in your 10th house of career, is also retrograde until the 12th. So, career issues need time to resolve. You may as well have fun.

Your financial planet Venus moves speedily this month, through three signs and houses of your chart. This signals much change in your financial attitudes and approaches. Until the 3rd, you're conservative in money matters. After then you're more experimental, but money comes the old-fashioned way, through work and productive service. After the 27th the financial intuition becomes important – as do your social contacts. Venus travels with Pluto on the 1st and 2nd. This transit favours buying, selling and trading. It also favours tax and insurance planning. On the 22nd Venus travels with Saturn, which brings a short-term attitude of conservatism. It can also bring some new financial responsibility.

The 4th and 5th bring spiritual insights and perhaps supernatural kinds of experiences. The 29th to the 31st can bring job opportunities.

Jupiter, your home and family planet, and a very slow-moving planet to boot, will have his solstice from the 1st to the 27th – this is a long time. He will be stationary in the heavens (in his latitudinal motion) and will then change direction. So, there is a pause in the family and domestic life and then a change of direction. Perhaps a family member is undergoing surgery or experiencing some other personal crisis. There is nothing much to be done right now, but a change of direction will happen by the 27th.

The New Moon of the 11th occurs in your 5th house, bringing a fun and creative kind of day. It is a good financial day for your friends. It also brings you spiritual insights. Issues involving your children or children figures in your life, and in your creativity, will clarify themselves in the coming weeks.

Health is basically good this month. After the 27th, you will need to rest and relax more, however.

February

Best Days Overall: 7, 8, 16, 17, 24, 25
Most Stressful Days Overall: 1, 14, 15, 20, 21, 27, 28
Best Days for Love: 2, 3, 12, 13, 20, 21, 22
Best Days for Money: 2, 3, 4, 5, 9, 10, 12, 13, 14, 15, 22, 23
Best Days for Career: 1, 8, 11, 18, 19, 27, 28

Health needs more attention this month – especially from the 18th onwards. There is nothing serious afoot, only short-term stress caused by the passage of short-term planets. Enhance the health with more rest and in the ways mentioned in the yearly report.

Health and work – mostly work – dominate the month until the 18th. With your spiritual planet the Sun in your 6th house until the 18th, spiritual healing will be beneficial for you.

Unusually, all the planets are moving forward this month, so events in your life and in the world in general are moving quickly. There is faster progress to your goals. Delays can happen but they are minimal.

There is some financial drama on the 1st and the 2nd. There is some financial disagreement with spouse, partner or current love on the 3rd and 4th – but this seems temporary. The 14th to the 16th brings fabulous financial intuition. There will be financial guidance from on high – from the spirit world. A friend is helpful financially.

Venus will have her solstice from the 21st to the 24th. She pauses in the heavens (in latitude) and then changes direction. And so it is with you. There is a pause in your financial life and then a change of direction. Venus moves into your 8th house on the 21st and will stay there for the rest of the month. You seem focused on prospering others now, especially the spouse, partner or current love. Your financial planet will be travelling with Jupiter at this time, although the aspect will be more exact next month. Still, you're feeling the influence now. Earnings increase – both personally and for the spouse, partner or current love.

The love life becomes more active from the 18th onwards. You begin a yearly love and social peak. The New Moon of the 20th also occurs in your 7th house, which will increase the social happiness even more. Even better, many issues to do with your relationship or love life in general will be clarified even after the New Moon actually occurs. The Moon is going to answer your questions as the weeks go by – until the next New Moon.

Mars is still in your 10th house all month (he's been there since the beginning of the year). This signals much activity in the career. Perhaps there are surgical procedures, deaths or near-death kinds of experience. These can affect bosses, parents, parent figures or people involved in your career.

March

Best Days Overall: 6, 7, 15, 16, 24, 25
Most Stressful Days Overall: 13, 14, 19, 20, 26, 27
Best Days for Love: 2, 4, 5, 11, 12, 19, 20, 24, 25, 29, 30
Best Days for Money: 4, 5, 11, 12, 13, 14, 21, 22, 24, 25, 31
Best Days for Career: 11, 12, 21, 26, 27, 31

A lot of changes are happening this month. Pluto moves into your 6th house on the 24th and changes your approach to health. It is only a short stay this year, but in the coming years you will feel the full brunt of these changes. More importantly, Saturn moves into your 7th house on the 8th and will stay there for the next two and a half years. You're in a yearly love and social peak (since February 18), coming off the back of a very strong social year (in 2022). Now, it's time to pull the horns in a little. Current relationships get tested to see if love is real. There is a need to focus on the quality of relationships rather than mere quantity. You are popular this month – especially from the 3rd to the 19th. You're very much there for others. You're there for your friends and current love. But Saturn is reminding you to focus on quality.

Health needs watching this month. The colon, bladder and sexual organs need more attention. Safe sex and sexual moderation are important. This might be difficult, as your 8th house of regeneration is unusually powerful, and libido is unusually high. However, listen to the messages of the body and you'll know when enough is enough. Detox regimes will be particularly effective at this time. Health and energy will improve from the 20th.

Your 8th house is supercharged this month – especially from the 20th onwards. Thus, it is a good time to focus on personal transformation – giving birth to the person you want to be, your ideal self. While this won't happen in one month, great progress will be made and that's what counts. Giving birth to one's ideal self is a work of many incarnations; making progress is the best we can hope for.

Finances should be good this month. Venus travels with Jupiter on the 1st and 2nd showing a nice (and happy) payday. Venus remains in your 8th house until the 17th, so, like last month, the object is to prosper others – to focus on their financial interest – and as you do so, your own prosperity will happen. It is still a good period to purge yourself of things you don't need or use. You seem a bit too speculative until the 17th – very much a risk taker. But you become more conservative after then (perhaps a few shocks or close calls prompt this conservatism).

April

Best Days Overall: 2, 3, 4, 12, 13, 30
Most Stressful Days Overall: 9, 10, 16, 17, 22, 23, 24
Best Days for Love: 3, 4, 8, 14, 16, 17, 22, 23, 26
Best Days for Money: 1, 3, 4, 5, 6, 10, 14, 19, 22, 23, 28, 29
Best Days for Career: 1, 12, 13, 21, 22, 23, 24, 30

A solar eclipse on the 20th occurs right on the border – the cusp – of your 8th and 9th houses and will impact on both these houses. It would be a good idea to reduce your schedule and relax over this period. Things that must be done should be done, but anything else – especially if it is stressful – is better off being postponed.

The impact on the 8th house affects the income of the spouse, partner or current love. He or she has been having a super prosperous period this year, especially last month and this month. So, there is a need to make some adjustments – their financial thinking might not have been realistic and course corrections are necessary. There can be encounters – usually psychological encounters – with death. Sometimes a friend calls you to tell of a death of someone close to them. Perhaps they tell you of a near-death kind of experience. Perhaps you have such a near-death experience. Often people have dreams of death. These events are the nudging of the spirit world, urging you to get more serious about life – it is short and can end at any time. Get down to the reason you have been incarnated.

The impact on your 9th house affects college-level students. There are changes in their educational plans (and good ones); perhaps obstacles to getting into a particular school are blasted away. Often there are changes of subjects and courses and disruptions at the college. There are disruptions at your place of worship and in the lives of worship leaders. Your religious beliefs will get tested as well. Some will be discarded; some will be modified. If you're involved in legal action, it takes a dramatic turn, one way or another (I would say a positive turn).

Pluto, the ruler of your 3rd house, is directly affected by this eclipse, which reinforces what we said earlier about encounters with death. But it also indicates dramas in the lives of siblings, sibling figures and neighbours. There can be disruptions in the neighbourhood too.

Every solar eclipse brings spiritual changes, and this one is no different. You could be changing your attitude, teachers or teachings. There are dramas in the lives of guru figures and disruptions in spiritual or charitable organizations that you're involved with.

May

Best Days Overall: 1, 9, 10, 17, 18, 19, 27, 28
Most Stressful Days Overall: 7, 8, 13, 14, 20, 21
Best Days for Love: 2, 3, 6, 9, 10, 13, 14, 17, 18, 19, 23, 24
Best Days for Money: 2, 3, 8, 9, 10, 16, 17, 18, 19, 24, 25, 30, 31
Best Days for Career: 1, 9, 10, 17, 18, 19, 20, 21, 27, 28

A lunar eclipse on the 5th occurs in your 3rd house, once again bringing personal dramas in the lives of siblings, sibling figures and neighbours. They should take a nice easy schedule over the eclipse period. Once again, like last month, there are disruptions in your neighbourhood. Students below college level are affected this time. They can change schools or change educational plans. Often there are disruptions at the school. Cars and communication equipment can behave erratically (this was true last month as well). Often repairs or replacements are necessary. It would be a good idea to drive more carefully over this period.

Every lunar eclipse impacts friends and tests friendships. Sometimes the dirty laundry in a friendship is revealed and it is either corrected or the friendship goes by the wayside. Sometimes the testing happens because of some personal drama in the friend's life and not necessarily because of the relationship. Computers, software and high-tech gadgetry get tested. They behave erratically. I've seen all kinds of things happen. Your software is updated and changes all your settings. Or there is a hack attack. Or the monitor goes out for no apparent reason.

So, in many cases, repairs or replacements are necessary. Keep your anti-virus and anti-hacking software up to date. Avoid opening emails from strangers. And even emails from friends can be hacked and have malicious links. Keep your important files backed up. A parent or parent figure has to make important financial changes. There is some financial drama going on. The money people in your life also have financial dramas.

Jupiter moves into your 9th house on the 17th, so college-level students – many of whom have had dramas last month thanks to the solar eclipse – are successful in their studies. Those applying to college also have good fortune. Health is generally good this month but needs more attention from the 21st onwards.

The Sun enters your 10th house of career on the 21st and you begin a yearly career peak. Enhance the career with involvement in charities and altruistic activities. Your spiritual life is very active as well.

June

Best Days Overall: 5, 6, 14, 15, 23, 24, 25
Most Stressful Days Overall: 3, 4, 9, 10, 16, 17
Best Days for Love: 2, 9, 10, 11, 19, 20, 21, 22, 29
Best Days for Money: 2, 5, 6, 11, 14, 15, 21, 22, 23, 24, 26, 27
Best Days for Career: 6, 16, 17, 26, 27

Health needs watching, but the month ahead is successful. You entered a yearly career peak last month and this continues until the 21st. More important than that is Mercury's entrance into your house of career on the 11th. This indicates personal elevation. You're honoured and appreciated not just for your professional skills but for who you are as a person. The ruler of your Horoscope is at the top of your chart. You're on top, in charge, above everyone in your world (in some cases, this is the aspiration). Personal appearance and overall demeanour are important factors in the career this month. Mercury will go 'out of bounds' on the 25th and stay that way until July 6. So, you're going outside your normal orbit. Perhaps career responsibilities are causing this. The New Moon of the 18th occurs in your 10th house and increases the success of the month. In addition, the New Moon will help clarify career issues as the weeks progress (until the next New Moon). Career questions and doubts will be answered.

A parent or parent figure has a super social month. Some have been divorced in recent years. And, if this is the case, a new romance is happening.

Love could be a lot better. The two planets involved in your love life – Neptune and Saturn – will both go retrograde this month. Also, the love planet is receiving stressful aspects. So, there is more work involved in keeping your relationship together. With these kinds of aspects time, and time alone, is the great healer.

Health improves after the 21st. In the meantime, as always, make sure to get enough rest. It is doubtful that you can ignore your career or social responsibilities but focus on the really important things and let lesser matters go. Enhance the health in the ways mentioned in the yearly report.

Mars will be in your 12th house of spirituality all month, signalling a desire to express your ideals in physical action. You can be more activist about these things. On a deeper level it shows a need to purge the mind and emotions of all that obstructs the spiritual energy.

July

Best Days Overall: 3, 4, 11, 12, 21, 22, 30, 31
Most Stressful Days Overall: 1, 2, 7, 8, 13, 14, 15, 28, 29
Best Days for Love: 2, 7, 8, 10, 17, 19, 20, 27, 29
Best Days for Money: 2, 3, 4, 10, 11, 12, 19, 20, 21, 22, 23, 24, 29, 30, 31
Best Days for Career: 8, 13, 14, 15, 18, 19, 30

The ruler of your Horoscope, Mercury, is still 'out of bounds' until the 6th. So, you continue to be 'off the reservation' in personal, career and social matters. You're seen this way by others. And perhaps you enjoy this designation.

You're still in a social month – but not necessarily a romantic one. These relationships seem more Platonic in nature. Still, these can be enjoyable. The New Moon of the 17th occurs in your 11th house of friends and it is an especially good social day. You're attracting spiritual people socially, and perhaps getting involved in spiritual or charitable groups.

The month ahead is very spiritual. The Sun enters your 12th house on the 23rd. Mercury has been there since the 11th and Venus since June 5. So, there are many messages here. The financial intuition is strong – though after the 23rd it needs some verification. Get right spiritually, and finances, personal appearance and the career will take care of themselves. You can expect a more active dream life and if strange, supernatural phenomena happen – it shouldn't surprise you.

Mars moves into your sign on the 11th. On the one hand this transit gives you more energy. Personal sex appeal – sexual magnetism – is unusually strong. You excel in exercise and sports (personal bests will be set). On the other hand, you can be too belligerent, argumentative, in a hurry. This can lead to confrontations, accidents or injury. It's not a good idea to be in a rush these days as retrograde activity is strong – 40 per cent of the planets are going backwards after the 23rd. Rushing won't make things happen faster.

Health is much improved over last month. Pluto is now out of your 6th house of health, but your health planet Uranus receives stressful aspects after the 23rd. So, you could be making changes to the health regime. The job situation seems more difficult as well.

Mercury moves into your own sign on the 29th. This brings self-esteem and confidence. It also brings career opportunity. People see you as successful.

August

Best Days Overall: 7, 8, 17, 18, 26, 27
Most Stressful Days Overall: 3, 4, 10, 11, 24, 25, 30, 31
Best Days for Love: 3, 4, 5, 6, 13, 14, 15, 23, 24, 25, 30, 31
Best Days for Money: 5, 6, 7, 8, 14, 15, 17, 18, 19, 20, 21, 24, 25, 26, 27
Best Days for Career: 7, 8, 10, 11, 17, 18, 26, 27

Mars remains in your sign almost all month, and planetary retrograde activity is increasing even further. By the end of the month 60 per cent of the planets will be retrograde – the maximum extent for the year.

This definitely is not a time to be in a rush. Feelings of frustration would be natural this month – but not very helpful. Practise the 'art of the possible' – whatever can be done should be done. But let go of what can't. Practise patience even when the stomach is churning and the neck overheats.

Though life is slowing down, the month ahead is happy. The Sun enters your sign on the 23rd and you begin a yearly personal pleasure peak. This is a time to enjoy the pleasures of the senses and to get the body and image into the shape that you want. The Sun is your spiritual planet. So don't be surprised if the body becomes more sensitive at this time. It is being raised in vibration. It is more refined and more sensitive to spiritual energies. This is a good month to make the changes you need to make for your happiness. The only problem is that with Mercury retrograde, you're not really sure what these changes should be.

Love needs a lot more work this month, but especially after the 23rd. Just ride it out and try to not make matters worse. Neither you nor the beloved are clear on things. Important love decisions shouldn't be made at this time. Wait until the planets start moving forward.

Finances are also complicated as Venus, your financial planet, is still retrograde. So verify your financial intuitions before leaping into action. Avoid major purchases or investments this month. If you must do these things, exercise strict 'due diligence'.

The New Moon of the 16th occurs in your 12th house of spirituality, so it is a particularly strong spiritual day. Insights and understandings come to you. The dream life is active and significant. Most importantly, spiritual issues will clarify themselves in the coming weeks.

September

Best Days Overall: 4, 5, 13, 14, 15, 23, 24
Most Stressful Days Overall: 6, 7, 21, 22, 27, 28
Best Days for Love: 1, 2, 3, 9, 10, 11, 12, 19, 21, 22, 27, 28, 30
Best Days for Money: 2, 3, 4, 5, 11, 12, 14, 15, 16, 17, 21, 22, 23, 24, 30
Best Days for Career: 4, 5, 6, 7, 13, 14, 15, 23, 24

Retrograde activity is still at fever pitch until the 16th, but now that Mars is out of your sign you're probably handling it better.

You remain in a yearly personal pleasure peak until the 23rd. Your spiritual planet in your sign gives a supernatural glow and glamour to the image. But in spite of this, love still needs a lot of work – a very confusing kind of area these days.

The good news is that finances are starting to straighten out. Your financial planet starts to move forward on the 4th and the financial intuition is more trustworthy. (It is always trustworthy, but you probably interpret it better.) On the 23rd the Sun enters your 2nd money house and you begin a yearly financial peak. You're definitely more charitable and generous now. You're experiencing 'miracle money' as opposed to 'natural money'. Miracle money is money that comes in unexpected ways and through unexpected means. When you experience it you'll know what we mean. Natural money is money that is earned from work, investments or through the family or spouse. The spirit world is letting you know that it desires your prosperity. It will guide you here as well.

Mars in the money house all month can make you take more risks in finance, so you need to be careful about this. Mars as ruler of your 8th house favours using spare cash to pay down debt. But if you need to borrow it is a good transit for that too. Also good for attracting outside investors to your projects if you have good business ideas. The spouse, partner or current love seems active in your financial life.

Mercury starts to move forward on the 15th. So, it is safer now to make the changes that need to be made for your happiness. Mercury in your sign improves the personal image and gives an aura of success

around you. You have the look of someone important or on the road to
it.

October

Best Days Overall: 1, 2, 11, 12, 20, 21, 28, 29
Most Stressful Days Overall: 3, 4, 18, 19, 24, 25
Best Days for Love: 7, 9, 10, 11, 17, 20, 21, 24, 25, 28, 29
Best Days for Money: 1, 2, 9, 10, 11, 12, 20, 21, 28, 29
Best Days for Career: 2, 3, 4, 24

Two eclipses dominate the month ahead. These eclipses are relatively
mild in their effects on you, as far as eclipses go, but if they hit a sensitive point in your actual Horoscope – the one cast especially for you –
they can be strong indeed. Eclipses have an impact on the world at
large and also a personal impact. For the global impact, just read the
newspapers this month. Here we will deal with the personal effects.

The solar eclipse of the 14th occurs in your money house and
provokes important financial changes – dramatic ones. Since you're in
the midst of a yearly financial peak (until the 23rd) I feel the shake-ups
and changes will be positive. They will add to your prosperity. But your
financial thinking and planning will need to be changed. As with any
solar eclipse, there are spiritual changes happening as well. You went
through a similar experience during the solar eclipse of April 20. So,
once again, important changes are happening in your spiritual life –
changes to your attitude, teachings, teachers and practice. Often some
new revelation comes to you that causes these things. This is natural
and normal. There are shake-ups and disruptions in spiritual or charitable organizations that you're involved with, and guru figures in your
life experience personal dramas. Siblings and sibling figures are also
experiencing these kinds of events.

The lunar eclipse of the 28th occurs in your 9th house, affecting
college-level students. There is a need to make dramatic changes to
educational plans. Perhaps a professor you like or a course you signed
up for is no longer available. Perhaps there is some disturbance at
school. Perhaps a change of courses. Since college students are in a
very fortunate period right now, these changes are good – but they're

not always comfortable while they're happening. Once again (just as in April) religious beliefs get tested. There is a need to modify them, and some will need to be discarded altogether. This lunar eclipse, like the one on May 5, affects friends and trade and professional organizations that you're involved with. There are shake-ups and dramas here. Computers and technical equipment can behave erratically. Back up important files and avoid opening emails from people you don't know. Avoid clicking on links even if they're from people you know.

November

Best Days Overall: 7, 8, 16, 17, 25, 26
Most Stressful Days Overall: 1, 14, 15, 21, 22, 27, 28
Best Days for Love: 3, 8, 9, 13, 18, 19, 21, 22, 27, 28, 30
Best Days for Money: 7, 8, 9, 10, 11, 16, 18, 19, 25, 27, 28
Best Days for Career: 1, 2, 3, 23, 24, 27, 28

Retrograde activity is starting to wind down. From the 4th onwards only 30 per cent of the planets are retrograde. This is within acceptable limits.

The love life is much improved this month. Saturn starts moving forward on the 4th and Neptune, though still retrograde, is getting ready to move forward. More importantly, Neptune is receiving very nice aspects – positive stimulation. So, relationships are starting to unfreeze. Clarity is coming in love – but you're not quite there yet.

Health is good but it needs keeping an eye on after the 22nd. Make sure to get enough rest – always important. With your health planet Uranus retrograde all month, be careful about making major changes to the health regime. Be extremely wary of miracle supplements or cures. These things need close study. Also avoid undergoing medical tests and procedures if you can – reschedule them for another time. With your health planet retrograde these things are prone to error. If you do have tests this period and the results are not happy, make sure to get a second opinion – but at a later date.

Finances seem good this month. Until the 8th Venus is in your sign – always a positive for finance. (She was in your sign last month too.) This brings windfalls and happy financial opportunities. Money chases you rather than vice versa. You spend on yourself and dress expensively. On the 8th Venus moves into your money house – her own sign and house. This too is good for finance as Venus is strong in her own sign and house. Earnings should be stronger.

Your 3rd house will be powerful until the 22nd. So, the focus is on intellectual interests – reading, studying, teaching, blogging and the like. This is a good time for students; learning goes well. The mental faculties are stronger than usual.

On the 22nd, as the Sun enters your 4th family house, you enter the midnight hour (symbolically speaking) of your year. The focus should be on your internal life – your home, family and emotional well-being. Even your career planet Mercury is in your 4th house from the 10th onwards. So home, family and emotional wellness is the mission – the real career – from the 10th.

December

Best Days Overall: 4, 5, 6, 14, 15, 22, 23, 31
Most Stressful Days Overall: 11, 12, 18, 19, 24, 25
Best Days for Love: 9, 10, 18, 19, 28, 30
Best Days for Money: 4, 7, 8, 9, 14, 18, 19, 22, 28, 30, 31
Best Days for Career: 4, 14, 22, 24, 25, 30

Your love planet Neptune moves forward on the 6th and clarity and confidence are returning to the love life. The social judgement is good. The only issue in love is that Neptune is receiving stressful aspects. A current relationship needs more work. This will change after the 22nd when the love planet starts to receive good aspects. Singles probably shouldn't marry just yet – though opportunities are there.

Health still needs some attention. Like last month, avoid undergoing tests or procedures if possible. Avoid making major changes to the health regime as well. Uranus, your health planet, is still travelling backwards. Make sure to get enough rest and enhance the health in the ways mentioned in the yearly report.

The power is still mostly in your 4th house of family this month. Mercury, your career planet, will spend time in Capricorn and Sagittarius. So home – and the children – are the real career this month. Mars spends the month in your 4th house, which signals many things. On a purely material level, this would show that you're in an excellent period for making renovations or major repairs about the house. There can be near-death experiences in the lives of family members too – perhaps surgery. On a deeper level, Mars in the 4th house signals a great opportunity to purge both the past and the emotional life of negative patterns. Mars, along with Pluto, rules detoxes. Emotional healing can be challenging as deep and traumatic, fear-based memories surface for cleansing. Hang in there. You will prevail and come out a better person. The New Moon of the 12th will occur in your 4th house and will further clarify emotional and family issues in the coming weeks.

With your financial planet in the sign of Scorpio from the 5th to the 30th, a detox is happening on the financial level as well. Best to coop-erate with it. Get rid of possessions that you don't need or use. Sell them or give them to charity. Start to 'declutter' the financial life. Less is more this period. You expand by cutting back – cutting waste and redundant accounts in the financial life. (We're not talking about cutting things that you need – just the extraneous.)

Libra

THE SCALES

Birthdays from
23rd September to
22nd October

Personality Profile

LIBRA AT A GLANCE

Element – Air

Ruling Planet – Venus
   Career Planet – Moon
   Love Planet – Mars
   Money Planet – Pluto
   Planet of Communications – Jupiter
   Planet of Health and Work – Neptune
   Planet of Home and Family Life – Saturn
   Planet of Spirituality and Good Fortune – Mercury

Colours – blue, jade green

Colours that promote love, romance and social harmony – carmine, red, scarlet

Colours that promote earning power – burgundy, red-violet, violet

Gems – carnelian, chrysolite, coral, emerald, jade, opal, quartz, white marble

Metal – copper

Scents – almond, rose, vanilla, violet

Quality – cardinal (= activity)

Qualities most needed for balance – a sense of self, self-reliance, independence

Strongest virtues – social grace, charm, tact, diplomacy

Deepest needs – love, romance, social harmony

Characteristic to avoid – violating what is right in order to be socially accepted

Signs of greatest overall compatibility – Gemini, Aquarius

Signs of greatest overall incompatibility – Aries, Cancer, Capricorn

Sign most helpful to career – Cancer

Sign most helpful for emotional support – Capricorn

Sign most helpful financially – Scorpio

Sign best for marriage and/or partnerships – Aries

Sign most helpful for creative projects – Aquarius

Best Sign to have fun with – Aquarius

Signs most helpful in spiritual matters – Gemini, Virgo

Best day of the week – Friday

Understanding a Libra

In the sign of Libra the universal mind – the soul – expresses its genius for relationships, that is, its power to harmonize diverse elements in a unified, organic way. Libra is the soul's power to express beauty in all of its forms. And where is beauty if not within relationships? Beauty does not exist in isolation. Beauty arises out of comparison – out of the just relationship between different parts. Without a fair and harmonious relationship there is no beauty, whether it in art, manners, ideas or the social or political forum.

There are two faculties humans have that exalt them above the animal kingdom: their rational faculty (expressed in the signs of Gemini and Aquarius) and their aesthetic faculty, exemplified by Libra. Without an aesthetic sense we would be little more than intelligent barbarians. Libra is the civilizing instinct or urge of the soul.

Beauty is the essence of what Librans are all about. They are here to beautify the world. One could discuss Librans' social grace, their sense of balance and fair play, their ability to see and love another person's point of view – but this would be to miss their central asset: their desire for beauty.

No one – no matter how alone he or she seems to be – exists in isolation. The universe is one vast collaboration of beings. Librans, more than most, understand this and understand the spiritual laws that make relationships bearable and enjoyable.

A Libra is always the unconscious (and in some cases conscious) civilizer, harmonizer and artist. This is a Libra's deepest urge and greatest genius. Librans love instinctively to bring people together, and they are uniquely qualified to do so. They have a knack for seeing what unites people – the things that attract and bind rather than separate individuals.

Finance

In financial matters Librans can seem frivolous and illogical to others. This is because Librans appear to be more concerned with earning money for others than for themselves. But there is a logic to this financial attitude. Librans know that everything and everyone is connected and that it is impossible to help another to prosper without also prospering yourself. Since enhancing their partner's income and position tends to strengthen their relationship, Librans choose to do so. What could be more fun than building a relationship? You will rarely find a Libra enriching him- or herself at someone else's expense.

Scorpio is the ruler of Libra's solar 2nd house of money, giving Libra unusual insight into financial matters – and the power to focus on these matters in a way that disguises a seeming indifference. In fact, many other signs come to Librans for financial advice and guidance.

Given their social grace, Librans often spend great sums of money on entertaining and organizing social events. They also like to help others when they are in need. Librans would go out of their way to help a friend in dire straits, even if they have to borrow from others to do so. However, Librans are also very careful to pay back any debts they owe, and like to make sure they never have to be reminded to do so.

Career and Public Image

Publicly, Librans like to appear as nurturers. Their friends and acquaintances are their family and they wield political power in parental ways. They also like bosses who are paternal or maternal.

The sign of Cancer is on Libra's 10th career house cusp; the Moon is Libra's career planet. The Moon is by far the speediest, most changeable planet in the horoscope. It alone among all the planets travels through the entire zodiac – all twelve signs and houses – every month. This is an important key to the way in which Librans approach their careers, and also to what they need to do to maximize their career potential. The Moon is the planet of moods and feelings – Librans need a career in which their emotions can have free expression. This is why so many Librans are involved in the creative arts. Libra's ambitions wax and wane with the Moon. They tend to wield power according to their mood.

The Moon 'rules' the masses – and that is why Libra's highest goal is to achieve a mass kind of acclaim and popularity. Librans who achieve fame cultivate the public as other people cultivate a lover or friend. Librans can be very flexible – and often fickle – in their career and ambitions. On the other hand, they can achieve their ends in a great variety of ways. They are not stuck in one attitude or with one way of doing things.

Love and Relationships

Librans express their true genius in love. In love you could not find a partner more romantic, more seductive or more fair. If there is one thing that is sure to destroy a relationship – sure to block your love from flowing – it is injustice or imbalance between lover and beloved. If one party is giving too much or taking too much, resentment is sure to surface at some time or other. Librans are careful about this. If anything, Librans might err on the side of giving more, but never giving less.

If you are in love with a Libra, make sure you keep the aura of romance alive. Do all the little things – candle-lit dinners, travel to exotic locales, flowers and small gifts. Give things that are beautiful, not necessarily expensive. Send cards. Ring regularly even if you have nothing in particular to say. The niceties are very important to a Libra. Your relationship is a work of art: make it beautiful and your Libran lover will appreciate it. If you are creative about it, he or she will appreciate it even more; for this is how your Libra will behave towards you.

Librans like their partners to be aggressive and even a bit self-willed. They know that these are qualities they sometimes lack and so they like their partners to have them. In relationships, however, Librans can be very aggressive – but always in a subtle and charming way! Librans are determined in their efforts to charm the object of their desire – and this determination can be very pleasant if you are on the receiving end.

Home and Domestic Life

Since Librans are such social creatures, they do not particularly like mundane domestic duties. They like a well-organized home – clean and neat with everything needful present – but housework is a chore and a burden, one of the unpleasant tasks in life that must be done, the quicker the better. If a Libra has enough money – and sometimes even if not – he or she will prefer to pay someone else to take care of the daily household chores. However, Librans like gardening; they love to have flowers and plants in the home.

A Libra's home is modern, and furnished in excellent taste. You will find many paintings and sculptures there. Since Librans like to be with friends and family, they enjoy entertaining at home and they make great hosts.

Capricorn is on the cusp of Libra's 4th solar house of home and family. Saturn, the planet of law, order, limits and discipline, rules Libra's domestic affairs. If Librans want their home life to be supportive and happy they need to develop some of the virtues of Saturn – order, organization and discipline. Librans, being so creative and so intensely in need of harmony, can tend to be too lax in the home and too permissive with their children. Too much of this is not always good; children need freedom but they also need limits.

Horoscope for 2023

Major Trends

Health is steadily improving this year, Libra. Pluto, who has been in stressful aspect with you for more than twenty years, is starting to move into a harmonious alignment. However, this is a two-year process. This year and next he will hover between Capricorn and Aquarius – between a harmonious and inharmonious aspect. Jupiter will move away from his stressful aspect on May 17, and by the end of the year only one long-term planet will be in stressful aspect. More on this later.

Pluto's movements – back and forth between Aquarius and Capricorn – also signals that important financial changes are beginning to happen. You will be less conservative and more experimental in finance. More details later.

Perhaps the main headline this year is love. Jupiter will be in your 7th house of love until May 17. This shows that major romance is happening – especially for singles. New friends are also coming into the picture. The whole social circle expands. There is much happiness in love and social matters in the year ahead. More on this later.

Your 6th house of health and work has been strong for many years. It was especially strong last year and remains so for the year ahead. Saturn moves into this house on March 8 and will be there for the next two and a half years, joining long-staying Neptune there. So there is a strong focus on health and there are job opportunities coming this year. Details below.

Uranus has been in your 8th house of regeneration for many years and will be there for a few more years to come. You've been sexually experimental as a result. You're learning what works for you personally. You get rid of all the 'how to' books and learn your own body. The spouse, partner or current love has been experimental in finances as well. This year, as Jupiter moves into your 8th house on May 17, he or she will see the positive results of this experimentation. There is a great prosperity for current love this year.

Your major interests this year are home and family (until March 24 and from June 12 onwards); children, fun and creativity (from January 1 to March 8 and from March 24 to June 12); health and work; love and romance (until May 17); sex, personal transformation and reinvention, and occult studies (from May 17 onwards).

Your paths of greatest fulfilment this year are love and romance (to May 17 and from July 18 onwards); and sex, personal transformation and reinvention, and occult studies.

Health

(Please note that this is an astrological perspective on health and not a medical one. In days of yore there was no difference, both these perspectives were identical. But these days there could be quite a difference. For a medical perspective, please consult your doctor or health practitioner.)

As we mentioned earlier, health is improving this year (and next year it will be even better). Sure, there will be periods where health and energy are less easy than usual – perhaps even stressful. But these are temporary blips caused by the transits of the short-term planets. They're not trends for the year. Health-wise, time is your friend. The long-term planets are moving in ever more harmonious relationship with you.

Good though your health is, you can make it better. Give more attention to the following – the vulnerable areas of your Horoscope this year (the reflex points are shown in the chart below):

- The kidneys and hips are always an important area for Libra as these areas are ruled by your sign. Regular hip massage will not only strengthen the hips and kidneys but the lower back as well.
- The feet. These too are always important for Libra, as Neptune is your health planet. Of late, with Neptune's long stay in your 6th house, they have become even more important. So regular foot massage should be a part of your health regime. You'll not only strengthen the feet by this but the whole body as well.
- The spine, knees, bones, teeth, skin and overall skeletal alignment. These become important from March 8 and remain so for the next two and a half years. Regular back and knee massage will be very beneficial, as will regular visits to a chiropractor or osteopath. The vertebrae need to be kept in right alignment. Exercises such as

Important foot reflexology points for the year ahead

Try to massage all of the foot on a regular basis – the top of the foot as well as the bottom – but pay extra attention to the points highlighted on the chart. When you massage, be aware of 'sore spots' as these need special attention. It's also a good idea to massage the ankles and below them.

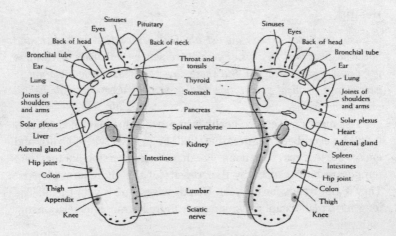

Pilates and Yoga are good – especially the asanas that deal with the spine. Therapies such as Alexander Technique, Rolfing or Feldenkrais are good. If you're spending time outside, use a good sunscreen. Good dental hygiene is more important than usual. Make sure to get enough calcium for the bones.

With Neptune as your health planet, you always benefit from spiritual healing methods. And now even more so. If you practise such techniques, you'll see absolute miracles in your health. Spirit controls the body absolutely (through the mind). If you feel under the weather, see a spiritual healer. You should read all you can on this subject – there is a lot of literature about it. Those who are interested can go to my website, www.spiritual-stories.com, where there is much information on this subject.

In your chart, health problems are never what they seem. If the Divine wants your attention, it will allow a health problem to develop. (It never sends these things.) When it gets your attention the health problem will dissolve of its own accord: it had no other reason for being there.

It is very important to pray and stay in a state of grace. This is good for its own sake but with you it's a health issue.

Home and Family

Pluto has been in your 4th house for many years – more than twenty, in fact. So, home and family life have been undergoing a long-term, cosmic detox. This hasn't been pleasant. Detoxing seldom is. Over the years there have been deaths in the family – perhaps of parents or parent figures. Some parents or parent figures might not have physically died but had near-death kinds of experiences – perhaps multiple surgeries as well.

Pluto, your financial planet, in the 4th house for so many years shows that your home has been a place of business as much as a home. You've installed a home office or other office equipment, and the trend continues this year (although it is weaker). Family support for finances seems good. You spend on the home and family, and they return the favour.

Your family planet, Saturn, makes a major move into your 6th house of health on March 8. This indicates that you're probably installing health equipment in the home and doing things to make the home a healthier place. The home will be as much a spa or gym as a home. (This transit also shows the importance of emotional health.)

There's nothing in your chart that is against a move this year, but if you do move it would be to some place near water or near a golf course or health spa or medical clinic.

If you're planning major renovations to the home, January 1 to March 24 and June 12 to the end of the year would be auspicious periods. If you're thinking of merely redecorating in a cosmetic kind of way, or buying art objects for the home, January 27–30, May 7–10 and December 4–7 would be good times.

A parent or parent figure seems more spiritual this year – softer, kinder, more gentle. He or she could move. If this figure is of child-bearing age, there is greater fertility this year. Children and children figures in your life are prospering but a move is not seen (there's nothing against it, however). They too – if they are of the appropriate age – are more fertile than usual. Grandchildren, or those who play that role in your life, have the urge for domestic change, but it's not likely this year. (It's more likely next year.)

Finance and Career

Though your money house is not prominent this year (which would normally show a tendency to the status quo) there are important long-term financial changes happening. These changes will not be abrupt but more like a process that will go on for many years. The beginnings of this process happen this year, from March 24 to June 12. Pluto, your financial planet, begins his two-year transition from Capricorn to Aquarius, from your 4th house to your 5th.

For many years now, you've been conservative in money matters. You avoided unnecessary risk. If you took risks, they were well calculated and well hedged. Your financial judgement was sound for the most part (though this could have been affected when Pluto received stressful aspects from the short-term planets or when your money planet was retrograde). You had a long-term view of wealth. Wealth is attained step by step in methodical ways. For the most part you avoided chasing the 'quick buck'. You spent on the home and family, and family support in financial matters was good. You earned money from home, and family and family connections were paramount in earnings. But now Pluto is starting to shift. His move into your 5th house indicates a change in your financial thinking and attitudes. You become more of a risk taker. You speculate more. You won't be hoarding cash but enjoying the wealth that you have. You will spend on joyful things. You will learn how to enjoy the act of making money. You will earn in fun ways. Those of you who invest will gravitate to companies that cater to the youth market – music, entertainment, video games, toymakers and the like.

You will spend more on your children and the children figures in your life. In many cases the children will actually supply material support. In other cases the children will motivate you to earn more. And, in some cases, they have profitable ideas to share.

Pluto moving into Aquarius favours the high-tech and online world – computers, software, websites, online commerce, etc.

This year (and next year) you waver between the sober, Capricorn approach and the more freewheeling Aquarius attitude.

Your 10th career house is not prominent this year. It is basically empty with only short-term planets moving through there, producing short-term effects. This tends to the status quo. You're more or less satisfied with things as they are and have no need to make major changes.

Your career planet, the Moon, is the fastest moving of all the planets. Where the other fast-moving planets (the Sun, Mercury and Venus) take a year to move through your chart, the Moon does this every month. During the year she will move through your chart at least twelve times, so there are many short-term career trends that depend on where the Moon is and the kinds of aspects she receives at any given time. These are best dealt with in the monthly reports. Generally speaking, the New and Full Moons tend to be important career days. The waxing Moon periods (when the Moon is growing) are better career-wise than the waning periods, when the Moon is getting smaller. You will have more energy and enthusiasm to achieve career goals during the waxing Moon periods than during the waning Moon periods.

A lunar eclipse on May 5 will bring both financial and career changes – perhaps upheavals. We will explain this further in that month's report.

Love and Social Life

Here we have the main headline of the year ahead, Libra. You're in a very strong love and social year – a happy one. So it is understandable that career and finance are less important this year. Your focus is on your first love – the social life – and being involved in romance. These are much more interesting to Libra than mundane matters such as money and career.

Jupiter is moving through your 7th house of love this year, which is a classic indicator of romance and social expansion in general. It denotes happiness and good fortune in these areas. So, singles are likely to meet that special someone this year. Marriages, or relationships that are like marriage, are likely. All of you, single or attached, will be socializing more, meeting new people, making new friends – and significant ones at that. You will be attending more weddings and other kinds of social gatherings.

With Jupiter in your 7th house you would find foreigners, professors and religious people alluring. You have the aspects of someone who falls in love with their professor, minister, priest or rabbi. Romantic meetings can happen in foreign lands or at religious or educational settings. You appreciate learned and highly educated people. You like people you can learn from.

With Mars as your love planet, you're naturally a 'love at first sight' kind of person, and this year more than ever. You know your feelings instantly. There is instant recognition. Perhaps you are too quick about this and will learn more caution from a few hard knocks. But when your intuition is correct, these 'instant recognitions' work out well.

Your love planet Mars is a relatively fast-moving planet, moving through seven signs this year. He is an 'in between' kind of planet. He moves faster than the long-term planets but slower than the really fast-moving ones like the Sun, Mercury and Venus. Thus, there are many short-term trends in love that depend on where Mars is and the kinds of aspects he receives. These are best dealt with in the monthly reports.

Self-improvement

Clare Martin, in her wonderful book *Alchemy: The Soul of Astrology*, posits that the transits of long-term planets – Pluto, Neptune, Uranus and Saturn – should be understood as a cosmic alchemy in a given area of life. Alchemy was never about making physical gold out of physical lead. These were only symbols of something deeper. Alchemy was about transforming psychological lead (negative experiences, habits and attitudes) into spiritual and psychological gold. It seems a natural process that happens automatically – but of course the results are better if one understands the process and cooperates with it. This transformation has been going on in your emotional life – your habits of mood, feeling and emotional responses – for over twenty years. Your emotional patterns have been completely (almost) transformed. You're emotionally healthier now than ever before. With Pluto now transitioning into Aquarius you are now going to see this alchemical process in your creative life, in your notions of pleasure and fun and in your dealings with children and children figures in your life. You're at the very beginning of this process and it will get stronger and stronger as the years go by.

Jupiter will move into your 8th house of regeneration on May 17 and spend the rest of the year there. This also furthers the cosmic alchemy going on. This is a period for purging – for going into the subconscious mind and clearing out the undesirable emotional and mental patterns there (what's left of them). It is also good for weight loss and physical detox regimes. But this period is really about giving birth to the person you want to be – to your ideal self. This ideal self is already there, but it is hidden behind masses of fear, worry, beliefs and perhaps the after-effects of traumatic experiences. Clear these out and what's left is your ideal self. Those who want to learn more about this can read my book *A Technique for Meditation*, or visit my website, www.spiritual-stories.com. There is much information on these subjects.

Your spiritual planet, Mercury, is a fast-moving planet, which means that the many short-term spiritual trends that depend on where Mercury is and the kinds of aspects he receives are best dealt with in the monthly reports.

Month-by-month Forecasts

January

Best Days Overall: 3, 4, 12, 13, 21, 22, 30, 31
Most Stressful Days Overall: 10, 11, 16, 17, 23, 24
Best Days for Love: 2, 3, 4, 12, 13, 16, 17, 21, 22, 30, 31
Best Days for Money: 2, 6, 7, 8, 11, 16, 19, 20, 23, 29
Best Days for Career: 2, 10, 11, 20, 21, 23, 24, 30, 31

You begin your year in the midnight hour of your chart (symbolically speaking); 60 per cent (and sometimes 70 per cent) of the planets are below the horizon this month and your 4th house of home and family is easily the strongest in the Horoscope. So, career is not high on the agenda now, but getting the domestic and emotional situation right is. This is a good month for planning future career moves and for working on the career by the methods of night – meditation, visualization, controlled daydreaming – putting yourself in the mood and feeling of where you want to be. Later, when the planets shift, you can take overt actions – and these actions will be powerful.

Health needs watching this month, especially until the 20th. Enhance the health with more rest, foot massage and through spiritual-healing techniques.

This is a great month for making psychological progress. Many psychological insights will come to you. This will happen whether you're in formal therapy or not. The cosmic therapist will bring up old, long-forgotten memories so that you can look at them from your present state of consciousness and understanding. You don't rewrite history, you just put a different interpretation on it.

Love is another major headline this month – and for months to come. Jupiter in your 7th house is a classic indicator of serious romance or marriage. Mars, your love planet, is 'out of bounds' all month and remains that way until May 4. So, in love matters you're going outside your normal sphere – your normal orbit. This can also indicate that you're attracted to people outside your normal sphere. Your love planet will be in your 9th house this month and will be retrograde until the 12th. There is indecision in love. But after the 12th love becomes clearer and all systems are go! Love opportunities can happen in educational settings, in foreign lands, and in religious settings and functions.

Finances are good this month. Your financial planet Pluto is moving forward and receives very nice aspects. The 1st, 2nd, 17th and 19th are good financial days. (This is aside from the days mentioned above.)

February

Best Days Overall: 1, 9, 10, 18, 19, 27, 28
Most Stressful Days Overall: 2, 3, 16, 17, 22, 23
Best Days for Love: 1, 2, 3, 9, 10, 12, 13, 18, 19, 22, 23, 27, 28
Best Days for Money: 4, 5, 8, 12, 13, 14, 15, 17, 22, 23, 25
Best Days for Career: 1, 2, 3, 9, 10, 20

Health and energy are much improved this month. Dramatically improved. And the month ahead is a happy one.

You began a yearly personal pleasure peak last month on the 20th and it continues this month until the 18th. It's time to dip into the joys of life. There is more involvement with children and children figures. They are good teachers about joy. We can learn a lot from them. Personal creativity is also very strong.

On the 18th, as the Sun enters your 6th house, you're more in the mood for work. Those of you who are unemployed will receive good job opportunities. But even if you're already employed there will be opportunities for overtime or second jobs. Many of you are involved in spiritual healing and this month great progress and insight will come – especially from the 14th to the 16th as Venus travels with your health planet Neptune. Good health will do more for your personal appearance than hosts of lotions and potions.

Love is still red hot. Jupiter is still in your 7th house of love and Venus, the ruler of your Horoscope, joins him on the 21st. You're very popular now and seem more aggressive in love. You put other people first and you know that as you do this, your good comes to you very naturally. Mars, your love planet, is even more 'out of bounds' this month than last – he is far outside his usual orbit. So, in matters of love and romance you're 'off the reservation' – you're exploring and finding. Being off the reservation is less safe, but much more exciting.

Venus has her solstice from the 21st to the 24th. She pauses in the heavens (in latitude) and then changes direction. So, there is a pause in your personal affairs and then a change of direction. This should not alarm you. It's natural. One cannot change direction abruptly. First one slows down, pauses, and then alters course.

The New Moon of the 20th occurs in your 6th house and brings healing to those who need it. Also job opportunities. More importantly, the Moon will bring clarity to health and work issues as the weeks progress.

March

Best Days Overall: 8, 9, 10, 17, 18, 26, 27
Most Stressful Days Overall: 1, 2, 15, 16, 21, 22, 28, 29, 30
Best Days for Love: 4, 5, 9, 10, 11, 12, 17, 18, 21, 22, 24, 25, 28
Best Days for Money: 4, 5, 7, 11, 12, 13, 14, 16, 21, 22, 25, 26, 31
Best Days for Career: 1, 2, 12, 20, 21, 28, 29, 30, 31

A momentous month ahead. Saturn, your family planet, makes a major move into your 6th house of health and work on the 8th and will remain there for the next two and a half years. You'll probably have to knuckle down at the job. Work harder. More will be demanded of you. More importantly, the health regime will change. Diet becomes more important. Good health means emotional and family harmony. Health will need more attention from the 20th onwards. Make sure, as always, to get enough rest.

Pluto, your financial planet, makes an important but brief move from your 4th house to your 5th house – from the sign of Capricorn to the sign of Aquarius. So financial attitudes change. You're less conservative than usual. You're more open to experimentation. This won't last long (only until June this year) but is a harbinger of things to come.

The main headline is the love life. On the 20th the Sun enters your 7th house and you begin a yearly love and social peak. For some of you, this will be a lifetime peak – much depends on your age. There is both romance and friendship happening. Singles are most likely involved in a serious relationship, but if not, there are many, many romantic opportunities now. You're still very popular. You're there for your friends and love interest. Romantic opportunities can happen in many ways and through a variety of people. Friends can decide they want to be more than that. Friends can play Cupid. Professors or worship leaders can play Cupid. The cosmos is conspiring to bring you love.

On the 20th the planetary power begins to shift to the upper half of your Horoscope – the day side. Dawn is breaking in your year. It is time to get up and be about the outer affairs of life. On the 26th your love planet Mars moves into your 10th house of career. So, you further the career by social means. You are attracted to high and powerful people. You will be meeting these kinds of people as well.

The New Moon of the 21st occurs in your 7th house and further enhances your red-hot love and social life. It brings high and mighty people into your social sphere. More importantly, it will clarify love and relationship issues in the coming weeks.

April

Best Days Overall: 5, 6, 14, 15, 22, 23, 24
Most Stressful Days Overall: 12, 13, 18, 19, 25, 26
Best Days for Love: 3, 4, 7, 8, 14, 16, 17, 18, 19, 22, 23, 25, 26
Best Days for Money: 1, 4, 5, 7, 8, 10, 13, 14, 19, 21, 22, 28, 29
Best Days for Career: 1, 10, 25, 26, 30

There is a powerful solar eclipse this month on the 20th that occurs right on the cusp of your 7th and 8th houses. All of you will feel its effects to some degree, but those born late in the sign of Libra – October 21–23 – will feel it strongest. If you're in this category take it nice and easy over this period.

Because this eclipse is on the border of two houses it will affect the affairs of both houses. So, the recent romantic encounters and social expansion will get tested. Only the real loves, the real friendships, will survive. Good relationships will be tested – usually long-suppressed grievances surface for resolution – but they tend to survive and get even better. Sometimes the testing is not because of the relationship itself, but because of personal dramas in the life of the beloved or friends. There could be surgery, or near-death experiences – close calls – that make them more temperamental.

The eclipse's impact in the 8th house of regeneration also shows psychological encounters with death; only rarely is it an actual physical death. If you, or a friend or the beloved, have been in dire health straits, a physical death can happen – the eclipse pushes the person over the edge – but it is not common. Often there are dreams of death or death touches you in oblique ways – a friend tells you of the passing of one of their acquaintances. Or you read of some grisly crime in the newspaper.

The spouse, partner or current love is forced to make important financial changes. There is some financial drama. And, because this eclipse is a direct hit on Pluto, your financial planet, you too have to make important financial changes. Financial thinking and planning haven't been realistic, as the events of the eclipse will show.

Computer, software and high-tech equipment can behave erratically. Sometimes these glitches are just temporary things but sometimes repairs or replacements are necessary. Make sure that important files are backed up and that your anti-virus, anti-hacking software is up to date.

May

Best Days Overall: 2, 3, 11, 12, 20, 21, 30, 31
Most Stressful Days Overall: 9, 10, 15, 16, 22, 23
Best Days for Love: 2, 3, 5, 6, 9, 10, 14, 15, 16, 17, 18, 19, 24, 25
Best Days for Money: 1, 2, 5, 6, 8, 10, 11, 16, 17, 19, 20, 24, 25, 29
Best Days for Career: 1, 9, 10, 18, 19, 22, 23, 30, 31

Your 8th house is strong all month. The Sun is there until the 21st, while Mercury and Uranus are there all month. On the 17th Jupiter enters this house of regeneration and will be there for the rest of the year ahead. So, the month ahead is erotic, but it is also good for projects involving personal transformation – giving birth to your ideal self. This doesn't happen overnight but progress will be made.

The lunar eclipse of the 5th occurs in your 2nd money house. So once again, like last month, important financial changes need to happen. Your financial thinking and planning haven't been realistic and a course correction is necessary. However, with Pluto, your financial planet, travelling backwards from the 1st (and he will be retrograde for many months) study the proposed changes carefully. Do your 'due diligence'.

The good news is that the spouse, partner or current love is having a banner financial month and seems very supportive.

Every lunar eclipse impacts your career because the eclipsed planet, the Moon, is your career planet. (In general, your career is sensitive to lunar phenomena.) So, career changes are happening and there are many scenarios. There can be a shake-up in your corporate hierarchy or industry. The government can change the rules regarding your industry. There can be dramas – personal dramas – in the lives of bosses, parents or parent figures. And, in rare cases, there can be an actual career change.

This eclipse sideswipes Uranus, your planet of children. So, they are affected here. Make sure they follow a relaxed schedule and avoid high-risk kinds of activities. They seem to be having personal dramas. A parent or parent figure also needs to make financial changes.

Health is good this month and will get even better after the 21st. Spiritual-healing methods are always beneficial, and this trend continues in the month ahead.

June

Best Days Overall: 7, 8, 16, 17, 26, 27
Most Stressful Days Overall: 5, 6, 11, 12, 18, 19, 20
Best Days for Love: 2, 3, 4, 11, 12, 21, 22
Best Days for Money: 1, 2, 5, 6, 7, 14, 15, 23, 24, 25, 28, 29
Best Days for Career: 7, 8, 17, 18, 19, 20, 28

A happy and successful month ahead, Libra. Enjoy. Your love goals have been more or less attained – the short-term ones at least – and the focus is now on travel, higher education and religious and theological studies. On a social level you're probably meeting foreign friends, which furthers your interest in other places and countries. It's the best way to learn about a foreign culture. Legal issues, if you're involved with such things, should go well. College students should also do well. The New Moon of the 18th occurs in your 9th house and is an excellent career day. From the 18th onwards you have more zest and enthusiasm for the career. This New Moon is also a good social day – not necessarily romantic but more about friendships and group activities. Religious, philosophical, theological and legal issues will become clearer in the coming weeks – the New Moon has effects beyond the actual event.

Health will need keeping an eye on from the 21st. This doesn't look like anything serious, merely short-term stress caused by the transits of short-term planets. As always, make sure to get enough rest and enhance the health in the ways mentioned in the yearly report.

The focus is on the career after the 21st and you seem successful. Friends also seem successful and are very much involved in your career. Your naturally good networking abilities are also helping the career.

On the 5th Venus, the ruler of your Horoscope, enters your 11th house of friends and will stay there for the next four months. This further reinforces the social trends that we mentioned. You're very focused on friends, groups, group activities and the online world. This transit will also enlarge your knowledge of computers, software, science, astronomy and astrology. Many people have their Horoscopes done under this kind of transit.

Your love planet Mars will also be in your 11th house all month. If there are still any single Libras left, romantic opportunity can come through your involvement with friends, groups, group activities and the online world. Be more mindful on the physical plane on the 24th and 25th (the beloved as well).

July

Though Pluto is retrograde (along with many other planets), a loose Grand Trine in the Earth signs should boost earnings this month (especially after the 11th). This can happen with delayed reactions, but it will happen.

Mars, your love planet, moves into your 12th house on the 11th and love becomes more idealistic – more spiritual. Spiritual compatibility is very important in love, as you will learn this month. With spiritual compatibility almost any problem can be worked out, but without it almost nothing can be resolved. Romantic opportunities happen in spiritual settings after the 11th – at a spiritual lecture or group meditation or prayer meeting. Perhaps at a charity event. If there are problems in the current relationship, cast the burden on the Divine and allow it to handle things. It will.

You're still in a very successful career period – a yearly career peak in fact. This continues until the 23rd. The New Moon of the 17th also occurs in your 10th house and further boosts the career. With the Moon as your career planet, lunar phenomena are very important in this area. New Moons and Full Moons tend to boost career. With this New Moon career questions and doubts will be resolved in the coming weeks. All the information you need to make good decisions will come to you.

Health and energy improve after the 23rd. You have plenty of energy. Any pre-existing conditions seem milder now.

Mercury is 'out of bounds' until the 6th. (He has been 'out of bounds' since June 25.) Thus, in your religious and spiritual life you're going outside your normal orbit. Perhaps in your travels as well. You like places outside the norm.

The month ahead is very social – even more so than last month. Your 11th house is chock-full of planets. So, it is good – and fun – to be involved with friends, groups and group activities. Also good to be involved with science, astronomy and astrology. Your knowledge of these things will increase.

August

Best Days Overall: 1, 2, 10, 11, 19, 20, 21, 29
Most Stressful Days Overall: 5, 6, 12, 13, 26, 27
Best Days for Love: 5, 6, 7, 8, 14, 15, 17, 18, 24, 25, 27, 28
Best Days for Money: 7, 8, 17, 18, 22, 23, 26, 27, 28
Best Days for Career: 5, 6, 12, 13, 15, 16, 26

Retrograde activity among the planets heats up this month and will reach the maximum extent for the year. By the 29th 60 per cent of the planets will be retrograde. But even before that half the planets will be travelling backwards, so life slows down. The pace of events, personally and in the world, slows down. You can't force events to happen, only time will do it. In the meantime, you can use this period to formulate goals in the various departments of life – see where improvements can be made – and then you can act on your plans when the planets start moving forward again. You move forward with the planets.

Despite all the retrogrades, it's still a very social month. Your 11th house remains strong until the 23rd. And the New Moon of the 16th occurs in your 11th house and boosts the social life and the career. It will clarify issues involving friends, technology, science and astrology as the weeks progress.

Venus, the ruler of your Horoscope, went retrograde on July 23 and will remain so for all of this month. So, though you're in a more independent period than usual – the Eastern sector of self in your chart is about as strong as it will ever be this year – you're not sure of what your personal goals are or what you really want. This will change next month, and it will be safer to make personal changes then.

Mars, your love planet, is still in your spiritual 12th house until the 28th. So, review our discussion of this last month. However, this month Mars will have his solstice. He pauses in the heavens (in latitude) and then changes direction. There is a pause in your love life –

nothing to be alarmed about – and then a change of direction. It is a healthy pause.

Health is good this month. Both the planets involved with your health – your health planet Neptune and Mercury, the generic ruler of health – are retrograde. So best to avoid elective tests and procedures: reschedule them for a later time if possible. Avoid making dramatic changes to the health regime as well. These changes need a lot more study.

Earnings should be good as Pluto receives even better aspects than last month. But he is still retrograde – so there can be glitches or delays. Earnings will happen though.

September

Best Days Overall: 6, 7, 16, 17, 25, 26
Most Stressful Days Overall: 2, 3, 8, 9, 10, 23, 24, 29, 30
Best Days for Love: 2, 3, 6, 11, 12, 16, 17, 21, 22, 25, 26, 29, 30
Best Days for Money: 4, 5, 14, 15, 18, 19, 23, 24
Best Days for Career: 4, 5, 8, 9, 10, 13, 14, 25

Libra, more than most other signs, doesn't mind a lack of independence. You enjoy relying on your social skills to attain your ends. But right now, you're at the most independent period of your year. In fact, you're rather spunky. Mars in your sign all month enhances independence and self-assertion. On the 23rd, the Sun enters your sign, which reinforces this even more, and the Eastern sector of self in your chart is still at its strongest for the year. So now is the time to make those changes that need to be made for your happiness. In addition, Venus starts to move forward on the 4th so there is clarity about what you want. It is safe to make these changes.

You begin a yearly personal pleasure peak (one of them) on the 23rd. A time to enjoy the pleasures of the body and the five senses. Also a good period to get the body and image in the shape that you want.

Mars, your love planet, is in your own sign all month, which is excellent for love. If you're in a relationship, the spouse, partner or beloved is very devoted to you – catering to you. If you're not yet in a relationship, it can easily happen this month – and there's nothing much that you need to do. Love pursues you. You just have to go about your daily business.

Mars continues his solstice on the 1st and 2nd. So there is a pause in love and then a change of direction.

Though Mars is wonderful for love, it does give a tendency to rush things and for impatience – wanting things done immediately. With 60 per cent of the planets still retrograde until the 16th – and 50 per cent still retrograde after then – rush is not advisable. Frustration is probably your biggest problem now.

Health is good. The main danger is injury or accident due to haste or impatience. So, slow down.

The month ahead – especially from the 23rd – is not only good for romance, but also for friendships. Friends seem very devoted to you.

October

Best Days Overall: 3, 4, 22, 23
Most Stressful Days Overall: 6, 7, 13, 14, 20, 21, 26, 27
Best Days for Love: 3, 4, 9, 10, 11, 15, 20, 21, 24, 25, 26, 27, 28, 29
Best Days for Money: 1, 2, 11, 12, 15, 16, 17, 20, 21, 28, 29
Best Days for Career: 3, 4, 6, 7, 24

The main headline this month is the two eclipses that happen. There is a solar eclipse on the 14th and a lunar eclipse on the 28th. Of the two, the solar eclipse of the 14th seems to affect you more powerfully, as it occurs in your own sign. Make sure you relax and reduce your schedule over this period. Sensitive people will feel this eclipse coming on for up to two weeks before it happens, although most of you will feel it a week before. This eclipse in your sign signals a need to redefine yourself for yourself. Don't let others do it. As you upgrade and update your opinion of yourself, image and wardrobe changes will happen very naturally, and this will go on in the coming months.

Every solar eclipse affects friendships and this one is no different. Friendships will get tested this month. If the relationship is basically flawed it can end, but good, solid friendships will survive the eclipse. Often this testing comes because of life-changing events in the lives of your friends. It's not the fault of the relationship per se. Computers, software and high-tech gadgetry can start to behave strangely. You can learn of an online hack of some company (your phone network provider or social media company or bank) where your personal information has been compromised. You might need to change your passwords and the like. Avoid opening emails from strangers; even emails from people you know can have harmful links so be more internet-security savvy now. Back up important files and keep your anti-hacking, anti-virus software up to date.

The lunar eclipse of the 28th is generally milder in its effects (but if it hits a sensitive point in your personal Horoscope – the one cast specifically for you – it can have a powerful impact). This eclipse occurs in your 8th house of regeneration, forcing the spouse, partner or current love to make important financial changes – a financial course correction is happening. There can be psychological confrontations with death – perhaps surgery or near-death experiences. Perhaps friends tell you of people they know who have passed from the scene. Sometimes people have dreams of death or find themselves in discussions about it. As we've said before, every lunar eclipse affects the career, and career changes are happening. There can be shake-ups in your corporate hierarchy or personal dramas in the lives of bosses, parents or parent figures. The government could issue new regulations for your industry. The rules of the game change.

November

Best Days Overall: 1, 9, 10, 11, 18, 19, 27, 28
Most Stressful Days Overall: 2, 3, 16, 17, 23, 24, 29, 30
Best Days for Love: 2, 3, 8, 9, 12, 13, 18, 19, 22, 23, 24, 27, 28
Best Days for Money: 7, 8, 12, 13, 16, 17, 25, 26
Best Days for Career: 2, 3, 12, 13, 23, 29, 30

Finances are much improved these days. For a start, Pluto, your financial planet, started to move forward on October 11, and will remain moving forward for many months to come. On October 23 the Sun entered your money house and you began a yearly financial peak, which is in effect until the 22nd of this month. In addition, Mars, your love planet, is in your money house until the 24th. All this spells prosperity. The spouse, partner or current love – and social contacts in general – are boosting your earnings. The only problem with Mars in your 2nd house is that you can become too reckless with money – too much of a risk taker. However, Mercury in the money house until the 11th signals financial increase too, and good intuition. The New Moon of the 12th also occurs in your money house and further boosts the finances – you begin a new career cycle that day too. This New Moon will bring clarity to financial issues for the next few weeks. Your questions will be answered, and your doubts assuaged. All very naturally and normally.

Love is more erotic and materialistic these days. Wealth is an important romantic allurement. That and sexual magnetism. Material support is how you give love and how you feel loved. For singles there are romantic opportunities with people involved in your financial life. Just focus on your financial goals and love opportunities will occur.

Health and energy are good this month. Now that Mars has moved out of your sign you're more mellow and less in a rush. Venus enters your sign on the 8th and boosts the health further. She boosts the personal appearance and beautifies the image, too.

Venus has her solstice from the 9th to the 13th, thus there is a pause in your personal life – your personal goals – and then a change of direction. This is a healthy pause and not something to be concerned about.

The Sun moves into your 3rd house of communication and intellectual interests on the 22nd and Mars moves in on the 24th. This is a good period for students, teachers, sales and marketing people – those of you who work with your intellect. Learning goes well and the mental faculties are enhanced. Mars's move makes you less materialistic about love and more into mental compatibility and intellectual harmony.

December

Best Days Overall: 7, 8, 16, 17, 24, 25
Most Stressful Days Overall: 14, 15, 20, 21, 27, 28
Best Days for Love: 2, 3, 9, 11, 12, 18, 19, 20, 21, 28, 29, 30
Best Days for Money: 4, 5, 6, 9, 10, 14, 15, 22, 23, 31
Best Days for Career: 2, 3, 11, 12, 21, 22, 27, 28, 29

Neptune, your health planet, finally moves forward again on the 6th and so it is safe now to make changes to the health regime or undertake medical tests or procedures. (However, avoid such tests if you can from the 13th onwards, as Mercury will be retrograde and results will more prone to error then.)

Health is basically good this month, but after the 22nd it will need more attention. Make sure to get more rest then, and enhance the health in the ways mentioned in the yearly report.

Venus's move into your money house on the 5th is a boost for earnings. The ruler of your Horoscope is always a friendly and beneficent planet. You spend on yourself. You cultivate an image of prosperity and dress the part. Others see you this way. Personal appearance and overall demeanour play an important role in earnings. More importantly, Venus's transit signals a personal interest in finance. It shows focus – and this is 90 per cent of success. Since Venus is both the ruler of your Horoscope and of your 8th house, her transit indicates a need to focus on the prosperity of others. To the degree that you prosper others, your own prosperity will happen.

Your 3rd house is still where the action is this month. So, it is a great time to pursue your intellectual interests. Good to read more or take courses. Some of you will teach and give seminars on your own. With the mental faculties supercharged these days it is good to make use of them.

Your love planet will be in your 3rd house all month. So, love is to be found in your neighbourhood and perhaps with neighbours. Romantic opportunities occur in educational-type settings – at school, a lecture or seminar, the bookshop or library. Mental ability and the gift of the gab are romantic turn-ons this month. Your love planet goes 'out of bounds' again this month (he spent over four months 'out of bounds' early in the year). So once again you're attracted to people who are outside your normal orbit. You like people who are 'off the beaten track'.

On the 22nd the Sun enters your 4th house and the focus is once again on home and family. Career issues can be let go of for a while. Focus on the home and especially on your emotional wellness.

Scorpio

♏

THE SCORPION

Birthdays from
23rd October to
22nd November

Personality Profile

SCORPIO AT A GLANCE

Element – Water

Ruling Planet – Pluto
   Co-ruling Planet – Mars
   Career Planet – Sun
   Love Planet – Venus
   Money Planet – Jupiter
   Planet of Health and Work – Mars
   Planet of Home and Family Life – Uranus

Colour – red-violet

Colour that promotes love, romance and social harmony – green

Colour that promotes earning power – blue

Gems – bloodstone, malachite, topaz

Metals – iron, radium, steel

Scents – cherry blossom, coconut, sandalwood, watermelon

Quality – fixed (= stability)

Quality most needed for balance – a wider view of things

Strongest virtues – loyalty, concentration, determination, courage, depth

Deepest needs – to penetrate and transform

Characteristics to avoid – jealousy, vindictiveness, fanaticism

Signs of greatest overall compatibility – Cancer, Pisces

Signs of greatest overall incompatibility – Taurus, Leo, Aquarius

Sign most helpful to career – Leo

Sign most helpful for emotional support – Aquarius

Sign most helpful financially – Sagittarius

Sign best for marriage and/or partnerships – Taurus

Sign most helpful for creative projects – Pisces

Best Sign to have fun with – Pisces

Signs most helpful in spiritual matters – Cancer, Libra

Best day of the week – Tuesday

Understanding a Scorpio

One symbol of the sign of Scorpio is the phoenix. If you meditate upon the legend of the phoenix you will begin to understand the Scorpio character – his or her powers and abilities, interests and deepest urges.

The phoenix of mythology was a bird that could recreate and reproduce itself. It did so in a most intriguing way: it would seek a fire – usually in a religious temple – fly into it, consume itself in the flames and then emerge a new bird. If this is not the ultimate, most profound transformation, then what is?

Transformation is what Scorpios are all about – in their minds, bodies, affairs and relationships (Scorpios are also society's transformers). To change something in a natural, not an artificial way, involves a transformation from within. This type of change is radical change as opposed to a mere cosmetic make-over. Some people think that change means altering just their appearance, but this is not the kind of thing that interests a Scorpio. Scorpios seek deep, fundamental change. Since real change always proceeds from within, a Scorpio is very interested in – and usually accustomed to – the inner, intimate and philosophical side of life.

Scorpios are people of depth and intellect. If you want to interest them you must present them with more than just a superficial image. You and your interests, projects or business deals must have real substance to them in order to stimulate a Scorpio. If they haven't, he or she will find you out – and that will be the end of the story.

If we observe life – the processes of growth and decay – we see the transformational powers of Scorpio at work all the time. The caterpillar changes itself into a butterfly; the infant grows into a child and then an adult. To Scorpios this definite and perpetual transformation is not something to be feared. They see it as a normal part of life. This acceptance of transformation gives Scorpios the key to understanding the true meaning of life.

Scorpios' understanding of life (including life's weaknesses) makes them powerful warriors – in all senses of the word. Add to this their depth, patience and endurance and you have a powerful personality. Scorpios have good, long memories and can at times be quite vindictive

– they can wait years to get their revenge. As a friend, though, there is no one more loyal and true than a Scorpio. Few are willing to make the sacrifices that a Scorpio will make for a true friend.

The results of a transformation are quite obvious, although the process of transformation is invisible and secret. This is why Scorpios are considered secretive in nature. A seed will not grow properly if you keep digging it up and exposing it to the light of day. It must stay buried – invisible – until it starts to grow. In the same manner, Scorpios fear revealing too much about themselves or their hopes to other people. However, they will be more than happy to let you see the finished product – but only when it is completely unwrapped. On the other hand, Scorpios like knowing everyone else's secrets as much as they dislike anyone knowing theirs.

Finance

Love, birth, life as well as death are Nature's most potent transformations; Scorpios are interested in all of these. In our society, money is a transforming power, too, and a Scorpio is interested in money for that reason. To a Scorpio money is power, money causes change, money controls. It is the power of money that fascinates them. But Scorpios can be too materialistic if they are not careful. They can be overly awed by the power of money, to a point where they think that money rules the world.

Even the term 'plutocrat' comes from Pluto, the ruler of the sign of Scorpio. Scorpios will – in one way or another – achieve the financial status they strive for. When they do so they are careful in the way they handle their wealth. Part of this financial carefulness is really a kind of honesty, for Scorpios are usually involved with other people's money – as accountants, lawyers, stockbrokers or corporate managers – and when you handle other people's money you have to be more cautious than when you handle your own.

In order to fulfil their financial goals, Scorpios have important lessons to learn. They need to develop qualities that do not come naturally to them, such as breadth of vision, optimism, faith, trust and, above all, generosity. They need to see the wealth in Nature and in life, as well as in its more obvious forms of money and power. When they develop generosity their financial potential reaches great heights, for Jupiter, the Lord of Opulence and Good Fortune, is Scorpio's money planet.

Career and Public Image

Scorpio's greatest aspiration in life is to be considered by society as a source of light and life. They want to be leaders, to be stars. But they follow a very different road than do Leos, the other stars of the zodiac. A Scorpio arrives at the goal secretly, without ostentation; a Leo pursues it openly. Scorpios seek the glamour and fun of the rich and famous in a restrained, discreet way.

Scorpios are by nature introverted and tend to avoid the limelight. But if they want to attain their highest career goals they need to open up a bit and to express themselves more. They need to stop hiding their light under a bushel and let it shine. Above all, they need to let go of any vindictiveness and small-mindedness. All their gifts and insights were given to them for one important reason – to serve life and to increase the joy of living for others.

Love and Relationships

Scorpio is another zodiac sign that likes committed, clearly defined, structured relationships. They are cautious about marriage, but when they do commit to a relationship they tend to be faithful – and heaven help the mate caught or even suspected of infidelity! The jealousy of the Scorpio is legendary. They can be so intense in their jealousy that even the thought or intention of infidelity will be detected and is likely to cause as much of a storm as if the deed had actually been done.

Scorpios tend to settle down with those who are wealthier than they are. They usually have enough intensity for two, so in their partners they seek someone pleasant, hard-working, amiable, stable and easy-going. They want someone they can lean on, someone loyal behind them as they fight the battles of life. To a Scorpio a partner, be it a lover or a friend, is a real partner – not an adversary. Most of all a Scorpio is looking for an ally, not a competitor.

If you are in love with a Scorpio you will need a lot of patience. It takes a long time to get to know Scorpios, because they do not reveal themselves readily. But if you persist and your motives are honourable, you will gradually be allowed into a Scorpio's inner chambers of the mind and heart.

Home and Domestic Life

Uranus is ruler of Scorpio's 4th solar house of home and family. Uranus is the planet of science, technology, changes and democracy. This tells us a lot about a Scorpio's conduct in the home and what he or she needs in order to have a happy, harmonious home life.

Scorpios can sometimes bring their passion, intensity and wilfulness into the home and family, which is not always the place for these qualities. These traits are good for the warrior and the transformer, but not so good for the nurturer and family member. Because of this (and also because of their need for change and transformation) the Scorpio may be prone to sudden changes of residence. If not carefully constrained, the sometimes inflexible Scorpio can produce turmoil and sudden upheavals within the family.

Scorpios need to develop some of the virtues of Aquarius in order to cope better with domestic matters. There is a need to build a team spirit at home, to treat family activities as truly group activities – family members should all have a say in what does and does not get done. For at times a Scorpio can be most dictatorial. When a Scorpio gets dictatorial it is much worse than if a Leo or Capricorn (the two other power signs in the zodiac) does. For the dictatorship of a Scorpio is applied with more zeal, passion, intensity and concentration than is true of either a Leo or a Capricorn. Obviously this can be unbearable to family members – especially if they are sensitive types.

In order for a Scorpio to get the full benefit of the emotional support that a family can give, he or she needs to let go of conservatism and be a bit more experimental, explore new techniques in childrearing, be more democratic with family members and try to manage things by consensus rather than by autocratic edict.

Horoscope for 2023

Major Trends

A lot of change is happening this year and much of it will be long-term change. Pluto, the ruler of your Horoscope and thus a very important planet in your chart, is beginning a two-year transition from Capricorn to Aquarius. You're feeling only the beginnings of it this year. But in the coming years (especially 2025) you will feel the effects much more strongly. For over twenty years Pluto has been revolutionizing the way you think, your mental patterns. This work is almost finished. When Pluto moves into Aquarius, your 4th house, a transformation of the home, family and emotional life will start to happen. More on this later.

Saturn makes a major move into your 5th house on March 8. This will impact on your children and the children figures in your life. There will be a need to discipline them properly – to set them proper limits. This is not about cruelty but is really for their benefit. You can harm them more (in the long term) by being too lax than by being too strict. Women of childbearing age could find pregnancy more difficult, too.

Jupiter will be in your 6th house of health and work until May 17. This indicates wonderful job opportunities opening up for you – and well-paying ones. Since Jupiter is your financial planet, it signals a new approach to earnings. You spend on your health and you can earn from it as well. More on this later.

Perhaps the major headline this year is Jupiter's move into your 7th house of love and romance on May 17. This is a tricky kind of transit. Uranus has been in your 7th house for many years now, and his presence has destabilized your marriage or relationship. There have probably been many divorces or break-ups for Scorpios in the past few years. Now Jupiter is moving into this house and this puts you in the marrying mood again. But this might not be advisable. Love is still very unstable. The good news is that the opportunity for marriage is there. More details later.

Your major interests this year will be intellectual interests and communication (until March 24 and from June 12 to the end of the year); home and family (until March 8 and from March 24 to June 12);

children, fun and creativity; health and work (until May 17); and love, romance and social activities.

Your paths of greatest fulfilment will be health and work (from January 1 to May 17 and from July 18 onwards); and love, romance and social activities.

Health

(Please note that this is an astrological perspective on health and not a medical one. In days of yore there was no difference, both these perspectives were identical. But these days there could be quite a difference. For a medical perspective, please consult your doctor or health practitioner.)

Health is reasonable this year. I won't say perfect – at times you'll have three long-term planets in stressful alignment with you (from May 17 to June 12), but other long-term planets (Saturn and Neptune) are making harmonious aspects to you. Also, the stress on health will be felt more by those born early in the sign of Scorpio – from October 23–25.

The good news is that you can do much to enhance your health and energy. Give more attention to the vulnerable areas of your chart – these are the areas most likely to cause problems (the reflex points are shown in the chart opposite). By giving them more attention – keeping them healthy and fit – you minimize the health dangers:

- The colon, bladder and sexual organs are always important areas for Scorpio and the reflex points are shown above. Safe sex and sexual moderation are very important. Listen to your body and not your mind and you'll know when enough is enough.
- The head, face and scalp. These too are always important for Scorpio, and regular scalp and face massage should be part of your normal health regime. You not only strengthen the given areas but the entire body as well (there are many meridian lines in the scalp and face). Craniosacral therapy is always beneficial for you.
- The musculature is another important area for you, Scorpio, as Mars, the planet that rules the muscles, is your health planet. So vigorous physical exercise is good for you – each according to their

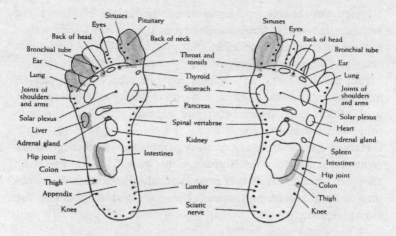

Important foot reflexology points for the year ahead

*Try to massage all of the foot on a regular basis – the top of the foot as well as
the bottom – but pay extra attention to the points highlighted on the chart.
When you massage, be aware of 'sore spots' as these need special attention.
It's also a good idea to massage the ankles, and especially below them.*

age and stage in life. It isn't necessary to be a bodybuilder, just to
have good muscle tone. Weak or flabby muscles can knock the
spine and skeleton out of alignment and upset your balance.

- The adrenals. The important thing here, as our regular readers
  know, is to avoid anger and fear, the two emotions that stress the
  adrenal glands out. Meditation is a big help here.
- The liver and thighs are important this year until May 17, with
  Jupiter in your 6th house of health. The liver reflex is shown in the
  chart above. Regular thigh massage will not only strengthen the
  liver and thighs but the lower back and colon as well.

Jupiter, your financial planet, in your 6th house shows that good health
for you also means good financial health. Financial ups and downs can
impact on your actual physical health – if you allow it. You shouldn't.
Health is health and finance is finance. Keep these things separate in
your mind. You are much more (and more important) than your bank
balance or net worth. Stay healthy, and money will take care of itself.

Long-term changes in your personal appearance and image are beginning this year. A lunar eclipse in your sign on May 5 adds to this. You will be changing your 'look', your presentation to the world, this year – and for many years to come.

Your health planet, Mars, spends many months 'out of bounds' – from January 1 to May 4. Thus, in health matters you're outside your usual orbit. You're exploring therapies and therapists that are outside your normal comfort zone.

Mars is a moderately fast-moving planet, moving through seven signs and houses of your Horoscope this year. So, there are many short-term health trends that depend on where Mars is at any given time and the aspects he receives. These are best dealt with in the monthly reports.

Home and Family

Your 4th house of home and family has been powerful for a few years now, and it will remain so for parts of the year ahead. In future years, though, it will become *very* powerful and important.

The past two years – and especially last year – have been challenging, both emotionally and in your family relationships. It has been a burden, a discipline, a cross to bear. By now you've learned the lessons, and on March 8 things get much easier.

A parent or parent figure has been very stressed out over the past two and a half years. There could have been health problems as well. Happily, by March 8 things improve for this parent figure. Health should improve as well.

With Uranus, your family planet, sitting in your 7th house for many years now you've been socializing more from the home and with family members. You've been beautifying the home – redecorating – and making the home as much a social centre as a home. This trend continues in the year ahead.

Pluto's brief flirtation into your 4th house, from March 24 to June 12, is a signal of things to come. You will be very focused on the home and family. You'll probably present an image of the 'family man' or 'family woman'. Your family will be an important part of your identity. More importantly, you will be delving into your past from a therapeutic perspective. Many of you will get involved in official therapeutic regimes – psychological or spiritual. You'll be sifting through your past, working to come to terms with it.

If you're planning house renovations, May 21 to July 11 would be a good period for this. If you're just redecorating (and you seem to be), January 3–27 seems a good time. This would also be a good time to buy art objects for the home.

A move could happen for you this year – but it's more likely next year. It seems happy and can happen suddenly. This year you're probably thinking about it or planning it. A parent or parent figure is likely to move this year. If this is a woman of childbearing age, she is very fertile. Siblings and sibling figures are likely to move this year. They also seem very fertile. Children and children figures seem rather pessimistic about their circumstances – not happy campers – but a move is more likely next year than this for them. Grandchildren (if you have them), or those who play that role in your life, are having a stable family year.

Finance and Career

The year ahead looks prosperous, Scorpio. Enjoy. Jupiter, your money planet, will be in Aries, your 6th house, until May 17. Jupiter is very comfortable in the sign of Aries and this indicates increased earnings. Jupiter in your 6th house also shows good fortune in the job market. If you're an employee, very happy job opportunities are coming to you – dream job opportunities – and they seem to be well paying.

Jupiter in impetuous Aries indicates a risk-taking mentality. When the intuition is on form, these risks pay off. When intuition is off, however, there can be losses. You have an urge for fast bucks. You want wealth in a hurry. Now. So you need to be careful of scam artists who prey on those with this kind of mentality.

Jupiter in your 6th house shows earnings happening through work – from productive service. Also, it indicates a good feeling for investments in the health field, especially pharmaceuticals that improve athletic performance. It favours investments in arms and munitions companies, athletic companies and companies that supply these sectors.

On May 17 Jupiter moves into Taurus and stays there for the rest of the year. This brings a more conservative approach to finance. You are less of a risk-taker. The financial judgement is sounder. Jupiter in Taurus favours investments in rural real estate, farm land and agricultural companies. Copper – the commodity – and copper mining and refining companies are also interesting investments. (But always do your due diligence, this is not automatic.)

Jupiter will be travelling near Uranus (although the transit is not exact) after May 17. This would favour residential real estate, hotels, motels, restaurants and the food business in general. This favourability increases next year.

Jupiter in your 7th house of love after May 17 gives many messages. This transit can bring opportunities for partnerships or joint ventures. (If you own a company, a sale or merger could happen.) It also signals the importance of your social contacts in finance. They seem very helpful.

In contrast to finance, your 10th career house is not a house of power this year. It is basically empty. Only short-term, fast-moving planets will move through there and their effect is short term. So, this is not a very strong career year and would tend to the status quo. This can be seen as a good thing. It denotes satisfaction with the way things are. You have no need to make dramatic changes.

Your career planet, the Sun, will be eclipsed twice this year. Once on April 20 and again on October 14. This will shake up the career and create changes. We will discuss this more fully in the monthly reports.

The Sun is a fast-moving planet and so there are many short-term trends in the career that depend on where the Sun is and the kinds of aspects he receives. These will also be discussed in the monthly reports.

Venus, your love planet, will spend over four months in your 10th house this year – an unusually long transit for Venus. (Her normal transit in a sign is a month.) So, from June 5 to October 9 the career would be best enhanced by social means – by attending or hosting the right kind of parties and gatherings. But I feel this transit is more about love than the career (and we will discuss this next).

Love and Social Life

The love life has been a major focus for many years. Uranus has been upending your whole social circle for years now. Getting used to (embracing) social change has been a major life lesson.

Uranus has destabilized the love and social life – and many of you have got divorced or experienced break-ups in recent years. On the other hand, the love life has become very exciting. Love and romantic opportunities can happen at any time in any place and in totally unexpected ways. You never know when Cupid will strike.

This year Jupiter will move through your 7th house from May 17 onwards. Generally, this is a classic signal for marriage. This year, however, I'm not so sure, as Uranus is still in the 7th house. So serious romance is happening – but marriage? I'm not so sure that it's even advisable. Enjoy love, but postpone commitment for a while. There's no rush.

Jupiter's move through your 7th house shows that much of your socializing is business related. Later, from June 5 to October 9, it seems career related. This year, really, you have the aspects of someone who likes to do business with friends, with people you socialize with. And you try to socialize with people you do business with. Business becomes just another extension of the social life. And the same happens with career later in the year.

Venus at the top of your chart in your 10th house from June 5 to October 9 signals an excellent love and social period. Her position shows that love is a high priority – perhaps your highest – and thus you pay attention. Also, it shows that singles are attracted to successful and high-status people – especially during that period. There are romantic opportunities with these kinds of people as well. And since Venus is also your spiritual planet, you're attracted to spiritual types of people as well.

There will be many short-term trends in love as well, as Venus is a fast-moving planet and many trends depend on where she is at any given time and the kinds of aspects she receives. These will be discussed in the monthly reports.

Self-improvement

Spiritual Neptune has been in your 5th house of fun and creativity for many years now and will be there for many more years to come. Those of you in the creative arts have been unusually inspired – inspired from on high. Children and children figures in your life have become more spiritual as well. They are having revelatory kinds of dreams and supernatural types of experiences. Their bodies are more sensitive as well. Their bodies are being refined and spiritualized. Thus, they should avoid alcohol and drugs as the body can overreact to these things. It is good for you to understand what is going on with them so that you can deal with them better. Try not to pooh-pooh their dreams and experiences. Listen without judgement.

This year Saturn will move into your 5th house on March 8 and will remain there for the next two and a half years. For those of you who are creative this signals a need for more structure and attention to detail in your creations. They can't just be formless and vague. Also, as we mentioned, there is a need to learn how to discipline the children or children figures in your life. Discipline doesn't mean cruelty – just the opposite. A right discipline – a setting of just limits – will help them now and in future years. Your tendency for many years has probably been to give them a free hand. But this won't work now. Dreaminess, fantasy, awareness of higher worlds are all wonderful things for children, but they also need to be able to handle the practical affairs of life. So, you need to get the balance just right.

Saturn rules your 3rd house of intellectual interests. His position in the sign of Pisces shows changes in your intellectual interests. They become more spiritual. Spiritual books and magazines are more alluring these days.

There are many short-term spiritual trends in the year ahead as well. Venus, your spiritual planet as well as your love planet, is a fast-moving planet as we've said. And the many short-term spiritual trends this year are best dealt with in the monthly reports.

Venus spending over four months in your 10th career house is good for the love life – as we've mentioned – but it is also good for the spiritual life. It becomes more important, more of a focus. So, her sojourn here is a period for much spiritual progress. In addition, it would show that you can boost the career through involvement in charitable and altruistic kinds of activities.

In some cases, Venus's transit can be read as your love life and your spiritual growth *being* the actual career – the actual mission – from June 5 to October 9.

Month-by-month Forecasts

January

Best Days Overall: 6, 7, 14, 15, 23, 24
Most Stressful Days Overall: 12, 13, 18, 19, 25, 26
Best Days for Love: 2, 3, 12, 13, 18, 19, 21, 22
Best Days for Money: 8, 9, 16, 23
Best Days for Career: 2, 10, 11, 20, 21, 25, 26, 30, 31

Health needs watching this month – especially from the 20th onwards. Your health planet Mars is retrograde until the 12th, so avoid making major changes to the health regime – also (if possible) avoid medical tests and procedures. After the 17th would be a better period for these things. Enhance the health in the ways mentioned in the yearly report, but also add arm and shoulder massage. Detox regimes are always good for you, but this month even more than normal.

Your health planet is 'out of bounds' all month (and will be that way until May 4). So, in health matters you're outside your normal orbit. People see you as 'off the reservation'. Your job situation also takes you out of your normal orbit.

With your financial planet Jupiter having his solstice this month – and it lasts for a long time, from the 1st to the 27th – there can be a long pause in your financial life, and then a change of direction. Finances are a bit stressful and complicated early in the month but will improve after the 20th.

Though this is not a strong career period now, there is a nice opportunity from the 17th to the 19th, as your career planet, the Sun, travels with Pluto. Venus, your love planet, travels with Pluto on the 1st and 2nd, making these very nice love and social days.

You begin the year with your 3rd house of intellectual interests very powerful. This has been an area of interest for many years, but even more so this month. Students should do well in school. Those who work with their intellect – writers, teachers, sales and marketing people – should also do well. Scorpio is not known for communication skills, but this period they're very much enhanced.

Your love planet Venus moves speedily this month, through three signs and houses of your chart. This shows social confidence. There is quick social and romantic progress. Venus in your 3rd house until the 3rd indicates love opportunities arising in your neighbourhood and perhaps with neighbours. Intellectuality is a romantic turn-on – especially so on the 22nd and 23rd. From the 3rd to the 27th Venus is in your 4th house of home and family. This brings more socializing from home and with the family. Family and family connections can be important in love. Often one meets up with an old flame under this kind of transit. Usually, the cosmos arranges these things to resolve old issues. On the 27th Venus moves into your 5th house and stays there for the remainder of the month. This transit favours non-serious love – love affairs and entertainment. (Marriage has not been advisable for some years now – so this is good.)

February

Best Days Overall: 2, 3, 12, 13, 20, 21
Most Stressful Days Overall: 4, 5, 6, 18, 19, 24, 25
Best Days for Love: 2, 3, 12, 13, 22, 24, 25
Best Days for Money: 4, 5, 14, 15, 22, 23
Best Days for Career: 1, 4, 5, 6, 9, 10, 20

Home and family have been a major area of interest – a major focus – since January 20 and this is so until the 18th. Your career planet the Sun is moving through the 4th house, signalling that home, family and emotional wellness are the real career, the real mission, this month. The month ahead is about building the foundations, the infrastructure upon which a successful career will be built. It does have career implications but more in terms of preparation for the future. If you're in a point of emotional harmony, you can be very successful in your career this month – from that point of harmony.

Health still needs watching, until the 18th. Keep in mind our discussion of this last month. Arm and shoulder massage should be added to your regular health regime. Your health planet Mars is even further 'out of bounds' than he was last month. So, you're really exploring new therapies, therapists and doctors.

The Sun travels with Saturn on the 15th and 16th – a good period for students and intellectual workers. On the 18th the Sun moves into your 5th house and you begin one of your yearly personal pleasure peaks. Time to enjoy life – to have fun. Even career pursuits should be fun. The New Moon of the 20th occurs in your 5th house, adding to the fun and boosting the career. Issues involving children, children figures in your life and your personal creativity will clarify themselves in the coming weeks.

The month ahead is prosperous. You've changed direction financially. You seem happy-go-lucky about finances, and perhaps overly risk-taking. Financial decision-making can be too quick – perhaps you need to sleep on things before making up your mind.

Though marriage is not advisable, love seems fun this month. Venus is still in your 5th house until the 21st. There is an important romantic connection from the 14th to the 16th. On the 21st Venus enters your 6th house of health and work and you're more a 'love at first sight' kind of person now – and you probably meet people who are also like this. Good health for you also means a healthy love life – good social health. You're attracted to therapists, health professionals and co-workers.

March

Best Days Overall: 1, 2, 11, 12, 19, 20, 28, 29, 30
Most Stressful Days Overall: 4, 5, 17, 18, 24, 25, 31
Best Days for Love: 4, 5, 11, 12, 24, 25
Best Days for Money: 4, 5, 13, 14, 21, 22, 31
Best Days for Career: 1, 2, 4, 5, 12, 20, 21, 31

Saturn moves away from his stressful aspect with you on the 8th and this improves the health in a dramatic way. Pluto will be making stressful aspects to some of you from the 24th onwards, when he moves into Aquarius – but only those born early in Scorpio, October 23–25, will feel this; most of you won't. So, health is good this month. Mars, your health planet, is still in your 8th house of regeneration, until the 26th, so detox regimes and arm and shoulder massage are still very good. After the 26th diet and good emotional health become important.

The New Moon of the 21st occurs in your 6th house, and this is an excellent day for the career and for those seeking jobs. It also favours health as there is great focus here. A good work ethic will impress your superiors on the 21st and beyond. Issues involving your health or job will become clearer as the weeks go by (until the next New Moon).

You're still in the midst of a yearly personal pleasure peak until the 20th. Leisure – and this is counter-intuitive – will actually benefit the career. People with this kind of aspect often make good career connections at parties or on the golf course or tennis court. The 15th and 16th are especially good for this – combining fun with the career.

Venus travels with Jupiter on the 1st and 2nd – these are spectacular days for both love and money. Venus is still in your 6th house, until the 17th, so love is shown through service – serving the practical needs of the beloved. This is how you show love and how you feel loved. There is still an allurement to health professionals and co-workers. On the 17th Venus enters your 7th house of love, her own house, where she is powerful on your behalf. Your social graces and magnetism are strong. The good news is that you're a bit more conservative about love. More cautious. There are short-term love dramas on the 15th, 16th, 30th and 31st.

The month ahead is prosperous. Money comes from the job, from giving practical service. There can be pay rises here as well. As has been the case all year, you should slow down financially. You're attracted to a 'quick buck' and this makes you vulnerable to all sorts of people who exploit this tendency. Still, this is a period – and it's been so since the beginning of the year – where you're learning financial fearlessness. The issue isn't whether you win or lose; it's conquering your fear.

April

Best Days Overall: 7, 8, 16, 17, 25, 26
Most Stressful Days Overall: 1, 14, 15, 20, 21, 27, 28, 29
Best Days for Love: 3, 4, 14, 20, 21, 22, 23
Best Days for Money: 1, 9, 10, 19, 28, 29
Best Days for Career: 1, 10, 27, 28, 29, 30

Health needs attention from the 20th onwards. Do your best to eat right and maintain harmonious moods and feelings. More important than what you eat is *how* you eat. Elevate meals into a spiritual act of worship – make this a spiritual experience.

A solar eclipse on the 20th occurs right on the border of your 6th and 7th houses. Thus it affects the affairs of both houses. If you were born early in the sign – October 23–25 – you will feel the effects of this eclipse the strongest, but all of you will feel it in some degree. This is really April's headline.

The eclipse's impact on the 6th house indicates job changes, perhaps disruptions at the workplace and dramas in the lives of co-workers. There will be changes – dramatic ones – in your health regime, and perhaps changes of doctors as well. The impact on the 7th house tests the love life. Now, the love life (especially for those of you who are married) has been tested for a few years now – this eclipse just tests it further. There can be personal dramas in the lives of the spouse, partner or current love.

Pluto, the ruler of your Horoscope, receives a direct hit from this eclipse, provoking a redefinition and reassessment of yourself and your image. You need to change the way you think of yourself and the way that you want others to think of you. Thus, you will be presenting a 'new you' in the coming months. If you haven't been careful in dietary matters, there can be a physical detox. This is not sickness – though the symptoms are similar. It is just the body cleansing itself of effete material.

Because the Sun is your career planet, every solar eclipse affects the career, and this one is no different. There can be shake-ups in your corporate hierarchy and in your industry. There can be personal dramas in the lives of bosses, parents and parent figures. There can be shake-ups in government regulations as well – the rules of the career change. You pursue it in a different way. Sometimes, albeit rarely, people change their careers.

Reduce your schedule from the 20th onwards – and especially around the eclipse period.

May

Best Days Overall: 13, 14, 22, 23
Most Stressful Days Overall: 5, 6, 11, 12, 17, 18, 19, 25, 26
Best Days for Love: 2, 3, 9, 10, 17, 18, 19
Best Days for Money: 7, 8, 16, 17, 24, 25
Best Days for Career: 1, 9, 10, 18, 19, 25, 26, 30, 31

Your personal image and self-concept get tested again this month, as a lunar eclipse on the 5th occurs in your sign. So, you still need to change your opinion of yourself – your self-concept – and the way you want others to think of you. Major changes to your image and presentation to the world will happen over the coming months.

This eclipse affects college-level students (or those applying to college). There are changes in educational plans – changes of subjects, courses and sometimes even changes of schools. There are disruptions in your college or university. If you're involved in legal issues, they take a dramatic turn one way or another. There are shake-ups in your place of worship and personal dramas in the lives of worship leaders. Perhaps more important than all of this is that your religious and theological beliefs will get tested. The events of the eclipse will test them. Some will get modified; some will get discarded. This process will have a profound effect on your outlook on life and on the way you live your life.

Uranus – your family planet – gets sideswiped by this eclipse, and so there can be family dramas and shake-ups. Emotions run high in the family. Sometimes repairs are needed in the home.

Health still needs attention this month – especially until the 21st. So, as always, make sure to get enough rest. Diet and good emotional health are still important until the 21st. After then, give more attention to the heart.

A happy career opportunity happens on the 20th and 21st.

The New Moon of the 19th occurs in your 7th house, making this a particularly good career and social day. More importantly, your love situation – your marriage or relationship – will be clarified as the weeks go by. All doubts and questions will get resolved, normally and naturally.

June

Best Days Overall: 1, 2, 9, 10, 18, 19, 20, 28, 29
Most Stressful Days Overall: 7, 8, 14, 15, 16, 21, 22
Best Days for Love: 2, 11, 14, 15, 21, 22
Best Days for Money: 3, 4, 5, 6, 14, 15, 23, 24
Best Days for Career: 7, 8, 17, 18, 21, 22, 28

Jupiter moved into your 7th house on May 17 and will be there for the rest of the year ahead. This is a wonderful aspect for love. Normally this would signal marriage or a serious committed relationship. But with Uranus still in your 7th house (and he's been there for many years now) this might not be advisable. One can enjoy love without legal commitments. This is also a nice transit for finance. It often shows a lucrative kind of business partnership (but this too should be kept informal) and the importance of social contacts in finance. Your social grace is a major factor in earnings. You like to do business with friends and like to make friends with those you do business with. Love is basically happy this month, but there are some challenges on the 4th, 5th, 10th and 11th.

Your 8th house of regeneration became powerful last month on the 21st and remains so until the 21st of this month. So, the month ahead should be happy. You're concentrating on the things you most like to do: sex, occult studies, research, managing money, detox and personal transformation. The New Moon of the 18th also occurs in this house, adding to these interests. Libido is stronger than usual. There is career success as well. Issues involving sex, personal transformation, your occult studies, tax and estate issues will clarify themselves as the weeks progress. All the information you need will come to you naturally and normally.

On the 5th Venus moves into your 10th house of career. Thus, your social contacts are boosting the career. Career is boosted by social means – by attending or hosting the right kinds of parties and gatherings and by meeting just the right people who can help you. With Venus in your 10th house, singles are allured to people with power and status – and there are romantic opportunities with such people this month.

Though Pluto moves away from his stressful aspect, health needs watching this month. The heart needs more attention, and it would be beneficial to massage the reflex point to it (see the chart in the yearly report above). Most importantly, make sure you don't get overtired.

Be more mindful on the physical plane on the 4th and 5th and from the 24th to the 28th. (A parent or parent figure should also be more mindful from the 24th to the 28th.)

July

Best Days Overall: 7, 8, 16, 17, 26, 27
Most Stressful Days Overall: 5, 6, 11, 12, 18, 19, 20
Best Days for Love: 2, 10, 11, 12, 19, 20, 29
Best Days for Money: 1, 2, 3, 4, 11, 12, 21, 22, 28, 29, 30, 31
Best Days for Career: 7, 8, 17, 18, 19, 20, 26

Love is happy but complicated this month. Your 7th house of love is very strong, but Uranus's presence there destabilizes things. However, it does add excitement – ups and downs! The main complication is Venus's rare retrograde on the 23rd. There is uncertainty in love – doubt as to the direction it takes.

Venus, your love planet, is still in your 10th house of career this month. So, like last month (and, indeed, for the next few months) you're attracted to people of power and prestige – people who can help you career-wise. The danger with this position is getting involved in relationships of convenience rather than true love.

Health is good but after the 23rd it becomes more stressful. So, as always, make sure to get enough rest. Your health planet Mars will be in your 10th house until the 11th, after which he moves into your 11th house. Enhance the health with chest massage (and massage of the heart reflex) until the 11th. After then, enhance the health with abdominal massage (and massage of the small intestine reflex – see the chart in the yearly report).

Your 9th house is very powerful until the 23rd. So, the month ahead is good for students – especially college-level students and for those applying to colleges. This is a period for gaining religious and theological insights. A foreign trip could also happen. The New Moon of the 17th occurs in your 9th house, bringing religious and theological insights. Issues involving education, foreign travel and religion will clarify as the weeks progress. The natural actions of the cosmos will answer your questions and resolve your doubts.

On the 23rd, as the Sun enters your 10th house of career, you begin a yearly career peak. And this looks very successful. The Sun will be in his own sign and house and thus more powerful than usual. This bodes well for the career.

Finances are good this month but become more challenging after the 23rd. Earnings will still happen, but you'll work harder for them. Your challenge is to decide what's more important – the bottom line or career prestige. Each pulls you in a different direction.

August

Best Days Overall: 3, 4, 12, 13, 22, 23, 30, 31
Most Stressful Days Overall: 1, 2, 7, 8, 14, 15, 16, 29
Best Days for Love: 5, 6, 7, 8, 14, 15, 24, 25
Best Days for Money: 7, 8, 17, 18, 24, 25, 26, 27
Best Days for Career: 5, 6, 14, 15, 16, 26

Health still needs a lot of attention until the 23rd. Keep in mind our discussion of last month. Your health planet is still in Virgo, so abdominal massage and massage of the small intestine reflex will enhance health. Most importantly, make sure to get enough rest. Your health and work planet Mars will have his solstice from the 27th to September 2. So, there is a pause and a change of direction in both your health attitudes and at the job.

You're still in the midst of a yearly career peak this month. You still seem successful. The main problem is balancing the home and family demands with the career. This seems a problem – especially on the 14th and 15th. But the focus should really be on the career now. The New Moon of the 16th occurs in your 10th house, which boosts the career even further – a successful day in a successful month. The New Moon has an effect long after it actually occurs; it clarifies issues as the weeks progress – until the next New Moon. So, career doubts and questions will get resolved over the weeks in natural and normal ways.

Love is still complicated this month as Venus is still retrograde. The 8th and 9th can bring love and family dramas. But these issues are short term.

Finances are still stressful. There are more challenges involved and you have to work harder for earnings. But they will come. You will see a big improvement in earnings after the 23rd. (Health will also improve after the 23rd.)

The Sun's move into Virgo on the 23rd signals a more social period – but it's more about friendships and Platonic kinds of relationships rather than romance. For as long as Venus is retrograde, avoid making important love decisions one way or another. The social judgement is not up to its usual standards.

By the end of the month 60 per cent of the planets will be retrograde – a huge percentage (and the maximum number for the year). Patience is called for. Dealing with frustration is perhaps your biggest challenge, Scorpio.

September

Best Days Overall: 8, 9, 10, 18, 19, 27, 28
Most Stressful Days Overall: 4, 5, 11, 12, 25, 26
Best Days for Love: 2, 4, 5, 3, 11, 12, 21, 22, 30
Best Days for Money: 4, 5, 14, 15, 21, 22, 23, 24
Best Days for Career: 4, 5, 11, 12, 13, 14, 25

Health is much improved this month, which is good news. Your health planet Mars is still in solstice mode until the 2nd, but after that his change of direction is established. So it is with your health regime and your job. Mars spends the month in Libra, your 12th house of spirituality. So, massage of the hips and the kidney reflexes will enhance health even further. But the real message here is that you respond well to spiritual healing. Many of you will go deeper into this during the month – especially after the 23rd.

Retrograde activity is strong all month. Until the 16th 60 per cent of the planets are retrograde, while after the 16th the figure is 50 per cent – still a very high percentage. So, life is slower now. Nothing much seems to be happening on the outside – but internally much is happening. It is just unseen.

Yet, in spite of all this, love is straightening out and career is moving forward. Venus starts moving forward on the 4th. So the social judgement is back to normal. There are romantic opportunities as you pursue your career goals and with people involved in your career. You're still very much attracted to people of power and prestige. Finance is important and love is important, and both areas vie for attention.

The Sun is now making good aspects with Jupiter, your money planet, and Uranus. So, finances should be good. Pay rises, official or unofficial, can happen (but with a delayed reaction). You can further the career by social means (which has been the case for the past few months) and through involving yourself with groups, trade and professional organizations. Good networking skills will advance the career.

The New Moon of the 15th occurs in your 11th house, and it also brings an excellent career day. It brings religious and theological insights too. It enhances your knowledge of science, computers, astronomy and astrology. A good social day as well.

On the 23rd the Sun enters your 12th house of spirituality, inaugurating an excellent period for meditation and spiritual practice. Your career is enhanced through involvement with charities and altruistic kinds of activities.

October

Best Days Overall: 6, 7, 15, 16, 17, 24, 25
Most Stressful Days Overall: 1, 2, 8, 9, 22, 23, 28, 29
Best Days for Love: 1, 2, 9, 10, 11, 20, 21
Best Days for Money: 1, 2, 11, 12, 18, 19, 20, 21, 28, 29
Best Days for Career: 3, 4, 8, 9, 24

Two eclipses shake up the world at large and your personal life this month. These shake-ups – though unpleasant – are often necessary. If one is on the wrong track, a good shake-up is needed. A person can veer 5 or 10 degrees off his or her life orbit. But if they veer more than that an eclipse comes along and brings them back in line.

There is a solar eclipse on the 14th and a lunar eclipse on the 28th. The lunar eclipse seems the stronger of the two – as it impacts you more directly.

The solar eclipse of the 14th occurs in your 12th house of spirituality, bringing dramatic changes to this area of your life. People change their spiritual attitudes, teachings or even teachers under this kind of eclipse. Often they change their practice as well. There are shake-ups in spiritual, charitable or altruistic organizations you're involved with. There are dramas in the lives of guru figures. The dream life is probably more active now, but probably not very reliable. (It is just psychic debris stirred up by the eclipse.) Friends can have financial dramas and are forced to make important financial changes. Every solar eclipse affects the career, as we've said, because the Sun is your career planet. So, career changes are happening. In rare cases people change their career and choose a completely different one. Usually there is a need to pursue the career in a different way: the government can change the rules and regulations of your industry or there are shake-ups in your industry or corporate hierarchy. There are personal dramas in the lives of bosses, parents or parent figures.

The lunar eclipse of the 28th occurs in your 7th house and will test your current relationship. Relationships have been tested for a few years now, but this eclipse will test them further. College-level students are dealing with disruptions at school and changes to their educational plans. Sometimes they actually change schools. There are dramas and disruptions at your place of worship and in the lives of worship leaders and in the congregation in general. More importantly, your religious and theological beliefs will get tested in the coming months. Some will be revised; some will be dropped. This is generally a healthy thing; it's good that our beliefs are tested and revised from time to time.

November

Best Days Overall: 2, 3, 12, 13, 21, 22, 29, 30
Most Stressful Days Overall: 4, 5, 6, 18, 19, 25, 26
Best Days for Love: 8, 9, 18, 19, 25, 26, 27, 28
Best Days for Money: 7, 14, 15, 16, 25
Best Days for Career: 2, 3, 4, 5, 6, 12, 13, 23

Though you still might be feeling the after-effects of last month's eclipses, the month ahead is basically happy. The Sun is in your own sign until the 22nd and you're in a yearly personal pleasure peak. You're enjoying all the pleasures of the physical body and getting the body and image into the shape that you want. Mars, your health planet, is also in your sign until the 24th. So, you're very much into physical fitness and health regimes. But these transits also have other effects. The Sun in your sign brings happy career opportunities to you – they chase you. You have the image of success and dress the part. (Perhaps you're overspending on this.) Job opportunities are also coming to you, with little effort on your part – they find you. Even if you're already employed, there can be offers from other companies or opportunities for overtime or second jobs.

Health is good. Your physical appearance mirrors your state of health. Since you are healthy you also look good. You're in a very good period for weight loss regimes, if you need them – also for detoxing.

On the 22nd the Sun enters your 2nd money house and you begin a yearly financial peak. The only issue is the retrograde of Jupiter, your financial planet. Earnings will be strong, but they come with delays or glitches. The Sun in the money house indicates the financial favour of bosses, parents and parent figures. They support your financial goals. Pay rises – official or unofficial – can happen. Earnings seem to come from work now. Be careful of too much risk taking in your finances from the 24th onwards. Mercury's move into the money house on the 10th makes it an excellent time to solicit outside investors if you have good business ideas. It is also a good time to pay down debt or take on loans – depending on your need. It is good for tax and insurance planning. For those of you of the appropriate age it is good for estate planning.

The New Moon of the 12th occurs in your own sign. This increases the personal pleasure and enhances physical appearance. The libido is higher on that day. It can bring an opportunity to travel or a career opportunity – or both. Any issues involving your personal appearance and image will become clearer as the weeks progress.

December

Best Days Overall: 9, 10, 18, 19, 27, 28
Most Stressful Days Overall: 2, 3, 16, 17, 22, 23, 29, 30
Best Days for Love: 9, 18, 19, 22, 23, 28, 30
Best Days for Money: 4, 11, 12, 14, 22, 31
Best Days for Career: 2, 3, 11, 12, 21, 22, 29, 30

Mars, your health planet, has spent a good part of the year 'out of bounds'. He was 'out of bounds' from January 1 to May 4 and this month he goes 'out of bounds' again, from the 22nd to the end of the month. So, in health matters you've been seriously outside your normal orbit, and this happens again. This is also true of your job situation.

The month ahead seems very prosperous. You're still in the midst of a yearly financial peak until the 22nd. But finances will be good even after then. Mars will be in your money house all month; Mercury will retrograde back in there on the 24th; and Venus will move in on the 30th. In addition, Jupiter, your financial planet, will start to move forward on the 31st. Finances are being clarified. Stuck projects and deals will start to move forward.

Health also looks good this month. With your health planet in Sagittarius, you can enhance it further with thigh massage and massage of the liver reflex. In the month ahead you will probably be more concerned with your financial health than with physical health.

If finances are not the way you want them, health can be impacted – but only if you allow it. You shouldn't.

Love seems happy – though the complications of having Uranus in your house of love are still active. Venus, your love planet, moves speedily this month through three signs and houses of your chart. There is social confidence, and your goals are attained quickly. But Venus's quick transit also shows a changeability in love and in your love needs. Until the 5th, as Venus is in your 12th house, love is more spiritual and spiritual compatibility with a partner is important. From the 5th to the 30th sexual magnetism seems the most important thing. Love also seems particularly happy this period. Love pursues you now, and if you're in a relationship the beloved is devoted to you. You come first. But even singles have love on their own terms. There's nothing much you need to do to attract love – it finds you. Just go about your daily business. On the 30th and 31st love is more material as Venus moves into your money house. Gifts and material support seem important. There are romantic opportunities as you pursue your financial goals and with people involved in your finances.

Sagittarius

THE ARCHER

Birthdays from
23rd November to
20th December

Personality Profile

SAGITTARIUS AT A GLANCE

Element - Fire

Ruling Planet - Jupiter
  Career Planet - Mercury
  Love Planet - Mercury
  Money Planet - Saturn
  Planet of Health and Work - Venus
  Planet of Home and Family Life - Neptune
  Planet of Spirituality - Pluto

Colours - blue, dark blue

Colours that promote love, romance and social harmony - yellow,
  yellow-orange

Colours that promote earning power - black, indigo

Gems - carbuncle, turquoise

Metal - tin

Scents - carnation, jasmine, myrrh

Quality – mutable (= flexibility)

Qualities most needed for balance – attention to detail, administrative and organizational skills

Strongest virtues – generosity, honesty, broad-mindedness, tremendous vision

Deepest need – to expand mentally

Characteristics to avoid – over-optimism, exaggeration, being too generous with other people's money

Signs of greatest overall compatibility – Aries, Leo

Signs of greatest overall incompatibility – Gemini, Virgo, Pisces

Sign most helpful to career – Virgo

Sign most helpful for emotional support – Pisces

Sign most helpful financially – Capricorn

Sign best for marriage and/or partnerships – Gemini

Sign most helpful for creative projects – Aries

Best Sign to have fun with – Aries

Signs most helpful in spiritual matters – Leo, Scorpio

Best day of the week – Thursday

Understanding a Sagittarius

If you look at the symbol of the archer you will gain a good, intuitive understanding of a person born under this astrological sign. The development of archery was humanity's first refinement of the power to hunt and wage war. The ability to shoot an arrow far beyond the ordinary range of a spear extended humanity's horizons, wealth, personal will and power.

Today, instead of using bows and arrows we project our power with fuels and mighty engines, but the essential reason for using these new powers remains the same. These powers represent our ability to extend our personal sphere of influence – and this is what Sagittarius is all about. Sagittarians are always seeking to expand their horizons, to cover more territory and increase their range and scope. This applies to all aspects of their lives: economic, social and intellectual.

Sagittarians are noted for the development of the mind – the higher intellect – which understands philosophical and spiritual concepts. This mind represents the higher part of the psychic nature and is motivated not by self-centred considerations but by the light and grace of a Higher Power. Thus, Sagittarians love higher education of all kinds. They might be bored with formal schooling but they love to study on their own and in their own way. A love of foreign travel and interest in places far away from home are also noteworthy characteristics of the Sagittarian type.

If you give some thought to all these Sagittarian attributes you will see that they spring from the inner Sagittarian desire to develop. To travel more is to know more, to know more is to be more, to cultivate the higher mind is to grow and to reach more. All these traits tend to broaden the intellectual – and indirectly, the economic and material – horizons of the Sagittarian.

The generosity of the Sagittarian is legendary. There are many reasons for this. One is that Sagittarians seem to have an inborn consciousness of wealth. They feel that they are rich, that they are lucky, that they can attain any financial goal – and so they feel that they can afford to be generous. Sagittarians do not carry the burdens of want and limitation which stop most other people from giving generously. Another reason for their generosity is their religious and philosophical idealism, derived from the higher mind. This higher mind is by nature generous because it is unaffected by material circumstances. Still another reason is that the act of giving tends to enhance their emotional nature. Every act of giving seems to be enriching, and this is reward enough for the Sagittarian.

Finance

Sagittarians generally entice wealth. They either attract it or create it. They have the ideas, energy and talent to make their vision of paradise on Earth a reality. However, mere wealth is not enough. Sagittarians want luxury – earning a comfortable living seems small and insignificant to them.

In order for Sagittarians to attain their true earning potential they must develop better managerial and organizational skills. They must learn to set limits, to arrive at their goals through a series of attainable sub-goals or objectives. It is very rare that a person goes from rags to riches overnight. But a long, drawn-out process is difficult for Sagittarians. Like Leos, they want to achieve wealth and success quickly and impressively. They must be aware, however, that this over-optimism can lead to unrealistic financial ventures and disappointing losses. Of course, no zodiac sign can bounce back as quickly as Sagittarius, but only needless heartache will be caused by this attitude. Sagittarians need to maintain their vision – never letting it go – but they must also work towards it in practical and efficient ways.

Career and Public Image

Sagittarians are big thinkers. They want it all: money, fame, glamour, prestige, public acclaim and a place in history. They often go after all these goals. Some attain them, some do not – much depends on each individual's personal horoscope. But if Sagittarians want to attain public and professional status they must understand that these things are not conferred to enhance one's ego but as rewards for the amount of service that one does for the whole of humanity. If and when they figure out ways to serve more, Sagittarians can rise to the top.

The ego of the Sagittarian is gigantic – and perhaps rightly so. They have much to be proud of. If they want public acclaim, however, they will have to learn to tone down the ego a bit, to become more humble and self-effacing, without falling into the trap of self-denial and self-abasement. They must also learn to master the details of life, which can sometimes elude them.

At their jobs Sagittarians are hard workers who like to please their bosses and co-workers. They are dependable, trustworthy and enjoy a challenge. Sagittarians are friendly to work with and helpful to their colleagues. They usually contribute intelligent ideas or new methods that improve the work environment for everyone. Sagittarians always look for challenging positions and careers that develop their intellect, even if they have to work very hard in order to succeed. They also work well under the supervision of others, although by nature they would rather be the supervisors and increase their sphere of influence. Sagittarians excel at professions that allow them to be in contact with many different people and to travel to new and exciting locations.

Love and Relationships

Sagittarians love freedom for themselves and will readily grant it to their partners. They like their relationships to be fluid and ever-changing. Sagittarians tend to be fickle in love and to change their minds about their partners quite frequently.

Sagittarians feel threatened by a clearly defined, well-structured relationship, as they feel this limits their freedom. The Sagittarian tends to marry more than once in life.

Sagittarians in love are passionate, generous, open, benevolent and very active. They demonstrate their affections very openly. However, just like an Aries they tend to be egocentric in the way they relate to their partners. Sagittarians should develop the ability to see others' points of view, not just their own. They need to develop some objectivity and cool intellectual clarity in their relationships so that they can develop better two-way communication with their partners. Sagittarians tend to be overly idealistic about their partners and about love in general. A cool and rational attitude will help them to perceive reality more clearly and enable them to avoid disappointment.

Home and Domestic Life

Sagittarians tend to grant a lot of freedom to their family. They like big homes and many children and are one of the most fertile signs of the zodiac. However, when it comes to their children Sagittarians generally err on the side of allowing them too much freedom. Sometimes their children get the idea that there are no limits. However, allowing freedom in the home is basically a positive thing – so long as some measure of balance is maintained – for it enables all family members to develop as they should.

Horoscope for 2023

Major Trends

Pluto, your spiritual planet, is still in your money house for most of this year, but is beginning to make the transition into your 3rd house of intellectual interests. This will be a two-year process. In 2025 he will enter your 3rd house for the long haul – for twenty or so years. This year, however, he moves in from March 24 to June 12. This has big implications for your taste in reading and education.

Saturn has been in your 3rd house for the past two and a half years, and on March 8 makes a major move into your 4th house, where he'll remain for the next two and half years. This brings important changes to the family and the emotional life. More on this later.

Jupiter, the ruler of your Horoscope, and thus a very important planet in your chart, will be in your 5th house of fun and creativity until May 17. This is a fun period in your life. It's party time. A happy-go-lucky period. Personal creativity will be strong. Women of childbearing age are more fertile, and in general there is more interest in children and children figures in your life.

On May 17 Jupiter enters your 6th house of health and work and stays there for the rest of the year. He joins Uranus, who has been in your 6th house for many years now. Jupiter's move here increases your interest in health and work. There are nice job opportunities coming. If there have been health problems, you should get best-case scenarios. More on this later.

Venus will spend over four months in your 9th house – an unusually long transit for her. (Her usual transit is a month.) So, this is a significant stay. It reinforces your love for foreign travel and higher education. There can be job opportunities in foreign lands (Venus is your planet of health and work). If there is a health problem, perhaps a foreigner or foreign hospital can be of help.

Your major interests this year are finance (until March 24 and from June 12 onwards); intellectual interests and communication (from January 1 to March 8 and from March 24 to June 12); home and family; fun, children and creativity (until May 17); and health and work.

Your paths of greatest fulfilment this year are fun, children and creativity (until May 17 and from July 18 onwards); and health and work.

Health

(Please note that this is an astrological perspective on health and not a medical one. In days of yore there was no difference, both these perspectives were identical. But these days there could be quite a difference. For a medical perspective, please consult your doctor or health practitioner.)

Saturn joining Neptune in stressful aspect to you makes the health more delicate this year. By itself this alignment would not be so bad, but when other short-term planets make stressful aspects in addition, you can be become vulnerable to problems. We will discuss these periods in the monthly reports.

The good news is that you're very focused on health – especially from May 17 onwards. Thus you're not likely to ignore things. You'll be on the case. This is a positive for health.

Also, as our regular readers know, there is much you can do to enhance the health and prevent problems from developing. Give more attention to the following – the vulnerable areas of your Horoscope this year (the reflex points are shown in the chart overleaf). Most of the time problems can be prevented. But even in cases where they can't be totally prevented, they can be softened to a great extent. They need not be devastating.

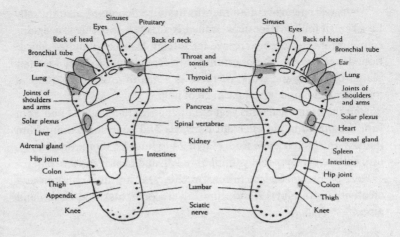

Important foot reflexology points for the year ahead

Try to massage all of the foot on a regular basis – the top of the foot as well as the bottom – but pay extra attention to the points highlighted on the chart. When you massage, be aware of 'sore spots' as these need special attention. It's also a good idea to massage the ankles and below them.

- The heart becomes an important area for you after March 8 and remains so for the next two and a half years. It becomes even more important from June 5 to October 9 as your health planet stays in Leo (the sign that rules the heart) for over four months. (The reflex point is shown above.) The important thing with the heart is to avoid worry and anxiety, the two emotions that stress it out. Replace worry with faith.

- The liver and thighs are always important for Sagittarius, as your sign rules these areas. These become even more important from May 17 onwards when Jupiter enters your 6th house. The liver reflex is shown above. Regular thigh massage is always beneficial for you; it not only strengthens the liver and thighs but the lower back as well.

- The neck and throat. These too are always important for Sagittarius, and regular neck massage should be a part of your normal health regime. Tension tends to collect in the neck and needs to be released. Craniosacral therapy is also very good for the neck.

- The ankles and calves have become an important area since 2019, when Uranus entered your 6th house. And they will remain important for another few years to come. The calves and ankles should be regularly massaged. Give the ankles more support when exercising as well.

Your health planet Venus is a fast-moving planet. During the year she will move through your entire Horoscope, so there are many short-term trends in health that depend on where Venus is and the kinds of aspects she receives. These are best dealt with in the monthly reports.

With Saturn making stressful aspects to you, don't be alarmed if you can't jog or run your usual distances. It's quite normal. It's like walking uphill. There's more resistance to deal with. More energy is needed than in walking on a level path or downhill. So, listen to the messages of the body and try not to push it beyond its capacity.

As mentioned, Uranus has been in your 6th house since 2019. So, some of the trends of recent years are still in effect this year. You're attracted to alternative therapies. You're more experimental in health matters. You're in the process of learning about yourself – how you function and what works for you.

When Jupiter enters your house of health on May 17, you'll learn that good health will do more to improve your personal appearance than hosts of lotions and potions. Just stay healthy and the physical appearance will reflect this.

Home and Family

Your 4th house of home and family has been an important focus for many years, and becomes even more important in the year ahead. The main headline is Saturn's move into this house on March 8. This can be stressful. You seem emotionally inhibited. Perhaps you don't feel safe expressing how you really feel, and the tendency will be to repress your feelings. This is dangerous. You need a safe way to express your feelings without repressing them or taking it out on others.

Last year your family circle expanded. In many cases this was through births: women of childbearing age were extremely fertile. This year we see the opposite. Pregnancy could be problematic. It can happen – especially until May 17 – but it will be more complicated.

Saturn is your financial planet, and his move into the 4th house in March shows that you spend more on the home and family, but you can earn from the home and family as well (more on this later).

If you did not move in the past year, this year is not a year for it. Better to make good use – more efficient use – of the space that you have. Many of you feel cramped in your present quarters. Try to be more creative in your use of space.

Family life this year seems a burden, a cross to bear, a duty and a discipline. The joy of family life doesn't seem to be there. You perform your duties, and others do as well, but you're all just going through the motions. You're not a depressive kind of person normally, but this year you'll have to work harder to avoid this.

If you're planning to renovate the home or carry out major repairs, May 1–21 and November 1–24 seem auspicious times. If you're just redecorating in a cosmetic kind of way, January 27 to February 20, May 7 to June 5 and December 6–29 would be good times. These periods are also good for buying art objects or other objects of beauty for the home.

A parent or parent figure seems sad and pessimistic. He or she feels older than their years. Things look black. A move is not likely this year – but could happen in 2024. Siblings and sibling figures could move this year (but later in the year) and next year as well. If the siblings are women of childbearing age, they are very fertile this year. Children and children figures in your life are prospering and living the high life, but a move is not likely this year. Grandchildren, or those that play that role in your life, are having a quiet, stable family year. A move is not likely.

Finance and Career

The year ahead is financially significant, Sagittarius. First off, as we mentioned earlier, Pluto is starting to make a transition out of your money house. It begins this year but will go on for a few more to come – Pluto is the slowest moving of all the planets. More important than that is the major move of your financial planet, Saturn, out of Aquarius and into Pisces on March 8.

Saturn's position in your 3rd house for the past two and a half years signalled earnings being derived from buying, selling, trading, advertising, PR, retailing and from your good communication skills. You were more experimental in financial matters. Start-ups, technology and online companies were alluring and profitable. Now Saturn's move into your 4th house brings new financial attitudes. For a start, your financial planet in spiritual Pisces highlights the importance of intuition in the financial life. You are naturally intuitive, Sagittarius, but now even more so than normal – and especially in money matters. Financial guidance comes to you in dreams, visions and hunches. Also from psychics, astrologers, tarot readers and spiritual channels. You are naturally a generous person, but in the coming years even more so. Charitable giving will increase.

Your financial planet in Pisces favours a new set of industries – oil, natural gas, water utilities, water bottlers and purifying companies, shipping, shipbuilders and the fishing industry. You will have a good intuition for these kinds of investments. It also favours certain kinds of pharmaceuticals – makers of mood enhancers and anaesthetics.

There are mutual funds that describe themselves as 'faith based' investments. Some call themselves 'social responsibility' investments. These would be attractive to you in the coming years.

Saturn in the 4th house also favours residential real estate, restaurants, the food business, hotels, motels and companies that cater to homeowners. Some of you will be attracted to psychology or psychiatry.

Family and family connections will play an important role in finance – more so than in previous years. Family support should be good. And it works both ways. You support the family and family members, and they support you.

More important than all of this is the fact that you'll be exploring the spiritual laws of supply – more of which later on.

Your 10th house of career is not prominent this year. Basically, it is empty. Only short-term planets will move through there and their effects are equally short term. Your family house is much more powerful than your career house and so this is not a strong career year. It will tend to the status quo.

Your career planet, Mercury, is a fast-moving planet (as our regular readers know) and will move through your whole Horoscope in any given year. Thus, there are many short-term career trends that depend on where Mercury is and the kinds of aspects he receives. These are best discussed in the monthly reports.

Love and Social Life

Your 7th house of love is not prominent this year. Only short-term planets will move through there and their effects will be short term, so this is not a strong romantic year. Again, this tends to the status quo. Your current relationship (if you are in one) will most likely continue, and those not in a relationship will most probably end the year this way too. Basically, you seem content with the way things are.

Next year, however, it will be a different story. Your 7th house becomes much more powerful in 2024 and singles are likely to experience major romance. I consider this year to be a year of preparation. Mental and emotional changes have to happen before you can meet that special someone. A romantic meeting – a serious one – doesn't just happen. Conditions have to be right for both parties. And that is what is going on this year.

Your love planet is Mercury – the same as your career planet. The fact that they are the same tells us much about your love life. It is very important to you. In many cases it is your real career. Even if you are involved in a worldly career, secretly your mission is your friends and marriage partner. In many cases, one chooses a worldly career based on the love and social opportunities that it offers – not so much about the work itself.

Mercury, as we've said, is a very fast-moving planet. He is also erratic in his movements. Sometimes he speeds through the heavens on winged sandals. Sometimes he slows down. Sometimes he stands still and sometimes he goes backwards. This is the nature of your love life. It tends to be erratic, mirroring Mercury's movements. And so there will be many short-term love trends that depend on where Mercury is at any given time and the kinds of aspects he receives. These are best dealt with in the monthly reports.

Usually, Mercury goes retrograde three times in a year. In the year ahead, however, he will be retrograde four times – from January 1–17; April 21 to May 14; August 23 to September 14; and December 13–31. Love can seem to go backwards during these periods. Your social judgement is not up to its usual standard. It is unwise to make important love decisions – one way or another – during these periods.

Self-improvement

Intuition has been important in your financial life for many years. Your spiritual planet, Pluto, has been in your money house for over twenty years and will be there still for most of the year ahead. But now your financial planet Saturn moves into Pisces on March 8, and the importance of intuition becomes even stronger. The year ahead is all about 'miracle money' and not so much about 'natural money'. You've been experiencing miracle money for many years, but now even more so. Natural money – money we get from our jobs, parents, spouses, investments, social security system, etc. – is also miracle money but more disguised. I define 'miracle money' as money that comes in unexpected ways – from ways that we never consciously imagined. The expression is money that comes from 'left field'. This is what happens when one operates the spiritual laws of wealth in a proper way – without doubt or subconscious denial.

Over the years you've been studying the spiritual laws of wealth and have gained a great understanding of them. This year you will go even deeper into the subject and will see remarkable results.

There is the Wall Street perspective on wealth and there is the spiritual perspective. There are similarities, but the differences are vast and often contradictory. Because we were all brought up to believe certain things – that matter is fact; that wealth comes from the 'sweat of our brow' – making the transition is a challenge. But you will do it.

In the Wall Street perspective, your wealth is defined by your bank statements and stock valuations. In the spiritual perspective, your wealth comes from the infinite resources of the Divine. How much you physically have is not an issue. In the Wall Street perspective, giving reduces your wealth. In the spiritual perspective, giving increases it. In the Wall Street perspective work creates wealth. In the spiritual perspective, it's just the opposite – wealth creates work. Work is involved (in the sense that physical motions are necessary) but the work itself is a side-effect of the flow of spiritual supply. So, continue with your efforts, you'll see good results. For more information on this subject, visit my website www.spiritual-stories.com. There is also much literature about spiritual wealth and you should continue to read all that you can about it.

Month-by-month Forecasts

January

Best Days Overall: 8, 9, 16, 17, 25, 26
Most Stressful Days Overall: 1, 2, 14, 15, 21, 22, 28, 29
Best Days for Love: 1, 2, 3, 10, 11, 12, 13, 18, 19, 21, 22, 28, 29
Best Days for Money: 4, 8, 10, 11, 12, 13, 16, 22, 23, 31
Best Days for Career: 1, 2, 10, 11, 18, 19, 28, 29

You begin your year in the midst of a yearly financial peak. It began last month on December 22, and it continues until the 20th. Prosperity is strong. (You will also end 2023 in a financial peak.) Finances will be good even after the 20th as your 2nd money house is still strong. Money can come from foreign investments, through social contacts and through good financial intuition (especially from the 17th to the 19th).

Health should be good this month. The long-term planets are mostly either in harmony with you or leaving you alone, although there is one long-term planet (and one short-term planet) in stressful alignment with you. You can enhance the health, however, with back and knee massage until the 3rd, with ankle and calf massage from the 3rd to the 27th and with foot massage from the 27th onwards. Spiritual-healing techniques and good emotional health seem important from the 27th.

Love is complicated this month. For a start, your love planet, Mercury, is retrograde until the 17th. The other planet involved in your love life, Mars, is retrograde until the 12th. So, things start off slow this year, and there are many doubts about your current relationship. However, love will improve after the 18th.

This is not a chart for marriage. Mars, sitting in your 7th house of love, rules your 5th house and so love seems more about fun and games – entertainment – rather than anything serious and committed. Jupiter's position in your 5th house reinforces this – you're in a mood for fun, for a happy-go-lucky kind of life.

Mercury spends the month in your money house, which indicates that singles are attracted to wealthy people. Love is about material support and material gifts. Singles can find love opportunities as they pursue their financial goals and with people involved in their finances.

Mars is 'out of bounds' this month and will remain so until early May. Children and children figures in your life are outside their normal orbits – and next month they'll be even further outside their normal orbits. Those of you in the creative arts are also going outside your normal sphere.

The New Moon of the 11th occurs in your money house and increases earnings even further. It would be a good day to pay off debt or to take out a loan, depending on your need. Religious and theological insights will come to you that period. As the weeks go by (until the next New Moon) financial issues will clarify themselves. Doubts will be resolved and questions answered, and all of this will be natural and normal.

February

Best Days Overall: 4, 5, 6, 14, 15, 22, 23
Most Stressful Days Overall: 1, 7, 8, 20, 21, 27, 28
Best Days for Love: 1, 2, 3, 8, 11, 12, 13, 18, 19, 22, 27, 28
Best Days for Money: 1, 4, 5, 10, 14, 15, 16, 17, 19, 22, 23, 28
Best Days for Career: 7, 8, 11, 18, 19, 27, 28

You love to travel but you should avoid it from the 3rd to the 5th – reschedule any trips for another time.

Last month on the 20th, as the Sun entered your 3rd house, your focus was on intellectual interests. This remains so until the 18th. Students should do well in school. Learning and teaching go easier as the mental faculties are greatly enhanced. This would also be a good month to catch up on the emails, letters and phone calls that you owe people.

Prosperity is still strong this month. Saturn, your financial planet, receives stimulating aspects especially on the 15th and 16th. The New Moon of the 20th occurs right on Saturn too – further increasing earnings.

The New Moon this month occurs in your 4th house of home and family. Women of childbearing age are more fertile that day. Issues involving the home and family will become clearer as the weeks progress – until the next New Moon.

Career is not a big issue this month – home and family and your emotional wellness seem much more important. But with your career planet in your 3rd house from the 11th onwards you can boost the career through good communications, sales and marketing. Pay rises – official or unofficial – can happen until the 11th. (They could have happened last month as well.)

Health becomes more delicate from the 18th onwards. Make sure to get more rest. Enhance the health with foot massage and spiritual techniques until the 21st. Spiritual-healing techniques are especially powerful from the 14th to the 16th. After the 21st scalp and face massage and physical exercise seem important. When Venus, your health planet, moves into Aries on the 21st you can enhance the health through joy. Just have fun – joy cures many issues.

Love opportunities occur as you pursue your financial goals, until the 11th, and can be found within your neighbourhood from the 11th onwards. Romantic opportunities happen in educational-type settings – at school, in lectures, seminars, the bookshop or library.

March

Best Days Overall: 4, 5, 13, 14, 21, 22, 31
Most Stressful Days Overall: 6, 7, 19, 20, 26, 27
Best Days for Love: 4, 5, 11, 12, 21, 24, 25, 26, 27, 31
Best Days for Money: 4, 5, 11, 13, 14, 15, 16, 19, 21, 22, 28, 31
Best Days for Career: 6, 7, 11, 12, 21, 31

On the 8th Saturn makes a major move into Pisces, your 4th house, which brings many changes. First off, your health will generally need more attention paid to it over the next two and a half years. In addition,

Saturn's transit signals that you will earn money from the home and spend more there. Family and family connections become very important in the financial life. Likewise, your financial intuition.

Keep monitoring the health this month, especially until the 20th. Enhance the health with scalp and face massage and physical exercise until the 17th. After then, neck and throat massage would be beneficial. Craniosacral therapy will also be good. Those of you on a spiritual path can enhance the health through mantra chanting and singing.

Health will improve dramatically after the 20th but still needs watching. Mars moves out of his stressful aspect with you on the 26th – which improves matters.

You love planet Mercury moves speedily this month through three signs and houses of your Horoscope. So, the love needs and allurements change equally quickly. On the flip side, Mercury's fast transit signals strong social confidence. Until the 3rd love is found close to home in your neighbourhood and you're attracted to intellectuals. A person's smarts turn you on. From the 3rd to the 19th love is more emotional and spiritual. Intellect is not enough for you now; you want a good emotional and spiritual connection. With your love planet in sensitive Pisces now, you are probably more easily hurt. You're more sensitive to voice tone and body language. (You could be meeting more sensitive people as well.) So be more careful about this. After the 19th love is about fun and games – it is another form of entertainment like the movies or theatre. This is not an aspect for marriage, but more about love affairs.

Mercury has his solstice on the 20th and 21st. He pauses in the heavens and then changes direction. So it is in your love life (and career). There is a pause (probably very needed) and then a change of direction.

Your 5th house of fun and creativity becomes very strong after 20th and you'll be enjoying a yearly personal pleasure peak (for some of you, depending on your age, it will be a lifetime personal pleasure peak). It's party time! Life is a party. You do what feels good and what gives you pleasure. Personal creativity is greatly enhanced.

April

Best Days Overall: 1, 9, 10, 18, 19, 27, 28, 29
Most Stressful Days Overall: 2, 3, 4, 16, 17, 22, 23, 24, 30
Best Days for Love: 1, 3, 4, 12, 13, 14, 21, 22, 23, 24, 30
Best Days for Money: 1, 7, 10, 12, 13, 16, 19, 25, 28, 29
Best Days for Career: 1, 2, 3, 4, 12, 13, 21, 30

A solar eclipse on the 20th is the main headline this month. Its effect is relatively mild on you as far as eclipses go, but it won't hurt to reduce your schedule at this time. (If this eclipse hits a sensitive point in your personal Horoscope – the Horoscope that is cast for your exact time and place of birth – it can be strong indeed.)

The eclipse occurs right on the border – the cusp – of your 5th and 6th houses and thus impacts on the affairs of both. Its impact on the 5th house indicates that children and children figures are affected by this eclipse. They experience personal dramas. Some of these dramas can be quite normal – sexual awakening, going off to school, moving away from home, etc. – the normal experiences of growing up. But other personal dramas could also happen, so it is advisable for them to stay out of harm's way and avoid dangerous or stressful activities. A love affair can get tested. Those of you involved in the creative or performing arts are making important changes in your area of creativity. A parent or parent figure is forced to make important financial changes. He or she should be more careful when driving during this period.

The impact of the solar eclipse on the 6th house signals job changes. Such change can be within your present situation or with a new company. Children and children figures in your life can experience financial dramas and need to make important changes here. If you hire others, there can be employee turnover over the coming months. There will be important changes to the health regime as well.

Since this eclipse impacts on your spiritual planet Pluto (a direct hit), spiritual changes are happening as well. You could change teachers, teachings or your spiritual practice. Some of this is quite normal. Certain practices are only valid for a certain time. When this is realized it is natural to change the practice. There are disruptions in a spiritual or charitable organization that you've involved with. Guru figures experience personal dramas as well. There will be changes in your philanthropic giving.

Because the Sun is the ruler of your 9th house, every solar eclipse affects students at college or postgraduate level. There are disruptions at your school and changes in your educational plans. There are disruptions and shake-ups in your place of worship and dramas in the lives of worship leaders. Your religious and theological beliefs will get tested in the coming months as well. Some will have to be modified, some will be discarded. The way you live your life will change. Avoid foreign travel during this eclipse period.

May

Best Days Overall: 7, 8, 15, 16, 25, 26
Most Stressful Days Overall: 1, 13, 14, 20, 21, 27, 28
Best Days for Love: 1, 2, 3, 9, 10, 17, 18, 19, 20, 21, 27, 28
Best Days for Money: 8, 9, 10, 13, 16, 17, 22, 24, 25
Best Days for Career: 1, 9, 10, 17, 18, 19, 27, 28

A lunar eclipse on the 5th once again disrupts your spiritual life, and spiritual and charitable organizations that you're involved with, and brings personal dramas in the lives of guru figures. This eclipse occurs in your spiritual 12th house. The dream life will tend to be hyperactive, and probably not pleasant either. But don't give these dreams any weight at this time – they will be just psychic debris stirred up by the eclipse. Friends have financial dramas and are forced to make important course corrections in finance. The spouse, partner or current love can experience job changes. He or she will change the health regime too in the coming months. Children or children figures in your life can have psychological encounters with death – perhaps near-death experiences. Actual physical death doesn't usually happen. Children should be kept out of harm's way this period, however. Aunts and uncles have their marriages tested.

Since the Moon rules your 8th house of regeneration, every lunar eclipse can bring psychological encounters with death. Sometimes you have a close brush with death, or you have dreams of death. One way or another, the cosmos forces you to confront the issue. This is not punishment, more about education. There is a need to understand this subject on a deeper level. Also, encounters with death tend to make us more serious about life. We focus on what's really important and what we came here to do.

The spouse, partner or current love could be experiencing financial dramas and is forced to make important financial changes.

Uranus is sideswiped by this eclipse. It is impacted but not in a very forceful way. So, cars and communication equipment can behave erratically – perhaps repairs are needed. It would be a good idea to drive more carefully during this eclipse period. Siblings, sibling figures and neighbours have personal dramas. They can be having career changes as well.

On the 17th Jupiter enters your 6th house of health and work and will remain there for the rest of the year ahead. The Sun has been in this house since April 21. The party is over now. You're in the mood to be more serious about life. You're in the mood for work.

June

Best Days Overall: 3, 4, 11, 12, 21, 22
Most Stressful Days Overall: 9, 10, 16, 17, 23, 24, 25
Best Days for Love: 2, 6, 11, 16, 17, 21, 22, 26, 27
Best Days for Money: 1, 5, 6, 9, 14, 15, 18, 23, 24, 28
Best Days for Career: 6, 16, 17, 23, 24, 25, 26, 27

Jupiter's move into your 6th house last month, and the overall power now in that house, bring happy job opportunities to you – dream jobs. If you employ others, you're expanding the workforce. If there have been health problems, you hear good news about them.

Health is stressful this month, though. You not only have Saturn in stressful alignment with you but other, short-term planets as well – the Sun and Mercury. Rest and relax more, when you can. Enhance the health with thigh, ankle and calf massage and by massage of the liver reflex point (shown in the chart in the yearly reports). Until the 5th diet and emotional harmony will be important. After the 5th give more attention to the heart. Massage the reflex to it and the chest. It would be a good idea to schedule more health treatments – massages and the like – until the 21st. Those of you in a good financial position can spend more time in a health spa. There will be improvement in health after the 21st – but with Saturn still in stressful alignment, wariness is a virtue.

The main headline this month is love. Last month, on the 21st, you began a yearly love and social peak. On the 11th Mercury, your love planet, enters your 7th house, where he is very powerful on your behalf. Love is going well. Singles have more social grace, are dating more and seem more serious about love. There seem to be two love interests this month. The New Moon of the 18th occurs in your 7th house of love, increasing your social grace. It brings increased libido and religious and theological insights as well. An opportunity to travel can also come. The New Moon will clarify love issues as the weeks progress. Your questions will be answered, and your doubts resolved.

Home and family still seem more important than career. But the short-term planets are shifting, and career is becoming more important than it has been this year. You can foster the career by social means after the 11th – by attending or hosting the right kinds of parties and gatherings. Another way to read this is that your love life is the real career – the real mission this month.

July

Best Days Overall: 1, 2, 9, 10, 18, 19, 20, 28, 29
Most Stressful Days Overall: 7, 8, 13, 14, 15, 21, 22
Best Days for Love: 2, 8, 10, 13, 14, 15, 18, 19, 20, 29, 30
Best Days for Money: 3, 4, 7, 11, 12, 16, 21, 22, 26, 30, 31
Best Days for Career: 8, 18, 19, 21, 22, 30

Retrograde activity among the planets increases this month; from the 23rd 40 per cent of the planets are retrograde, but we're not at the maximum extent for the year. That will happen in the next two months. But things are beginning to slow down. More patience is needed.

You begin the month with a strong 8th house of regeneration. So, this is a good period to get rid of the extraneous and effete in your life – in your possessions and in your mental and emotional patterns. It is good for projects involving personal transformation, for giving birth to your ideal self. The spouse, partner or current love is prospering. Your personal finances are good, but your financial planet Saturn is retrograde: earnings do come but perhaps more slowly than usual – there are delays and payment glitches. Avoid speculations after the 11th.

Health is good this month, though after the 11th it will need keeping more of an eye on. Mars joins Saturn and Neptune in stressful aspect with you. It is important to listen to the messages of your body. If you're working out and feel a pain or some discomfort, take a break. Avoid pushing the body beyond its limits. This month enhance the health with massage of the heart reflex and chest massage. Your health planet will start to travel backwards on the 23rd (this is one of Venus's rare retrogrades), so you should avoid making major changes to the health regime or taking tests or procedures (if you can) after that date. Reschedule such tests if they are elective. If you must undergo these things and the results don't seem right, get a second opinion.

Your 9th house – your favourite house – becomes very powerful from the 23rd onwards. This is an excellent time for travel, higher education and religious and theological studies. All kinds of insights will come to you.

Love seems happy. Your love planet moves speedily this month, through three signs and houses of your chart. You make good progress in love and have confidence. Until the 11th sexual chemistry with potential partners seems most important. From the 11th to the 29th you're attracted to people who can show you a good time. Philosophical compatibility is important too. After the 29th you find power and prestige alluring.

August

Best Days Overall: 5, 6, 14, 15, 16, 24, 25
Most Stressful Days Overall: 3, 4, 10, 11, 17, 18, 30, 31
Best Days for Love: 5, 6, 7, 8, 10, 11, 14, 15, 17, 18, 24, 25, 26, 27
Best Days for Money: 3, 7, 8, 12, 17, 18, 22, 26, 27, 30
Best Days for Career: 7, 8, 17, 18, 26, 27

Being a fire sign, Sagittarius, you like a fast-paced life. You like to get things done in a hurry. This month, when retrograde activity will hit its maximum extent for the year – 60 per cent of the planets will be retrograde after the 29th – patience is the spiritual lesson. The delays that are happening are not your fault. And rushing and forcing matters won't speed things up. Only time will do that. This is the case next month as well.

Health and energy could be a lot better – especially after the 23rd. So, rest and relax more. The career demands are strong this month and you probably can't avoid them. Try to focus on the really important things in your life and let the lesser things go. Don't sweat the small stuff, as they say.

Finances could also be better. Your financial planet, Saturn, is still retrograde and receives stressful aspects. So, you have to work harder for earnings and delays and glitches are possible.

On the 23rd the Sun enters your 10th house and you begin a yearly career peak. The only problem is that Mercury, your career planet, goes retrograde on the same day. So though there is success happening, there are delays involved. A lot of things are going on behind the scenes. There can be career-related travel happening, and, if so, allow more time to get to and from your destination. There are career opportunities coming to you, but these need more study and research. Avoid making important decisions about the career while Mercury is heading backwards.

Mars will spend most of the month in your 10th house. This signals a lot of activity, but it also shows that children and children figures are successful and that they seem involved in your career. It can also show that children or children figures in your life *are* the actual career – the actual mission – this month.

The New Moon of the 16th occurs in your 11th house, making it a good social day. As always, the New Moon brings religious and theological insights to you. Issues involving friends, technology, science, astronomy and astrology will be clarified as the weeks unfold.

September

Best Days Overall: 2, 3, 11, 12, 21, 22, 29, 30
Most Stressful Days Overall: 6, 7, 13, 14, 15, 27, 28
Best Days for Love: 2, 3, 4, 5, 6, 7, 11, 12, 13, 14, 15, 21, 22, 23, 24, 30
Best Days for Money: 4, 5, 8, 14, 15, 18, 23, 24, 27
Best Days for Career: 4, 5, 13, 14, 15, 23, 24

Retrograde activity is still at its maximum extent for the year until the 16th, with 60 per cent of the planets travelling backwards. And even after the 16th half the planets will still be retrograde – still a very large percentage. So again, patience, patience, patience. You probably won't eliminate delays in your life, but you can minimize them by being as perfect as you can be in all that you do. Handle the details of life perfectly. Use this slowdown to review the different areas of life and see where improvements can be made. Don't take action on these things yet, though, but when the planets start to move forward you can move forward with them.

Health still needs attention until the 23rd. So, as always, be sure to get enough rest. Enhance the health in the ways mentioned in the yearly report and give special attention to the heart. Venus will start to move forward again on the 4th, so it is safer to take tests or undergo procedures. It is also safer to make changes to the health regime from that date. With your health planet remaining in your 9th house for several months (unusually), prayer therapy is very effective.

You're still in a yearly career peak until the 23rd. Mercury, your career planet, will start to move forward on the 15th and will begin to clarify things there. In addition, the New Moon of the 15th occurs in your 10th house, and this will further clarify career issues in the coming weeks. This New Moon is an excellent career day and can also bring career-related travel.

Mercury in his own career house for the second month (he was there all of August) shows success. You're honoured and appreciated. The problem has been a lack of clarity and direction in the career, but this should clear up from the 15th when Mercury starts to move forward. The 3rd to the 8th seems a particularly successful period.

Finances have been challenging lately, but there should be some improvement after the 23rd. Health, too, improves after the 23rd.

October

Best Days Overall: 8, 9, 15, 16, 17, 26, 27
Most Stressful Days Overall: 3, 4, 11, 12, 24, 25
Best Days for Love: 2, 3, 4, 9, 10, 11, 20, 21, 24, 28, 29
Best Days for Money: 1, 2, 6, 11, 12, 15, 20, 21, 24, 28, 29
Best Days for Career: 1, 2, 3, 4, 11, 12, 24

An eventful month ahead. Two eclipses this month ensure that there will be much change and excitement. The good news is that health is much improved this month – though the eclipse on the 28th could test things.

We have a solar eclipse on the 14th and a lunar eclipse on the 28th. These eclipses seem to be mild in their effects on you – as far as eclipses go. Still, it won't hurt to relax your schedule at these times. If either of these eclipses hits a sensitive point in your own Horoscope – the one cast specifically for you, based on the actual date, time and place of your birth – they can be strong indeed.

The solar eclipse of the 14th occurs in your 11th house and affects friendships. They get tested. Sometimes it's the fault of the relationship, but not always. Friends can be experiencing personal, life-changing dramas that impact on your relationship. There are disruptions and shake-ups in trade or professional organizations that you're involved with. A parent or parent figure has financial dramas and is forced to make a course correction in finance. Computers and high-tech equipment can behave erratically. Important files should be backed up and your anti-virus, anti-hacking software should be kept up to date. You're a traveller by nature, but it's not a good idea to be travelling this period. Every solar eclipse tends to affect your place of worship and the lives of worship leaders. They have personal dramas. College-level students can experience disruptions at school or change their educational plans. Sometimes they change colleges.

The lunar eclipse of the 28th occurs in your 6th house and can bring job changes, disruptions in your place of work and changes in the health regime. Sometimes such eclipses bring health scares, but your health looks good this period and any such drama will probably be no more than a scare. If you employ others there can be employee turnover in the coming months. This eclipse can also bring psychological encounters with death. Some people hear of deaths or have dreams about it. The thousand-eyed angel knows how to alert you to his presence. It tends to make a person more serious about life. Less frivolous.

November

Best Days Overall: 4, 5, 6, 14, 15, 23, 24
Most Stressful Days Overall: 1, 7, 8, 21, 22, 27, 28
Best Days for Love: 1, 2, 3, 8, 9, 18, 19, 23, 24, 27, 28
Best Days for Money: 2, 7, 12, 16, 17, 25, 29
Best Days for Career: 2, 3, 7, 8, 23, 24

With the excitement of the eclipses last month winding down a bit, the month ahead seems happy. You begin November in a strong spiritual period, which is good for your spiritual practice and for involving yourself in charitable and idealistic kinds of activities. Much progress will be made. The New Moon of the 12th occurs in your 12th house of spirituality as well. This is an especially good day for your spiritual practice. It not only brings spiritual insights but religious and theological ones as well. Spiritual issues will clarify themselves long after the New Moon actually happens – it will go on for the next few weeks, until the next New Moon. Questions and doubts will be dealt with normally and naturally.

On the 22nd the Sun enters your own sign and you begin a yearly personal pleasure peak – very good for enjoying all the pleasures of the body. Weight will need watching this period, though. Women of child-bearing age are more fertile than usual. Health will be good. With Mars also in your sign from the 24th you have plenty of energy, although you shouldn't overdo things as Saturn is still stressing you out. Mars will also bring more fun into your life and children and children figures seem devoted to you.

Retrograde activity among the planets is winding down this month, and by the end of November retrograde activity will be just half of its peak in August and September, with only 30 per cent travelling back-wards. Life is moving more quickly, and blocked projects are starting to move forward.

With the Sun in your own sign foreign travel is likely. It can even happen before then – until the 22nd there are travel opportunities that are religious or spiritually oriented. Perhaps your place of worship organizes a trip. Perhaps you go on a pilgrimage to visit a holy site. This kind of travel appeals to you now.

Love seems happy as well. Until the 10th romantic opportunities happen in spiritual-type venues. After the 10th, as Mercury moves into your sign, there's nothing special you need to do to find love – love will find you. Just go about your daily business. Career opportunities are also finding you after the 10th.

December

Best Days Overall: 2, 3, 11, 12, 20, 21, 29, 30
Most Stressful Days Overall: 4, 5, 6, 18, 19, 24, 25, 31
Best Days for Love: 4, 9, 14, 18, 19, 22, 24, 25, 28, 30
Best Days for Money: 4, 9, 14, 15, 18, 22, 26, 27, 31
Best Days for Career: 4, 5, 6, 14, 22, 30, 31

Finances have improved ever since Saturn, your money planet, started to move forward on November 4. But right now, you have to work harder for earnings than usual. This will improve after the 22nd and the month ahead looks both happy and prosperous.

You're still in the midst of a yearly personal pleasure peak until the 22nd. Though Saturn is still in adverse aspect with you, health remains good this month – the short-term planets are supporting you. Also, you seem focused on health (and have been ever since May 17). So, you're on the case. Foreign travel is still likely this month. College-level students hear good news, and your personal appearance shines – though you still need to watch the weight. The New Moon of the 12th occurs in your own sign. A New Moon in a person's own sign is one of the highlights of any month. It gives energy, enhances libido and over-all personal appearance, and gives self-confidence and self-esteem. So personal pleasure is increased. Further, any issues involving personal appearance and the overall image will clarify as the weeks progress – until the next New Moon.

Love is more complicated this month. Mercury goes retrograde again on the 13th and stays that way for the rest of the month. So your normally good social graces could be better. On the 24th your love planet moves back into your sign. This is normally a good love aspect but the retrograde complicates things. Love pursues you, but there is much hesitancy and doubt about it. Mercury will also be 'out of bounds' until the 14th. And so, in both love and career you're outside your normal boundaries – in uncharted territory. This could explain the hesitancy in love. Clarity in love should happen next month as both Mercury and Jupiter, the ruler of your Horoscope, will be moving forward. (Jupiter starts to move forward on the 31st.)

On the 22nd the Sun moves into your 2nd money house and you begin a yearly financial peak. Prosperity is happening. The Sun, as ruler of your 9th house, is very beneficent in your chart, and so there is good fortune in finance. The 2nd house also rules possessions, not just money – so holiday gifts should be ample.

Capricorn

♑

THE GOAT

Birthdays from
21st December to
19th January

Personality Profile

CAPRICORN AT A GLANCE

Element – Earth

Ruling Planet – Saturn
   Career Planet – Venus
   Love Planet – Moon
   Money Planet – Uranus
   Planet of Communications – Neptune
   Planet of Health and Work – Mercury
   Planet of Home and Family Life – Mars
   Planet of Spirituality – Jupiter

Colours – black, indigo

Colours that promote love, romance and social harmony – puce, silver

Colour that promotes earning power – ultramarine blue

Gem – black onyx

Metal – lead

Scents – magnolia, pine, sweet pea, wintergreen

Quality – cardinal (= activity)

Qualities most needed for balance – warmth, spontaneity, a sense of fun

Strongest virtues – sense of duty, organization, perseverance, patience, ability to take the long-term view

Deepest needs – to manage, take charge and administrate

Characteristics to avoid – pessimism, depression, undue materialism and undue conservatism

Signs of greatest overall compatibility – Taurus, Virgo

Signs of greatest overall incompatibility – Aries, Cancer, Libra

Sign most helpful to career – Libra

Sign most helpful for emotional support – Aries

Sign most helpful financially – Aquarius

Sign best for marriage and/or partnerships – Cancer

Sign most helpful for creative projects – Taurus

Best Sign to have fun with – Taurus

Signs most helpful in spiritual matters – Virgo, Sagittarius

Best day of the week – Saturday

Understanding a Capricorn

The virtues of Capricorns are such that there will always be people for and against them. Many admire them, many dislike them. Why? It seems to be because of Capricorn's power urges. A well-developed Capricorn has his or her eyes set on the heights of power, prestige and authority. In the sign of Capricorn, ambition is not a fatal flaw, but rather the highest virtue.

Capricorns are not frightened by the resentment their authority may sometimes breed. In Capricorn's cool, calculated, organized mind all the dangers are already factored into the equation – the unpopularity, the animosity, the misunderstandings, even the outright slander – and a plan is always in place for dealing with these things in the most efficient way. To the Capricorn, situations that would terrify an ordinary mind are merely problems to be managed, bumps on the road to ever-growing power, effectiveness and prestige.

Some people attribute pessimism to the Capricorn sign, but this is a bit deceptive. It is true that Capricorns like to take into account the negative side of things. It is also true that they love to imagine the worst possible scenario in every undertaking. Other people might find such analyses depressing, but Capricorns only do these things so that they can formulate a way out – an escape route.

Capricorns will argue with success. They will show you that you are not doing as well as you think you are. Capricorns do this to themselves as well as to others. They do not mean to discourage you but rather to root out any impediments to your greater success. A Capricorn boss or supervisor feels that no matter how good the performance there is always room for improvement. This explains why Capricorn supervisors are difficult to handle and even infuriating at times. Their actions are, however, quite often effective – they can get their subordinates to improve and become better at their jobs.

Capricorn is a born manager and administrator. Leo is better at being king or queen, but Capricorn is better at being prime minister – the person actually wielding power.

Capricorn is interested in the virtues that last, in the things that will stand the test of time and trials of circumstance. Temporary fads and fashions mean little to a Capricorn – except as things to be used for profit or power. Capricorns apply this attitude to business, love, to their thinking and even to their philosophy and religion.

Finance

Capricorns generally attain wealth and they usually earn it. They are willing to work long and hard for what they want. They are quite amenable to forgoing a short-term gain in favour of long-term benefits. Financially, they come into their own later in life.

However, if Capricorns are to attain their financial goals they must shed some of their strong conservatism. Perhaps this is the least desirable trait of the Capricorn. They can resist anything new merely because it is new and untried. They are afraid of experimentation. Capricorns need to be willing to take a few risks. They should be more eager to market new products or explore different managerial techniques. Otherwise, progress will leave them behind. If necessary, Capricorns must be ready to change with the times, to discard old methods that no longer work.

Very often this experimentation will mean that Capricorns have to break with existing authority. They might even consider changing their present position or starting their own ventures. If so, they should be willing to accept all the risks and just get on with it. Only then will a Capricorn be on the road to highest financial gains.

Career and Public Image

A Capricorn's ambition and quest for power are evident. It is perhaps the most ambitious sign of the zodiac – and usually the most successful in a worldly sense. However, there are lessons Capricorns need to learn in order to fulfil their highest aspirations.

Intelligence, hard work, cool efficiency and organization will take them a certain distance, but will not carry them to the very top. Capricorns need to cultivate their social graces, to develop a social style, along with charm and an ability to get along with people. They need to bring beauty into their lives and to cultivate the right social contacts. They must learn to wield power gracefully, so that people love them for it – a very delicate art. They also need to learn how to bring people together in order to fulfil certain objectives. In short, Capricorns require some of the gifts – the social graces – of Libra to get to the top.

Once they have learned this, Capricorns will be successful in their careers. They are ambitious hard workers who are not afraid of putting in the required time and effort. Capricorns take their time in getting the job done – in order to do it well – and they like moving up the corporate ladder slowly but surely. Being so driven by success, Capricorns are generally liked by their bosses, who respect and trust them.

Love and Relationships

Like Scorpio and Pisces, Capricorn is a difficult sign to get to know. They are deep, introverted and like to keep their own counsel. Capricorns do not like to reveal their innermost thoughts. If you are in love with a Capricorn, be patient and take your time. Little by little you will get to understand him or her.

Capricorns have a deep romantic nature, but they do not show it straight away. They are cool, matter of fact and not especially emotional. They will often show their love in practical ways.

It takes time for a Capricorn – male or female – to fall in love. They are not the love-at-first-sight kind. If a Capricorn is involved with a Leo or Aries, these Fire types will be totally mystified – to them the Capricorn will seem cold, unfeeling, unaffectionate and not very spontaneous. Of course none of this is true; it is just that Capricorn likes to take things slowly. They like to be sure of their ground before making any demonstrations of love or commitment.

Even in love affairs Capricorns are deliberate. They need more time to make decisions than is true of the other signs of the zodiac, but given this time they become just as passionate. Capricorns like a relationship to be structured, committed, well regulated, well defined, predictable and even routine. They prefer partners who are nurturers, and they in turn like to nurture their partners. This is their basic psychology. Whether such a relationship is good for them is another issue altogether. Capricorns have enough routine in their lives as it is. They might be better off in relationships that are a bit more stimulating, changeable and fluctuating.

Home and Domestic Life

The home of a Capricorn – as with a Virgo – is going to be tidy and well organized. Capricorns tend to manage their families in the same way they manage their businesses. Capricorns are often so career-driven that they find little time for the home and family. They should try to get more actively involved in their family and domestic life. Capricorns do, however, take their children very seriously and are very proud parents – particularly should their children grow up to become respected members of society.

Horoscope for 2023

Major Trends

This year a series of very important and long-term changes are happening in your life. No doubt you're feeling the stirrings even now. Pluto has been in your sign for more than twenty years. Thus, your whole image, personality, mode of dress and self-concept have been changed. They are completely different than they were twenty years ago. You've been giving birth to your ideal image and personality. It's been rough going – Pluto can be very intense and extreme. But the work is almost finished. Pluto will still be mostly in your sign this year, but he makes a brief foray into Aquarius, from March 24 to June 12. This is a harbinger of things to come. Pluto will hover in and out of your sign next year, too, before he moves into Aquarius in 2025 for the long haul (at least another twenty years). In recent years there have been surgeries (perhaps cosmetic-type surgeries as well) and near-death sorts of experiences. There was much sex appeal to the image as well. Soon, however (and you're in the beginning stages now), Pluto is going to transform your financial life – make it ideal. Thus, there will be all kinds of crises happening there. These should be regarded not as punishments but as educational. More on this later.

The other major change – and an important one for you – is Saturn's move out of Aquarius and into Pisces on March 8 – from your money house into your 3rd house of intellectual interests. This is a good transit for students – especially those below college level. They will focus on their studies – pay attention – and this spells success. The intellectual and communication faculties will also be sharper than usual.

Jupiter will be in your 4th house until May 17. This can bring a move and enhanced fertility for women of childbearing age. More on this later.

Life becomes more fun after May 17, as Jupiter moves through your 5th house of fun and creativity. Uranus has been in this house for many years now (and remains here this year). Children have been difficult to handle as they seem more rebellious. This year things seem easier, however.

Your major interests this year will be the body, image and personal appearance (until March 24 and from June 12 to the end of the year); finance (until March 8 and from March 24 to June 12); intellectual interests and communication; home, family and emotional wellness (from January 1 to May 17); and children, fun and creativity.

Your paths of greatest fulfilment this year are home and family (until May 17 and from July 18 to the end of the year); and children, fun and creativity.

Health

(Please note that this is an astrological perspective on health and not a medical one. In days of yore there was no difference, both these perspectives were identical. But these days there could be quite a difference. For a medical perspective, please consult your doctor or health practitioner.)

Health is basically good this year, Capricorn. Pluto in your sign for most of the year shouldn't be much of a problem, as you've been dealing with this for over twenty years and by now know how to handle it. Aside from Pluto, Jupiter will make a stressful aspect from January 1 to May 17. After May 17 the only stressful planet will be Pluto, however.

Your 6th house of health is basically empty as well, with only short-term planets moving through there and their effects are short term. I read this as a positive for health. You don't pay undue attention here as there's nothing wrong.

Of course, there will be periods where your health and energy are less easy than usual – perhaps even stressful. These come for the transits of the short-term, fast-moving planets and are temporary and not trends for the year. When they pass your normally good health and energy return.

Good though your health is, you can make it better. Give more attention to the following – the vulnerable areas of your Horoscope this year (the reflex points are shown in the chart below):

- The spine, knees, teeth, bones and overall skeletal alignment. These are always important for Capricorn; regular back and knee massage should be part of your normal health regime. Regular visits to a chiropractor or osteopath are also good – the vertebrae need to be kept in alignment. Exercises such as Yoga (especially the postures that deal with the spine) and Pilates are good. Therapies such as Rolfing, Alexander Technique and Feldenkrais are also beneficial. The Alexander Technique is especially recommended, and it is as much educational as therapeutic. One is trained in proper posture, the proper way to sit and get up from a

Important foot reflexology points for the year ahead

Try to massage all of the foot on a regular basis – the top of the foot as well as the bottom – but pay extra attention to the points highlighted on the chart. When you massage, be aware of 'sore spots' as these need special attention. It's also a good idea to massage the ankles and below them.

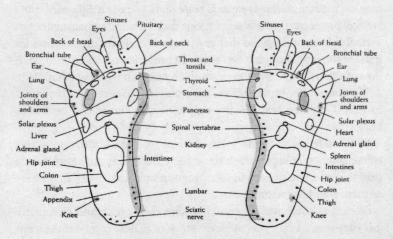

chair – to do these simple things in ways that don't throw the spine out of alignment. Good dental hygiene is also important for you, and make sure you get enough calcium for the bones.

- The lungs, arms, shoulders and respiratory system. These areas are also always important for Capricorn, as Mercury, the planet that rules these areas, is your health planet. Regular massage of the arms and shoulders would be wonderful. Tension tends to collect in the shoulders and needs to be released.

Mercury, your health planet, is a very fast-moving planet. He moves through your entire Horoscope during the year and so there are many short-term health trends that depend on where Mercury is and the kinds of aspects he receives. These are best dealt with in the monthly reports.

Home and Family

Your 4th house is strong this year and it seems a happy area of life. Benevolent Jupiter is moving through there from January 1 to May 17. This brings moves, the purchase of additional homes or access to additional homes. Sometimes people don't literally move, but they renovate or expand the existing home in a way that is more comfortable. The effect is 'as if' they have moved. This transit often shows the fortunate purchase or sale of a home.

The family circle expands in the year ahead as well. Usually this happens through births or marriages, but not necessarily. Sometimes you meet people who are 'like' family to you – who fulfil that function. As we mentioned earlier, women of childbearing age are unusually fertile all year.

This is a year for emotional healing. Knotty emotional problems get sorted out. There is a feeling of optimism and well-being on the emotional level. Those of you in formal types of therapy will make much progress and receive much insight in the year ahead. Generally, people are afflicted by their past, but this year your past seems kind to you. Perhaps you remember the good times. Sure, there has been pain in the past, but there were good times too. It is good to remember this.

A parent or parent figure is prospering this year, living the high life – the good life. Weight needs keeping an eye on. If this parent figure is a woman of childbearing age, she is more fertile. Children and children figures in your life are also prospering and seem to be enjoying their freedom. There could have been multiple moves in recent years as they seem restless. There might not be a formal move this year, but they could live in different places for long periods of time. Grandchildren (or those who play that role in your life) are having a quiet, stable family year. Probably they feel like moving, but next year seems more likely for this.

If you're planning renovations or major repairs to the home, July 11 to August 28 and November 24 to December 31 would be good times. If you're redecorating or buying objects of beauty for the home, February 20 to March 16 seems good for this.

Finance and Career

A lot of financial changes are going on this year but, in the end, we see prosperity. Next year looks even more prosperous than this one. Your money house, which has been prominent for the past two years, becomes a little less prominent this year. Saturn moves out of the 2nd house on March 8. Pluto moves in briefly from March 24 to June 12, but after June 12 the money house will be empty. Nevertheless, Jupiter will be travelling with your financial planet Uranus from May 17, so there is prosperity even though there is less attention on financial matters.

The planetary behaviour suggests a lot of shifting around of assets – a lot of shifting around of plans and strategies.

Saturn's move out of your money house suggests that your short-term financial goals have been achieved and you're now ready to focus on learning, on building up your intellectual capital. This is the fruit of financial success. Money buys freedom to grow and study.

While your ruling planet has been in your money house (and he's still there until March 8) you have been cultivating the image of wealth and prosperity. You've been dressing the part and spending on yourself. People have seen you as a 'money person'. But now you're cultivating a different image – an image of an intellectual, of a student or teacher. Looking smart seems more important than looking wealthy.

Your financial planet Uranus has been in your 5th house for many years and will remain there for a few more years to come. Thus, you've been more speculative than usual – and this trend is even more pronounced in the year ahead, especially after May 17. Uranus as the financial planet favours the high-tech and online world. You have a good intuition for these sectors. The electronic media is very good for you too.

Uranus in Taurus favours agriculture (companies and commodities), rural real estate, copper and copper-mining companies and refiners.

The financial planet in the 5th house produces many signals. You spend more on children or the children figures in your life, but you can also earn from them. If they are of an appropriate age, they can help in a material way. If they are young, they can inspire you to earn more. Young children can often have profitable ideas. This aspect also favours companies and industries that cater to the youth market – music, entertainment, streaming videos, toymakers. The 5th house also rules casinos.

Perhaps the most important aspect of the financial planet in the 5th house is that you enjoy the wealth that you have. It is an aspect for happy wealth. Money is earned easily and in happy ways and spent on happy things. (This is as it should be.) It indicates a kind of happy-go-lucky attitude to wealth. You will see this all year but especially after May 17.

With regards to career, Capricorns are always ambitious, but this year less so than usual. The action is more in your 4th house of home and family, which is strong, and not in your 10th house of career which is basically empty. I would describe this as a year for building the foundations – the infrastructure – for future career success. A period of preparation for the future rather than overt career success. Career tends to the status quo this year.

There will be a solar eclipse on October 14 that occurs in your career house. This will shake things up a bit. Perhaps you change your career, or pursue it in a different way.

Your career planet is Venus, a fast-moving planet. She will move through your entire Horoscope in any given year, and so there are many short-term trends in the career that depend on where Venus is and the kinds of aspects she receives. These are best dealt with in the monthly reports.

Fast moving though Venus is, she spends over four months in Leo, your 8th house of regeneration. This can show personal dramas – perhaps surgery or near-death experiences in the lives of parents, parent figures, bosses and people involved in your career. It indicates a kind of purging happening in your company or industry.

Love and Social Life

Your 7th house of love is not prominent this year – it is not a house of power. Only short-term planets move through there and their effects are short term. Thus, love tends to the status quo this year. Those who are married will tend to stay married, and singles will tend to stay single. You seem basically satisfied with things the way they are and have no need to make dramatic changes.

Your love planet is the Moon, the fastest moving of all the planets. Where the other fast-moving planets take a year to move through your Horoscope, the Moon does this every month. So, there are many short-term love trends that depend on where the Moon is and the kinds of aspects she receives. These will be discussed in the monthly reports.

In general, however, we can say that the New and Full Moons tend to be excellent love and social days. Also, you will have more energy and enthusiasm for romance (and social activities) when the Moon is waxing and growing in size. When the Moon is waning there is less enthusiasm.

Though marriage for singles isn't likely this year there will be many opportunities for love affairs – especially from May 17 onwards.

The social life is happy, but not very serious, and friends are devoted to you. Opportunities for friendship seek you out without you having to do much. This has been the case for many years now. However, this is soon to change. Pluto, your planet of friends, will this year start to make a two-year-long transition from your own sign into Aquarius. So, your taste in friends is undergoing change, and this will be a long-term trend for many, many years. This year Pluto will be in your money house briefly, from March 24 to June 12, and friendship opportunities will come as you pursue your financial goals. You will be attracted to rich friends during this period, and friends will be helpful in your financial life.

Self-improvement

Spiritual Neptune has been in your 3rd house of intellectual interests for many years and is there this year too. So, your intellectual tastes are being elevated and refined. You've been gravitating to spiritual types of literature. This continues in the year ahead and gets even stronger with Saturn's move into this house on March 8.

With Neptune (and Saturn) in your 3rd house you express yourself more poetically – in a more inspired way. This is a wonderful transit for creative writers.

Jupiter is your spiritual planet. Generally, this favours the mystical side of your native religion. There's no need to travel far and wide for spiritual truth; it's all there close to home. You don't need to discard your native religion, just go deeper into it.

Jupiter will move through two houses this year. Until May 17 he will be in your 4th house of home, family and the emotional life. This produces a few interpretations. It signals the importance of your emotional state in spiritual matters. There is a need to be in the right emotional state if you want to see progress. It would favour the Bhakti path – the path of exalting the emotions to a high, high pitch. So, you could be attracted to drumming, singing, dancing, the chanting of mantras – things that elevate the emotions. And your spiritual under-standing will help you emotionally and in dealing with your family. (The family as a whole seems more spiritual this year.)

While Jupiter is in your 4th house, you will also favour Karma Yoga – the path of action. You will have a need to express your spiritual ideals in action. Abstractions are not enough for you. This can make you an activist in altruistic causes. In some cases, it can lead to militancy.

After May 17 Jupiter moves into your 5th house. This transit still favours mantra chanting, drumming and dancing, but it also favours the path of creativity. This is a valid spiritual path. By creating – whether it be pottery, or painting, or music – you learn the laws of the

Great Creator, for the same laws apply, though on a much smaller scale. Jupiter in your 5th house also favours the path of joy and bliss. Joy, say the sages, is a special wisdom. You're very close to the Divine when you're happy.

Month-by-month Forecasts

January

Best Days Overall: 1, 2, 10, 11, 18, 19, 28, 29
Most Stressful Days Overall: 3, 4, 16, 17, 23, 24, 30, 31
Best Days for Love: 2, 3, 10, 11, 12, 13, 20, 21, 22, 23, 24, 30, 31
Best Days for Money: 1, 2, 8, 10, 11, 12, 13, 16, 18, 19, 23, 28, 29
Best Days for Career: 2, 3, 4, 12, 13, 21, 22, 30, 31

A happy and prosperous month ahead, Capricorn. Enjoy.

You start the year in the midst of a yearly personal pleasure peak (one of them) as your 1st house of self is the strongest in the Horoscope. Health is good. You look good. There is more sex appeal to the image. This is a good period for weight-loss and detox regimes. The New Moon of the 11th occurs in your own house, adding to all of this. It also brings happy romantic and social experiences. The current love is very much on your side and is devoted to you. Any issues involving the image and personal appearance will be clarified in the coming weeks. Questions will be answered, and doubts settled.

The month ahead is a very 'me'-oriented period. There's nothing wrong with this. It's just the cycle you're in. It's about having things your way and designing your life the way you want it. You're in a period of maximum personal independence. Personal initiative matters. If there are changes that need to be made for your future happiness, now is the time to make them. Later on, as the planets move to the West and the social sector of your chart, it will be more difficult.

This is not an especially strong career month. Your 10th house is empty: only the Moon moves through there on the 3rd, 4th, 30th and 31st. Your 4th house of home and family, in contrast, is very strong and 90 per cent (and sometimes all) the planets are on the night side of your chart. Home and family issues – and especially your emotional wellness – are far more important than the career now. Having said this, there are interesting things happening in the career. Happy opportunities can come until the 3rd. From the 3rd to the 27th pay rises – official or unofficial – can happen. On the 22nd and 23rd your career planet Venus travels with Saturn, the ruler of your Horoscope, and this brings career success and opportunity.

On the 20th the Sun moves into your money house and you begin a yearly financial peak. A prosperous period. This is a good period to pay off debt or to take out loans – depending on your need. It is good for tax and insurance planning, and for dealing with estates as well. Good for detoxing the financial life and getting rid of possessions that you don't need or use.

February

Best Days Overall: 7, 8, 16, 17, 24, 25
Most Stressful Days Overall: 2, 3, 9, 10, 22, 23
Best Days for Love: 1, 2, 3, 9, 10, 12, 13, 20, 22
Best Days for Money: 4, 5, 7, 8, 14, 15, 16, 17, 18, 19, 22, 23, 24, 25
Best Days for Career: 2, 3, 9, 10, 12, 13, 22

Health is excellent this month and prosperity is still happening. You're in the midst of a yearly financial peak until the 18th and the trends we wrote of last month are still in effect until then. Mercury moves into your money house on the 11th and further boosts finances. Money comes from work and perhaps from foreign investments or foreigners. Another way to read this is that your work creates good fortune. (Mercury is a fortunate planet in your Horoscope.)

Love seems quiet. Your 7th house is basically empty (only the Moon moves through there on the 2nd and 3rd) while your 1st house of self is strong. You seem generally satisfied in the love department and have no need to make dramatic changes or to pay undue attention to it. Love and social matters will go better from the 20th to the 28th as your love planet waxes. You have more enthusiasm and confidence in this department. In addition, the New Moon of the 20th occurs right on Saturn, the ruler of your Horoscope – this brings both romance and erotic love.

Mars has been in your 6th house of health since the beginning of the year. This would indicate that health can be enhanced with scalp and face massage and by vigorous exercise.

Your 3rd house of intellectual interests and communication was strong last month and becomes even stronger after the 20th. It is an excellent period in which to read, study, teach and write and to attend seminars and lectures. The intellectual faculties are much enhanced now and you may as well take advantage of this. Students will do well in school.

Jupiter has been in your 4th house of home and family since the beginning of the year. Moves could happen. There could be a fortunate purchase or sale of a home. Women of childbearing age are unusually fertile. The family circle expands. On the 21st, your career planet Venus enters your 4th house and home and family become the mission – the real career. This month is also good for entertaining from home, socializing with family members and for beautifying the home.

March

Best Days Overall: 6, 7, 15, 16, 24, 25
Most Stressful Days Overall: 1, 2, 8, 9, 10, 21, 22, 28, 29, 30
Best Days for Love: 1, 2, 4, 5, 11, 12, 20, 21, 24, 25, 28, 29, 30, 31
Best Days for Money: 4, 5, 6, 7, 13, 14, 15, 16, 17, 18, 21, 22, 24, 25, 31
Best Days for Career: 4, 5, 8, 9, 10, 11, 12, 24, 25

An eventful month, Capricorn. *All* the planets are moving forward this month and if you're starting a new project or launching a new venture, this is a great month to do it. Especially from the 21st onwards. You have many cosmic trends helping you. Both the cosmic and your personal solar cycles are waxing. The Sun will be in Aries then, which is the best starting energy of the year. And the Moon will also be waxing. You will have a lot of 'oomph' behind you.

Health is good, but after the 20th it will need a bit more attention. There is nothing serious amiss, just short-term stress caused by the short-term planets. But make sure to get enough rest and enhance the health in the ways mentioned in the yearly report. Vigorous exercise and scalp and face massage will be beneficial until the 26th.

Saturn, the ruler of your Horoscope and a very important planet in your chart, makes a major move out of your 2nd house and into your 3rd on the 8th. He will remain there for the next two and a half years. Finance is less of a priority now, therefore. Probably your financial goals have been achieved and you're more interested now in the life of the mind – the pleasures of the mind. This transit of Saturn especially benefits students (especially below the college level). They will be focused on their studies and probably enjoying them too. This spells success. It is also a good signal for sales and marketing people, teachers, writers and traders. You will be changing the personal appearance in the coming months and years. There will be more glamour to the image. You will project a more spiritual type of image – softer, more accessible, less stern and aloof.

Home and family are the main headlines this month. Jupiter and Venus are already in your 4th house at the start of the month. Mercury enters on the 19th and the Sun on the 20th. So this is where the action is this month, especially after the 20th. Career issues can be de-emphasized – the focus is on the home and family. Yet, in spite of this lack of attention, there is career success on the 1st and 2nd as Venus travels with Jupiter. Friends seem helpful in the career.

This is a great period (all month – but especially after the 20th) for emotional healing, for healing of old traumas. Many psychological insights will be revealed to you this month. Observe without judgement the many memories that surface spontaneously.

April

Best Days Overall: 2, 3, 4, 12, 13, 20, 21, 30
Most Stressful Days Overall: 5, 6, 18, 19, 25, 26
Best Days for Love: 1, 3, 4, 10, 14, 22, 23, 25, 26, 30
Best Days for Money: 1, 3, 4, 10, 12, 13, 14, 15, 19, 21, 28, 29, 30
Best Days for Career: 3, 4, 5, 6, 14, 22, 23

You're still in an excellent time for starting new projects or launching new ventures. All the planets are moving forward, the Sun will still be in Aries and, until the 6th, the Moon will be waxing.

The main headline this month is the solar eclipse of the 20th. It affects all of you strongly, but especially those with birthdays from January 18-20. This eclipse occurs on the exact cusp of your 4th and 5th houses, and so it has an influence on both these houses. The impact in the 4th house is likely to be something positive – a move, the birth of a child, some renovation of the home. Keep in mind that good things can be just as disruptive as bad things. Whatever the event is it shakes up the status quo. It breaks up your routine and comfort zone. There can be personal dramas in the lives of parents and parent figures. A family member can have a near-death kind of experience.

The impact on your 5th house affects children and children figures in your life. They too have personal dramas. If you're into the creative arts, there are dramatic changes in your creativity and creative life in general. A parent or parent figure needs a financial course correction.

Pluto, the planet of death, and the Sun, the ruler of your 8th house of regeneration, are both impacted directly by this eclipse. As a result, there are psychological encounters with death. Perhaps near-death experiences – close calls. The thousand-eyed one lets you know that he's around. The eclipse brings financial changes for the spouse, partner and current love. Children and children figures should be more careful driving.

Friends also experience personal dramas, and these can cause some disruptions or testing of your friendship. Computer equipment and high-tech gadgetry can behave erratically (and often repairs or replacement are necessary). Do your best to maintain online safety. Beware of suspicious emails and links. Beware of people who use names or accounts of friends to do mischief.

May

Best Days Overall: 1, 9, 10, 17, 18, 19, 27, 28
Most Stressful Days Overall: 2, 3, 15, 16, 22, 23, 30, 31
Best Days for Love: 1, 2, 3, 9, 10, 17, 18, 19, 22, 23, 30, 31
Best Days for Money: 1, 8, 9, 10, 11, 12, 16, 17, 18, 19, 24, 25, 27, 28
Best Days for Career: 2, 3, 9, 10, 17, 18, 19, 30, 31

In spite of the lunar eclipse that occurs on the 5th, the month ahead is basically happy and healthy. The eclipse just adds some spice and excitement to things. As far as eclipses go, this one only has a mild effect on you. However, if it hits some sensitive point in your Natal Horoscope – the one cast for your exact date, time and place of birth – it can be powerful. So, it won't hurt to take a more relaxed schedule anyway.

This eclipse occurs in your 11th house of friends. There are personal dramas in their lives as a result, and they should take it nice and easy this period too. A parent or parent figure has to make financial course corrections. And since this eclipse sideswipes Uranus, the impact on friends is even stronger. Computers and high-tech equipment can behave erratically, and repairs or replacement can be necessary. Make sure important files are backed up and that you're more careful about suspicious emails or links. Even if you know the person who sent the email, it might not actually be from them but from a hacker. There are disruptions and shake-ups in trade or professional organizations that you're involved with too.

Since Uranus is your financial planet, you are also forced to make financial changes. These don't seem too serious though, as Uranus is only grazed by the eclipse – it's not a direct hit.

As the Moon is your planet of love and relationships, every lunar eclipse shakes up your love life and tests romantic relationships. This one is no different. You go through this twice a year and by now you know how to handle it. Good relationships go through these periods and will get even better. Flawed ones can be in trouble. The eclipse will bring up the repressed grievances in the relationship – the dirty laundry – so that you can deal with them. Often, we're oblivious to the existence of such problems. Now you find out. There can also be personal dramas in the life of the current love, and these too would test the relationship.

This eclipse happens in the midst of a yearly personal pleasure peak. This pleasure peak will be much stronger than usual, as Jupiter moves into your 5th house on the 17th. One can have fun and not be irresponsible.

June

Best Days Overall: 5, 6, 14, 15, 23, 24, 25
Most Stressful Days Overall: 11, 12, 18, 19, 20, 26, 27
Best Days for Love: 2, 7, 8, 11, 17, 18, 19, 20, 21, 22, 28
Best Days for Money: 5, 6, 7, 8, 14, 15, 23, 24, 25
Best Days for Career: 2, 11, 21, 22, 26, 27

Happiness cures many health issues – especially until the 11th. Spiritually speaking, health and harmony are synonymous. Health is not about your blood chemistry or blood pressure – it's about your state of harmony. So, enjoy life and stay in harmony. This is especially important after the 21st when health becomes more stressed. There's nothing serious afoot, however, just short-term stress caused by short-term planets.

Your 6th house of health and work is powerful until the 21st, so your focus on health will stand you in good stead for afterwards. The power in the 6th house also signals job opportunities for job-seekers. Those already employed have opportunities for overtime and second jobs. You're in the mood for work. The New Moon of the 18th occurs in your 6th house, adding to this focus. This should be an erotic and romantic day too. Health and job issues will be clarified in the coming weeks – until the next New Moon. Your questions will be answered, normally and naturally.

Mercury, your planet of health and work, goes 'out of bounds' on the 25th and remains so until July 6. So, in health matters (and perhaps at the job) you're outside your normal sphere – your normal orbit. You're searching for solutions outside your orbit.

On the 21st the Sun moves into your 7th house of love and you begin a yearly love and social peak. Singles are allured by sexual magnetism. Co-workers, health professionals and foreigners are also alluring. There are two love interests this month for singles.

Finances should be good. Jupiter is travelling near Uranus, your financial planet – a classic signal of prosperity. They are still far apart at the moment but are getting closer to each other day by day. You're feeling the influence of financial expansion. (This aspect will become very exact next year.)

You and family members should be more mindful on the physical plane from the 24th to the 28th.

July

    Best Days Overall: 3, 4, 11, 12, 21, 22, 30, 31
    Most Stressful Days Overall: 9, 10, 16, 17, 23, 24
    Best Days for Love: 2, 7, 8, 10, 16, 17, 19, 20, 26, 29
    Best Days for Money: 3, 4, 5, 6, 11, 12, 21, 22, 30, 31
    Best Days for Career: 2, 10, 19, 20, 23, 24, 29

Mercury, your health planet, is still 'out of bounds' this month, until the 6th. So review our discussion of this last month.

Health still needs attention, but you'll see improvement after the 23rd. In the meantime, make sure to get enough rest.

A Grand Trine in the Earth signs from the 11th onwards sharpens your already strong managerial and organizational skills. It also improves the finances – though you have to work harder for them this month. There's more challenge, but despite this there is prosperity.

Career is gradually becoming more important. Last month the planetary power shifted from the night side of your Horoscope to the day side. So, dawn is breaking in your year. It is time to be up and about and focused on the activities of the day – outer activities. This month you seem to be preparing for a career push. Your career planet, Venus, goes retrograde on the 23rd. So, it would be beneficial to gain more clarity in career matters. Get more facts. Things aren't as they seem.

You're still in the midst of a yearly love and social peak until the 23rd and the focus remains on the social life. Romance is on your mind. Like last month, sexual magnetism is the main attraction for singles. And even for those already in relationships. Good sex covers many sins in a relationship, but it's not everything. Other needs are also important. The New Moon of the 17th occurs in your 7th house, adding to the romantic, erotic nature of the period. In addition, the waxing Moon will help clarify relationship issues as the weeks progress.

On the 23rd the Sun enters your 8th house and so sex maintains its importance. The libido is very strong in the month ahead. Regardless of your age or stage in life, libido is stronger than usual. And while your finances are challenging, the spouse, partner or current love's finances are excellent.

August

Best Days Overall: 7, 8, 17, 18, 26, 27
Most Stressful Days Overall: 5, 6, 12, 13, 19, 20, 21
Best Days for Love: 5, 6, 12, 13, 14, 15, 16, 24, 25, 26
Best Days for Money: 1, 2, 7, 8, 17, 18, 26, 27, 29
Best Days for Career: 5, 6, 14, 15, 19, 20, 21, 24, 25

Your 8th house is still very strong this month – even your career planet is in this house. This is a month to work on personal transformation. This is about giving birth to the person you want to be, the person you were meant to be. An alchemical process is happening this month. And though things can be stormy, the purpose is to purge the mind and emotions of patterns that don't belong there. During this purge you'll see starkly the patterns that were holding you back. It is also good for physical detox regimes and weight-loss regimes (if you need them). The work of personal transformation doesn't happen overnight – the sages say that it is the work of many lifetimes – but no matter. You make progress towards it and that's what counts. The New Moon of the 16th occurring in your 8th house just adds to the above. The 16th is also a strong love, social and erotic day. Issues involving personal transformation (a complex subject) will clarify themselves in the coming weeks – likewise issues involving the spouse's income, investors, tax and insurance issues. All the information you need will come to you very naturally.

Things become less stormy after the 23rd as the Sun moves into a harmonious aspect with you in Virgo. The Earth element is very strong all month, but especially after the 23rd, and you're even more practical, more organized, more managerial than usual. The transit is also good for health. Earth is a comfortable element for you.

The Grand Trine in Earth is wonderful for your finances. Earnings should increase and the financial judgement is sound. But, Uranus, your financial planet, will go retrograde on the 29th and will remain that way for many months to come. Try to wrap up important purchases or investments before then.

Your career planet Venus is still retrograde (all month), which indicates that career is still in preparation.

In fact, with 60 per cent of the planets retrograde after the 29th, there's not much happening in the world right now. But you, more than most, know how to handle these slowdowns. Practise the 'art of the possible'.

September

Best Days Overall: 4, 5, 13, 14, 15, 23, 24
Most Stressful Days Overall: 2, 3, 8, 9, 10, 16, 17, 29, 30
Best Days for Love: 2, 3, 4, 5, 8, 9, 10, 13, 14, 21, 22, 25, 30
Best Days for Money: 4, 5, 14, 15, 23, 24, 25, 26
Best Days for Career: 2, 3, 11, 12, 16, 17, 21, 22, 30

Though retrograde activity is still at its maximum extent for the year for the first half of this month – 60 per cent of the planets are travelling backwards until the 16th – certain things are opening up for you, namely the career. Venus moves forward on the 4th and the Sun will enter your 10th house of career on the 23rd. You begin a yearly career peak. You have confidence and clear direction. Mars will also be in your 10th house all month, signalling much activity in the career – a more aggressive posture. Your family planet in the career house shows that the family is supporting your career goals. You don't have the usual conflict of family and career. They seem to work together. There can be dramas in the lives of parents, parent figures and bosses this month.

The 8th house appears prominent in the career this month. Your career planet Venus occupies the 8th house and the ruler of the 8th house, the Sun, moves into your 10th house. There can be much dealing with surgery or death issues – perhaps estates – towards the end of the month.

Your 9th house is powerful until the 23rd. This is good for college-level students. It shows a focus on their studies. With Mercury retrograde until the 15th (and in your 9th house), avoid making important changes in educational plans before he moves forward. Also, avoid foreign travel that period as well. Jupiter retrogrades on the 4th and, with Mercury retrograde as well, the two planets involved in foreign travel are both retrograde at the same time. Foreign travel will go better after the 15th but still allow more time for getting to and from your destination.

The New Moon of the 15th occurs in your 9th house. As with every New Moon it brings romance and enhanced eroticism, and this month the waxing Moon is especially good for religious studies and the study of scripture. It brings insights and deeper understanding penetration. Additionally, issues involving higher education, travel, religion, theology and legal issues will be clarified in the coming weeks.

Health is good, but after the 23rd you should rest and relax more. You can enhance the health in the ways mentioned in the yearly report, but you can also add massage of the lower abdomen to the list.

You have more energy and enthusiasm for romance and social activities from the 15th to the 29th. Romance will go better that period.

October

Best Days Overall: 1, 2, 11, 12, 20, 21
Most Stressful Days Overall: 6, 7, 13, 14, 26, 27
Best Days for Love: 3, 4, 6, 7, 9, 10, 11, 20, 21, 24
Best Days for Money: 1, 2, 11, 12, 20, 21, 22, 23, 28, 29
Best Days for Career: 8, 9, 10, 11, 20, 21, 28, 29

With two eclipses happening, the month ahead is guaranteed to be eventful. There is a solar eclipse on the 14th and a lunar eclipse on the 28th. Of the two, the solar eclipse seems stronger on you. But keep in mind that if any eclipse hits a sensitive point in your birth chart – the one cast specifically for your date, time and place of birth – it can be powerful indeed. So it would be a good idea to reduce your schedule over both eclipse periods.

The solar eclipse of the 14th occurs in your 10th house and brings career changes. Usually this is not a complete change of career (although sometimes it happens) but changes in the rules of the game – changes in your approach to the career. There can be personal dramas in the lives of bosses, parents and parent figures. There can be shake-ups in the corporate hierarchy and in your industry. The government can change the rules and regulations affecting your industry. But you seem ready to handle all this. Health needs keeping an eye on until the 22nd, but especially during this eclipse period. With the Sun ruling your 8th house, every solar eclipse can bring psychological encounters with death (generally not actual physical death). Thus, a parent, parent figure or boss can have a brush with death – perhaps some surgery or a near-death experience. Sometimes someone you know tells you of the death of an acquaintance. Sometimes people have dreams of death. There is a spiritual agenda behind this. There is a need to understand death better. To understand death is to understand life, and one lives differently when this happens.

The lunar eclipse of the 28th occurs in your 5th house of fun, children and creativity. Children and children figures in your life are thus affected and should also take a more relaxed schedule. There should be no daredevil antics this period. Those of you in the creative arts make important changes to your creativity. A parent or parent figure is forced to make important financial changes. Every lunar eclipse tests your relationship, and this one is no different. So, the dirty laundry in the relationship – the repressed grievances – surface so that they can be dealt with. The spouse, partner or current love can be experiencing personal dramas, and this can test the relationship. Be more patient with him or her at this time.

November

Best Days Overall: 7, 8, 16, 17, 25, 26
Most Stressful Days Overall: 2, 3, 9, 10, 11, 23, 24, 29, 30
Best Days for Love: 2, 3, 8, 9, 12, 13, 18, 19, 23, 27, 28, 29, 30
Best Days for Money: 7, 8, 16, 17, 18, 19, 25, 26
Best Days for Career: 8, 9, 10, 11, 18, 19, 27, 28

The career is still good, though your yearly career peak is over. On the 8th Venus enters your career house. She occupies her own sign and house and thus will be more powerful on your behalf. Your career planet has her solstice from the 9th to the 13th. She pauses in the heavens – in her latitudinal motion – and then changes direction (in latitude). So it is with the career. There is a pause and then a change of direction – and a positive change.

Health is good this month. There is only one long-term planet in stressful alignment with you – Pluto – and only those of you born late in the sign are really affected by this. All the other planets are either in harmonious aspect or leaving you alone. Only the Moon will sometimes (and for very brief periods) make stressful aspects. All systems are go health-wise.

The power this month is in your 11th house of friends, groups and group activities. Thus, the social life is more about Platonic kinds of friendships rather than romantic ones. It signals the friendship of people with similar interests. The New Moon of the 12th occurs in your 11th house, making it an even stronger social day than before. This New Moon also shows a more romantic kind of day as well. Your romantic energy will be strongest from the 12th to the 27th as the Moon waxes. The New Moon will clarify issues with friends and organizations you're involved with, and this will go on over the next few weeks. Mars's presence in the 11th house indicates that you could be installing high-tech gadgetry in the home.

You and family members should be more mindful on the physical plane on the 10th and 11th. There can be some financial dispute with a family member.

On the 22nd the Sun enters your 12th house of spirituality. Mars will enter there on the 24th while Mercury is there from the 10th.

You're in a very spiritual period this month. The presence of your health planet in the 12th house shows an affinity for spiritual healing. You get more results from it than from conventional approaches. With your health planet 'out of bounds' from the 16th onwards, you're now more likely to explore spiritual-healing techniques as well.

December

Best Days Overall: 4, 5, 6, 14, 15, 22, 23, 31
Most Stressful Days Overall: 7, 8, 20, 21, 27, 28
Best Days for Love: 2, 3, 9, 11, 12, 18, 19, 21, 22, 27, 28, 29, 30
Best Days for Money: 4, 5, 6, 14, 15, 16, 17, 22, 23, 31
Best Days for Career: 7, 8, 9, 18, 19, 28, 30

The planetary power is now mostly in the Eastern sector of self. Saturn, the ruler of your Horoscope, is moving forward again and you are in a period of great personal independence. The month ahead is 'me'-oriented. You know what's best for you. Your way is the best way. So, make the changes that need to be made for your personal happiness. Your happiness is up to you these days.

You remain in a strong spiritual period this month. Your 12th house of spirituality is where the power is right now, so focus on your spiritual practice and spiritual goals. Your spiritual understanding will help health-wise, and in family and emotional issues. The New Moon of the 12th occurs in your 12th house as well. This enhances the spiritual energy and brings spiritual insights and progress. It will probably bring revelatory kinds of dreams and supernatural kinds of experiences. In addition, it will help clarify spiritual issues in the coming weeks. This New Moon is also a good love and social day. Love is very idealistic around this period.

Health is excellent this month. Only Pluto is in stressful alignment with you – and most of you won't feel it (only those born very late in the sign of Capricorn – January 17–20 – will feel it). The Moon will occasionally make stressful aspects but these are of very short duration. All the other planets are either in harmonious aspect or leaving you alone. With more energy there is more optimism and enlarged horizons. Things that seemed impossible before become eminently possible.

Your financial planet Uranus is still retrograde. This won't stop earnings but it does slow things down a bit. Earnings are stronger after the 22nd.

Love does not seem a big issue this month. Your social energy and personal magnetism are strongest from the 12th to the 27th as the Moon waxes. The Full Moon of the 27th occurs in your 7th house and this is an especially good love and social day.

On the 22nd the Sun enters your own sign and you begin a yearly personal pleasure peak. A good time to enjoy all the pleasures of the body and the five senses. It will also be beneficial for detox and weight-loss regimes.

Aquarius

≈≈≈

THE WATER-BEARER

Birthdays from
20th January to
18th February

Personality Profile

AQUARIUS AT A GLANCE

Element – Air

Ruling Planet – Uranus
   Career Planet – Pluto
   Love Planet – Sun
   Money Planet – Neptune
   Planet of Health and Work – Moon
   Planet of Home and Family Life – Venus
   Planet of Spirituality – Saturn

Colours – electric blue, grey, ultramarine blue

Colours that promote love, romance and social harmony – gold, orange

Colour that promotes earning power – aqua

Gems – black pearl, obsidian, opal, sapphire

Metal – lead

Scents – azalea, gardenia

Quality – fixed (= stability)

Qualities most needed for balance – warmth, feeling and emotion

Strongest virtues – great intellectual power, the ability to communicate and to form and understand abstract concepts, love for the new and avant-garde

Deepest needs – to know and to bring in the new

Characteristics to avoid – coldness, rebelliousness for its own sake, fixed ideas

Signs of greatest overall compatibility – Gemini, Libra

Signs of greatest overall incompatibility – Taurus, Leo, Scorpio

Sign most helpful to career – Scorpio

Sign most helpful for emotional support – Taurus

Sign most helpful financially – Pisces

Sign best for marriage and/or partnerships – Leo

Sign most helpful for creative projects – Gemini

Best Sign to have fun with – Gemini

Signs most helpful in spiritual matters – Libra, Capricorn

Best day of the week – Saturday

Understanding an Aquarius

In the Aquarius-born, intellectual faculties are perhaps the most highly developed of any sign in the zodiac. Aquarians are clear, scientific thinkers. They have the ability to think abstractly and to formulate laws, theories and clear concepts from masses of observed facts. Geminis might be very good at gathering information, but Aquarians take this a step further, excelling at interpreting the information gathered.

Practical people – men and women of the world – mistakenly consider abstract thinking as impractical. It is true that the realm of abstract thought takes us out of the physical world, but the discoveries made in this realm generally end up having tremendous practical consequences. All real scientific inventions and breakthroughs come from this abstract realm.

Aquarians, more so than most, are ideally suited to explore these abstract dimensions. Those who have explored these regions know that there is little feeling or emotion there. In fact, emotions are a hindrance to functioning in these dimensions; thus Aquarians seem – at times – cold and emotionless to others. It is not that Aquarians haven't got feelings and deep emotions, it is just that too much feeling clouds their ability to think and invent. The concept of 'too much feeling' cannot be tolerated or even understood by some of the other signs. Nevertheless, this Aquarian objectivity is ideal for science, communication and friendship.

Aquarians are very friendly people, but they do not make a big show about it. They do the right thing by their friends, even if sometimes they do it without passion or excitement.

Aquarians have a deep passion for clear thinking. Second in importance, but related, is their passion for breaking with the establishment and traditional authority. Aquarians delight in this, because for them rebellion is like a great game or challenge. Very often they will rebel strictly for the fun of rebelling, regardless of whether the authority they defy is right or wrong. Right or wrong has little to do with the rebellious actions of an Aquarian, because to a true Aquarian authority and power must be challenged as a matter of principle.

Where Capricorn or Taurus will err on the side of tradition and the status quo, an Aquarian will err on the side of the new. Without this virtue it is doubtful whether any progress would be made in the world. The conservative-minded would obstruct progress. Originality and invention imply an ability to break barriers; every new discovery represents the toppling of an impediment to thought. Aquarians are very interested in breaking barriers and making walls tumble – scientifically, socially and politically. Other zodiac signs, such as Capricorn, also have scientific talents. But Aquarians are particularly excellent in the social sciences and humanities.

Finance

In financial matters Aquarians tend to be idealistic and humanitarian – to the point of self-sacrifice. They are usually generous contributors to social and political causes. When they contribute it differs from when a Capricorn or Taurus contributes. A Capricorn or Taurus may expect some favour or return for a gift; an Aquarian contributes selflessly.

Aquarians tend to be as cool and rational about money as they are about most things in life. Money is something they need and they set about acquiring it scientifically. No need for fuss; they get on with it in the most rational and scientific ways available.

Money to the Aquarian is especially nice for what it can do, not for the status it may bring (as is the case for other signs). Aquarians are neither big spenders nor penny-pinchers and use their finances in practical ways, for example to facilitate progress for themselves, their families, or even for strangers.

However, if Aquarians want to reach their fullest financial potential they will have to explore their intuitive nature. If they follow only their financial theories – or what they believe to be theoretically correct – they may suffer some losses and disappointments. Instead, Aquarians should call on their intuition, which knows without thinking. For Aquarians, intuition is the short-cut to financial success.

Career and Public Image

Aquarians like to be perceived not only as the breakers of barriers but also as the transformers of society and the world. They long to be seen in this light and to play this role. They also look up to and respect other people in this position and even expect their superiors to act this way.

Aquarians prefer jobs that have a bit of idealism attached to them – careers with a philosophical basis. Aquarians need to be creative at work, to have access to new techniques and methods. They like to keep busy and enjoy getting down to business straight away, without wasting any time. They are often the quickest workers and usually have suggestions for improvements that will benefit their employers. Aquarians are also very helpful with their co-workers and welcome responsibility, preferring this to having to take orders from others.

If Aquarians want to reach their highest career goals they have to develop more emotional sensitivity, depth of feeling and passion. They need to learn to narrow their focus on the essentials and concentrate more on the job in hand. Aquarians need 'a fire in the belly' – a consuming passion and desire – in order to rise to the very top. Once this passion exists they will succeed easily in whatever they attempt.

Love and Relationships

Aquarians are good at friendships, but a bit weak when it comes to love. Of course they fall in love, but their lovers always get the impression that they are more best friends than paramours.

Like Capricorns, they are cool customers. They are not prone to displays of passion or to outward demonstrations of their affections. In fact, they feel uncomfortable when their other half hugs and touches them too much. This does not mean that they do not love their partners. They do, only they show it in other ways. Curiously enough, in relationships they tend to attract the very things that they feel uncomfortable with. They seem to attract hot, passionate, romantic, demonstrative people. Perhaps they know instinctively that these people have qualities they lack and so seek them out. In any event, these relationships do seem to work, Aquarian coolness calming the more passionate partner while the fires of passion warm the cold-blooded Aquarius.

The qualities Aquarians need to develop in their love life are warmth, generosity, passion and fun. Aquarians love relationships of the mind. Here they excel. If the intellectual factor is missing in a relationship an Aquarian will soon become bored or feel unfulfilled.

Home and Domestic Life

In family and domestic matters Aquarians can have a tendency to be too non-conformist, changeable and unstable. They are as willing to break the barriers of family constraints as they are those of other areas of life.

Even so, Aquarians are very sociable people. They like to have a nice home where they can entertain family and friends. Their house is usually decorated in a modern style and full of state-of-the-art appliances and gadgets – an environment Aquarians find absolutely necessary.

If their home life is to be healthy and fulfilling Aquarians need to inject it with a quality of stability – yes, even some conservatism. They need at least one area of life to be enduring and steady; this area is usually their home and family life.

Venus, the generic planet of love, rules the Aquarian's 4th solar house of home and family, which means that when it comes to the family and child-rearing, theories, cool thinking and intellect are not always enough. Aquarians need to bring love into the equation in order to have a great domestic life.

Horoscope for 2023

Major Trends

You're coming out of a banner financial year, Aquarius. There was great prosperity and great expansion. Perhaps you over-expanded, which often happens when the mood is ebullient. This year, as Saturn moves into your money house on March 8, it is a time for consolidation, for pulling in your horns, for stabilizing the gains of the previous year. More on this later.

Pluto has been in your 12th house of spirituality for many, many years – over twenty years. During this time your spiritual life has been totally transformed. This process is still happening, but it is mostly over with by now. Pluto will move into your own sign on March 24 and stay there until June 12. This is an announcement of things to come. Your image, personal appearance and self-definition are beginning to undergo radical change. This won't happen overnight but as a long, multi-year process.

Saturn leaving your sign on March 8 (after a stay of two and a half years) removes some of the personal gloom and pessimism you've been feeling. It should improve the love and social life as well. Your overall energy should improve too, but health still needs keeping an eye on from May 17 onwards. More on this later.

Neptune has been in your money house for many years. This year, from March 8, he is joined by your spiritual planet, Saturn. So, the financial intuition is extra super this year. You've made great progress in understanding and applying the spiritual laws of wealth, and this progress continues in the year ahead (and next year too).

Jupiter will be in your 3rd house of communication and intellectual interests until May 17, signalling a good period for students. The intellectual faculties are expanded and they should do well in their studies. School and studying bring great satisfaction.

Jupiter moves into your 4th house on May 17 and stays there for the rest of the year. This can bring a move and enhanced fertility for women of childbearing age. More details later.

Your major interests this year are spirituality (until March 24 and from June 12 onwards); the body, image and personal appearance (until March 8 and from March 24 to June 12); finance; intellectual interests and communication (until May 17); home, family and emotional wellness; and love and romance (from June 5 to October 9).

Your paths of greatest fulfilment are intellectual interests and communication (until May 17 and from July 18 onwards); and home and family.

Health

(Please note that this is an astrological perspective on health and not a medical one. In days of yore there was no difference, both these perspectives were identical. But these days there could be quite a difference. For a medical perspective, please consult your doctor or health practitioner.)

Health generally will improve this year, as Saturn moves out of your sign on March 8. However, after May 17 you will have two long-term planets in stressful alignment with you and health will need more attention. By themselves these stressful aspects are not serious, but when other short-term planets join the party, it can make you more vulnerable. Your 6th house of health is not powerful this year and so the tendency is to not pay attention to your health. But after May 17 you might need to force yourself to do so.

There is much you can do to enhance the health and prevent problems from developing. Give more attention to the following – the vulnerable areas of your Horoscope this year and the likely trouble

Important foot reflexology points for the year ahead

Try to massage all of the foot on a regular basis – the top of the foot as well as the bottom – but pay extra attention to the points highlighted on the chart. When you massage, be aware of 'sore spots' as these need special attention. It's also a good idea to massage the ankles and below them.

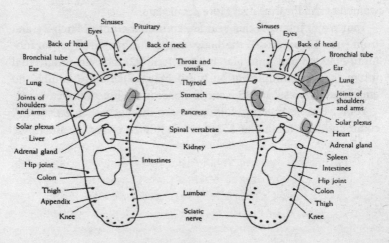

spots. Most of the time, if one is diligent, problems can be prevented. But even in cases where they can't be totally prevented, they can be softened to a great extent and need not be devastating.

Here are the areas to focus on this year (the reflex points are shown in the chart opposite):

- The heart has only been an important area for you for the past two years, remaining so until March 8 (especially for those born between February 10 and February 18). It becomes significant for your health again after May 17. The important thing with the heart is to avoid worry and anxiety, the two emotions that stress it out. Replace worry with faith. Meditation is a big help.
- The ankles and calves. These are always important for Aquarius as your sign rules these areas. Regular ankle and calf massage will be wonderful. Sometimes tension and tightness collect in the calves and need to be released. Stretching exercises for the calves will be good. Give the ankles more support when exercising.
- The stomach and breasts. These areas are also always important for Aquarius as the Moon, the planet that rules these areas, is your health planet. Diet is an important issue for you – more so than for others. What you eat is important and should be checked with a professional, but *how* you eat is just as important. There is a need to elevate the act of eating from mere animal appetite to an act of worship and gratitude. It is good, therefore, to make eating a ritual. Grace, in your own words, should be said before and after meals. Food should be blessed (in your own words). If possible, have nice soothing music playing as you eat. These practices will elevate the energy vibrations of the food you eat and also of the body and digestive system. You will get the highest and best from the food and it will digest better. Women should have regular breast check-ups.

There are many short-term health trends every month, as your health planet is the fastest moving of all the planets. (She moves through your whole Horoscope every month.) These are best covered in the monthly reports. In general, we can say that the New and Full Moons tend to be good health days. When the Moon is waxing (growing) it is good to take vitamin supplements and the like – add to the body what it needs. And the periods when the Moon is waning are good for detox regimes.

Home and Family

Your 4th house has been an important focus for you for many years now and in the year ahead becomes even more important. This area of life becomes very happy from May 17 onwards as Jupiter enters this house. So, as we mentioned, moves can happen. Often there is the fortunate purchase or sale of a home. The family as a whole seems more prosperous and family support will be good.

Sometimes people don't literally move under this transit. Sometimes they buy additional homes or gain access to additional homes. Or they renovate the existing home or buy expensive items for the home – the effect is 'as if' they have moved. Living conditions improve with beneficent Jupiter in your 4th house.

The family circle gets enlarged this year. Usually this happens through birth or marriage, but not always. (However, as we mentioned, women of childbearing age are extremely fertile this year, especially from May 17 onwards.) Sometimes you meet people who become like family to you. Sometimes a friend decides to play this role in your life.

Family members have been prone to wild and sudden mood swings for some years now. This year it seems more optimistic. The swings will tend to be happy ones.

This is a year for great psychological progress. Those of you in formal therapy will make great progress, but even if you're not in any formal therapy all kinds of psychological insights will come to you. It is a year for emotional healing.

There are many short-term home and family trends as Venus, your family planet, is very fast moving. These are best dealt with in the monthly reports.

Venus will spend an unusual amount of time in your 7th house this year, from June 5 to October 9 – quadruple her usual transit. This period would be a good time to redecorate or otherwise beautify the home. There will be more socializing from home and with the family too.

A parent or parent figure prospers this year. He or she will need to watch their weight. If this parent figure is a woman of childbearing age, she is very fertile after May 17. This parent figure will probably travel more this year, but a move is not likely. The other parent or parent figure feels restless with the winds of change, but a move is not likely this year. Siblings and sibling figures in your life are prospering, but their home and family life tends to the status quo. Children, children figures and grandchildren (if you have them) are having a stable home and family year.

Finance and Career

As we mentioned earlier, 2022 was a major financial year for you. Prosperity was great. Earnings, and opportunities to earn, expanded tremendously. Now it is time to consolidate your gains and make them more stable and secure. There is an alternation to life – to nature. One doesn't expand and expand indefinitely. You can't keep breathing in all the time. The in breath is followed by an out breath, night follows day. Bull markets don't last for ever.

This year we see this in the financial life. You're still prosperous and your financial intuition is still super. But there's a need to thin out earnings opportunities, investments and assets. Choose the quality ones and let the lesser ones go. There is a financial reorganization and consolidation happening. I feel this is healthy.

Saturn in your 2nd money house after March 8 indicates that you're taking on more financial responsibilities. Often this makes a person feel a sense of 'lack' – but this is only a feeling and not a reality. If you reorganize your finances, shift things around here and there, you'll have more than enough resources to handle these extra responsibilities.

Saturn's purpose is not to punish you. His transit through your money house over the next two and a half years is to ensure that the wealth you have is stable and enduring, and he will guide you on this path.

Though your financial intuition is still very good, you become more conservative this year. You take a more realistic, long-term approach to wealth. Wealth is attained (and maintained) in a step-by-step methodical way. This is a great year to set up disciplined savings and investment plans – and to stick to them. It is also a good period to explore money management more deeply. This year is not so much about increasing your earnings – though this will probably happen – but about managing what you have in a good way. Good money management will probably do more for you than just increasing earnings.

You're basically a generous person. Very charitable. This year it would be good to keep your charity within bounds. Tithing is always an excellent practice for you, but especially nowadays. Tithing puts a limit, a sense of proportion, on your giving.

Jupiter will be travelling near Uranus, the ruler of your Horoscope, after May 17, although the aspect won't be exact until next year. But you will feel the influence now, and it tends to prosperity. Friends seem helpful. Jupiter in your 3rd house until May 17 indicates a likelihood of a new car and communications equipment.

With regards to career, Aquarius, your 10th house is not prominent this year. Not a house of power. It is basically empty; only short-term planets, with short-term effects, will move through there. Yet we see the beginnings of major change here. Your career planet, Pluto, is beginning a two-year transition from Capricorn into your own sign, and this will be very positive for you. Though you feel it weakly this year and next, in 2025 and beyond you'll feel it strongly. Pluto will bring happy career opportunities to you. He will also give you the image of success and prominence.

A lunar eclipse on May 5 occurs in your 10th house. This too will shake things up in your career. It can produce job changes as well. We will cover this more fully in the monthly report.

Love and Social Life

Though your 7th house is empty for the most part (excepting Venus, who will spend over four months there), the love life is pretty much stable. Those of you who are married will tend to stay married, and singles will tend to stay single.

The period from June 5 to October 9 (Venus's transit through the 7th house) will be an active love and social period. There is a love interest there for singles. It can be someone from your past – an old flame – or someone who comes to you by means of the family or family connections. Will it end in marriage? Unlikely. This relationship seems very complicated. It goes forwards and backwards and there is much doubt and indecision about it.

Your love planet, the Sun, is a fast-moving planet, as our regular readers know. Thus, there are many short-term love trends that depend on where the Sun is and the kinds of aspects he receives. These are best covered in the monthly reports.

Friendships and group activities seem happy this year, especially from May 27 onwards. This area gets really happy next year, but you're already feeling the effects in the year ahead.

Parents and parent figures have social happiness from June 12 onwards. Things get even better socially next year. Children and children figures in your life are looking for someone spiritual from May 17 onwards. If they are single, they should look in spiritual venues – not the usual bars and clubs. Marriage is not likely for them this year. Siblings and sibling figures have a quiet, stable love year. If they are married or in a relationship, it will get tested by the solar eclipse of October 14. Grandchildren (if you have them) will have a fabulous social year – especially from January 1 to May 17. If they are of an appropriate age, there can be serious romance – even marriage.

Self-improvement

Saturn, your spiritual planet, makes a major move into your money house on March 8. This has great impact on both the finances and your spirituality. Saturn is perhaps the most down to earth and practical of the planets. His move into your money house shows that for you, spirituality is not something abstract. It's not about spouting clichés at cocktail parties. It is the most down to earth and practical thing in the world – except the approach is different. It has practical, bottom-line consequences. Now spirituality has been important in your finances for many years – it has always been important in finance but especially in recent years. Spirit is guiding your financial life – and even more so this year. If there are financial problems, it would be good to surrender the whole situation – and your whole financial life – to the Divine and to let it handle things. This will straighten out the knottiest problem if it is done sincerely.

Financial guidance will come through psychics, astrologers, spiritual channels, ministers, dreams and hunches. When your intuition is firing, guidance can come through a road sign, a phrase in the newspaper, or from some offhand remark made by someone. They may not have realized the import, but you do.

You've been experiencing miracle money for many years now. This year even more so. You will see-know-feel the hand of the Divine in your financial affairs.

This is a year where there is a need for financial management. For pruning the investments and opportunities that come. Where to prune? How to prune? Spirit will guide you.

With spiritual Neptune sitting in your money house for many years now, you've been a charitable giver. This is a great thing. But most likely it was overdone. Now that Saturn will be in your 2nd house as well, your giving will be more proportional and organized. Right proportion is the essence of beauty and health - and we should have it in our finances as well. Thus, as we mentioned, tithing would be an excellent practice to adopt over the next few years.

Month-by-month Forecasts

January

Best Days Overall: 3, 4, 12, 13, 21, 22, 30, 31
Most Stressful Days Overall: 6, 7, 18, 19, 25, 26
Best Days for Love: 2, 3, 10, 11, 12, 13, 20, 21, 22, 25, 26, 30, 31
Best Days for Money: 7, 8, 14, 15, 16, 23, 24
Best Days for Career: 2, 6, 7, 11, 19, 20, 29

A happy and healthy month ahead. Enjoy! You begin the month in a strong spiritual period. Spirituality has been important in your life for many years, and even more so this month. So, progress and insights are happening. The New Moon of the 11th also occurs in your 12th house of spirituality, further emphasizing this area. It is an especially good day for spiritual healing and spiritual-healing techniques. It is also a good love and social day. As the weeks go by (until the next New

Moon) spiritual issues will become clearer for you. Many questions will be answered. What you need to know will be shown to you.

Health is excellent this month. There is only one long-term planet in stressful alignment with you; all the others, except the Moon (and that only occasionally) are either in harmonious aspect or leaving you alone. So, you have plenty of energy to achieve whatever you set your mind to. When you think about it, health is another form of wealth.

Love also seems happy. Until the 20th your love planet is in your spiritual 12th house. Thus, romantic opportunities for singles happen in spiritual-type venues – the yoga studio, the spiritual lecture or seminar, the meditation class. Love is idealistic, and very pure. On the 20th the Sun moves into your own sign, which brings romantic opportunities without you having to do much – just show up! Love pursues you. The 4th and 5th bring romantic opportunity. The 17th to the 19th likewise. Though this latter period seems more about the career, or perhaps with someone involved in your career.

On the 20th you enter a yearly personal pleasure peak. You look good and the social grace is strong (Venus in your sign from the 3rd to the 27th just adds to this). You'll be enjoying the pleasures of the body and the five senses. This is a time to pamper the body, but also to get it into the shape that you want.

Finances are OK, but next month they will be a lot better.

February

Best Days Overall: 1, 9, 10, 18, 19, 27, 28
Most Stressful Days Overall: 4, 5, 6, 12, 13, 24, 25
Best Days for Love: 1, 2, 3, 4, 5, 6, 9, 10, 12, 13, 20, 22
Best Days for Money: 3, 4, 5, 13, 14, 15, 20, 21, 22, 23
Best Days for Career: 8, 12, 13, 17, 25

All the planets are moving forward this month. The Universal solar cycle is in its waxing phase, and when your birthday happens, your personal solar cycle will also be waxing. So you're in a beautiful period of cosmic energy for starting new projects or launching new ventures into the world, from your birthday onwards. During this period the 20th to the 28th is especially good, as the Moon will also be waxing.

Next month will also be good for starting new projects. There's a lot of cosmic support.

The month ahead is still happy, healthy and prosperous. Saturn is still affecting some of you, but mostly those born late in your sign – February 17-19. All the other planets are either in harmonious aspect or leaving you alone. Only the Moon will sometimes – briefly – make a stressful aspect. So, health is excellent.

You're still in the midst of a yearly personal pleasure peak until the 18th. So, by all means, pamper the body and show it appreciation for all the selfless service it gives you.

Love is still happy. Until the 18th love pursues you. If you're in a relationship the spouse, partner or current love is eager to please; he or she seems devoted to you. After the 18th the partner seems financially supportive – seems involved in your financial goals.

After the 18th, as the Sun moves into your money house, you enter a yearly financial peak. Earnings are strong. The financial intuition – always good – is even better than usual. Social contacts are playing a big role. Family support for finances seems strong (and this works both ways), and it seems especially strong from the 14th to the 16th. The New Moon of the 20th occurs in your money house and impacts on your spiritual planet Saturn. Thus, your financial intuition is exceptionally strong that day. This New Moon is good for finances and will clarify financial issues in the coming weeks – until the next New Moon. Your questions get answered and doubts resolved.

Jupiter has been in your 3rd house of intellectual interests since the beginning of the year. On the 21st Venus, your family planet, joins him. So, students are doing well in school. Learning is easy. The mental faculties are stronger than usual.

March

Best Days Overall: 8, 9, 10, 17, 18, 26, 27
Most Stressful Days Overall: 4, 5, 11, 12, 24, 25, 31
Best Days for Love: 1, 2, 4, 5, 11, 12, 20, 21, 24, 25, 31
Best Days for Money: 2, 4, 5, 12, 13, 14, 19, 20, 21, 22, 29, 30, 31
Best Days for Career: 7, 11, 12, 16, 25, 26

Saturn's move into your money house on the 8th increases your already strong financial intuition. It also improves the overall health and energy levels. Saturn has been in adverse aspect to you for the last two and a half years and has now finally moved out of his stressful aspect and health will be better than it has been for that entire period.

Saturn's move into your money house can bring additional financial responsibilities to you. It can create feelings of lack – but these are just feelings, not reality. There is a need now to reorganize the finances, however. Shift things around. If you do this, you'll have all the resources that you need.

Pluto makes a short move into your own sign on the 24th but it is only a brief flirtation – he will retrograde out of Aquarius again on June 12. Only those of you born early in the sign – January 20-21 – will feel the effect of this short transit. Most of you won't. But it does announce the start of a long-term personal transformation in your physical image and personality, which will begin in earnest in 2025.

You're still in a yearly financial peak, which began on February 18 and will go on until the 20th of this month. Earnings will be strong. Trust your intuition – it is the short cut to wealth.

Venus travels with Jupiter on the 1st and 2nd. This can make women of childbearing age more fertile than usual. It can also bring a foreign trip. There is prosperity for a parent or parent figure.

On the 20th your 3rd house becomes even more powerful than it has been (and it's been strong all year), as the Sun moves into it. Students and intellectual workers shine.

Love also seems happy. Until the 20th romantic opportunities happen as you pursue your financial goals and perhaps with people involved in your finances. After the 20th, with your love planet's move into your 3rd house, you're attracted by intellectuals. The mind is as alluring to you as the body. You can be a love-at-first-sight kind of person during this period. You jump into relationships very quickly – perhaps too quickly.

April

Best Days Overall: 5, 6, 14, 15, 22, 23, 24
Most Stressful Days Overall: 1, 7, 8, 20, 21, 27, 28, 29
Best Days for Love: 1, 3, 4, 10, 14, 22, 23, 27, 28, 29, 30
Best Days for Money: 1, 8, 10, 16, 17, 19, 26, 28, 29
Best Days for Career: 4, 5, 7, 8, 13, 14, 21, 22

With your love planet still in Aries until the 20th the spiritual lesson is to be fearless in love. Whether a relationship works out or not isn't really important. The fact that you overcame your fears is what counts. Love opportunities can happen at the gym, bookshop, library, school, lecture or seminar.

A solar eclipse on the 20th occurs right on the border of your 3rd and 4th houses. Thus, it impacts on the affairs of both houses. Those born early in your sign – January 19–21 – will feel the effects of this eclipse very strongly (although all of you will feel it). Make sure you take it nice and easy during this period.

The eclipse's impact on your 3rd house indicates that students will be changing their educational plans, perhaps even changing schools. There are disruptions at the school. Siblings, sibling figures and neighbours will experience personal dramas. There will be disruptions in the neighbourhood.

The impact on the 4th house signals dramas at home and in the lives of family members – especially a parent or parent figure. Repairs could be needed in the home. You probably didn't know that anything was wrong until the eclipse came along and revealed it to you. The dream life will most likely be very active, overactive in fact, but these dreams shouldn't be given much weight. What you see is just psychic debris stirred up by the eclipse.

This solar eclipse scores a direct hit on Pluto, your career planet, provoking changes and upheavals in the career. There can be shake-ups in your company hierarchy or in your industry. The government can change the regulations governing your industry. The rules of the game change. Sometimes people actually change careers completely.

With the Sun as your love planet, every solar eclipse tests your relationship, and this one is no different. You go through this twice a year

(usually) and know how to handle it by now. Generally repressed grievances (real or imagined) – dirty laundry – surface so that they can be
dealt with. Good relationships weather these things, but flawed ones
are in danger.

May

Best Days Overall: 2, 3, 11, 12, 20, 21, 30, 31
Most Stressful Days Overall: 5, 6, 17, 18, 19, 25, 26
Best Days for Love: 1, 2, 3, 9, 10, 17, 18, 19, 25, 26, 27, 28
Best Days for Money: 6, 8, 13, 14, 16, 17, 23, 24, 25
Best Days for Career: 1, 2, 10, 11, 19, 20, 29

We have another eclipse this month, on the 5th, that has a strong
effect on all of you, Aquarius. So, reduce your schedule and take things
nice and easy over that period. The cosmos will signal when you should
start doing this. Some strange event happens and you'll know you're
in the eclipse period. You should be reducing your schedule anyway
this month (until the 21st) but especially during the eclipse period.

This eclipse is a lunar eclipse, and it occurs in your 10th house of
career. So, more career changes and upheavals are coming your way.
Bosses, parents and parent figures experience personal dramas –
perhaps health dramas. There is still upheaval in your corporate hierarchy. Your industry is changing. The spouse, partner or current love
has dramas in their family. Siblings and sibling figures can have
surgery or near-death kinds of experiences – confrontations with
death.

The Moon is your health planet, which means your health is very
sensitive to lunar phenomena – not just eclipses. There can be a health
scare thanks to this eclipse, but your health is basically good (although
this month is not your best health month) and it is likely to be nothing
more than a scare. In the coming months you'll be making important
changes to the health regime. Job changes are also likely. These
changes can be within your present company (they shift you from one
position to another) or with a new one. There are disruptions at the
workplace. If you employ others there can be high levels of employee
turnover and dramas in the lives of employees.

This eclipse grazes Uranus, the ruler of your Horoscope and a very important planet in your chart. So, you'll find there is a need to redefine yourself and your image. In the coming months you'll be making important changes to the way you dress and present yourself. You'll be modifying your presentation to the world.

Health will improve after the 21st. In the meantime, enhance the health with more rest and in the ways mentioned in the yearly report.

June

Best Days Overall: 7, 8, 16, 17, 26, 27
Most Stressful Days Overall: 1, 2, 14, 15, 16, 21, 22, 28, 29
Best Days for Love: 2, 7, 8, 11, 17, 18, 21, 22, 28
Best Days for Money: 5, 6, 9, 10, 14, 15, 23, 24, 25
Best Days for Career: 1, 2, 6, 7, 15, 25, 28, 29

Now that the excitement generated by the eclipses is over, you're in a happy, fun kind of period. On May 21 you entered a yearly personal pleasure peak and this continues until the 21st of this month. A time for fun and recreation. A time to explore the rapture side of life.

Health is much improved this month. There are two long-term planets in stressful aspect to you, but the short-term planets are either in harmony with you or leaving you alone. Pluto moving back out of your sign on the 12th is another positive for health.

Last month on the 17th, Jupiter moved into your 4th house, and he will be there for the rest of the year ahead. So, a move can happen or a renovation. Women of childbearing age are unusually fertile. There is much happiness at home now.

Love is happy this month – kind of happy-go-lucky. Love is not serious but is about having fun – entertainment. Singles are attracted to those who can show them a good time. This kind of attitude is not conducive to serious relationships and love affairs are more likely. After the 21st, the love planet moves into your 6th house of health and work and you become more serious about love (and life in general). There is more socializing at home and with the family. There is a need for emotional bonding and sharing with potential partners. Singles will find themselves attracted to co-workers or health professionals.

In general, there is a greater focus on health after the 21st – especially on emotional health.

The New Moon of the 18th occurs in your 5th house and is a fun kind of day. A nice day for romance, but not the serious kind. Issues involving your personal creativity and the children or children figures in your life will be clarified as the weeks progress.

Financial intuition needs more verification from the 17th onwards, but earnings should be good after the 21st. Your financial planet Neptune starts to travel backwards on the 30th and will be retrograde for many months to come – so try to finalize important purchases or investments before then.

July

Best Days Overall: 5, 6, 13, 14, 15, 23, 24
Most Stressful Days Overall: 11, 12, 18, 19, 20, 26, 27
Best Days for Love: 2, 7, 8, 10, 17, 18, 19, 20, 26, 29
Best Days for Money: 3, 4, 7, 8, 11, 12, 17, 21, 22, 27, 30, 31
Best Days for Career: 4, 12, 22, 26, 27, 31

Your strong focus on health until the 23rd will stand you in good stead for after then. You are building up 'health reserves' which will carry you through later periods where your health seems stressed. Make sure to rest and relax more after the 23rd. Enhance the health in the ways mentioned in the yearly report. This stress on health is a temporary situation caused by the movements of short-term planets. It doesn't seem particularly serious, but when energy is low a person can become more vulnerable to other problems.

The main headline this month is love. Your 7th house of love is chock-full of planets. And, on the 23rd, the Sun enters this house and you begin a yearly love and social peak. Singles will have many romantic opportunities and with a variety of people. The problem this month can be having too much of a good thing – but it's a nice problem to have. The social grace is unusually strong as your love planet is in his own sign and house, where he is powerful. Those already in a relationship are socializing more – attending parties and gatherings and perhaps weddings.

Home and family life is happy these days, but there is more stress here. Happy things can bring as much stress as challenging things. Still, it is a good kind of stress. Venus, your family planet, goes retrograde on the 23rd (a rare retrograde, one that only happens every two years). So, family issues need more thought and study – there are no quick solutions here, time alone will sort things out.

The two planets involved in your finances, Saturn and Neptune, are both retrograde all month (and will be for many more months), so earnings are slower. They happen but with more delays and glitches involved. You can minimize delays (though you probably won't eliminate them) by handling the details of your finances perfectly. Make sure invoices are dated and submitted properly. Double-check names and account numbers when making payments, etc. Earnings are stronger before the 23rd than after.

The New Moon of the 17th occurs in your 6th house of health. It is both a good social and romantic day and good for dealing with health issues. Health issues (and job issues) will clarify themselves as the weeks progress – until the next New Moon.

August

Best Days Overall: 1, 2, 10, 11, 19, 20, 21, 29
Most Stressful Days Overall: 7, 8, 14, 15, 16, 22, 23
Best Days for Love: 5, 6, 14, 15, 16, 24, 25, 26
Best Days for Money: 3, 4, 7, 8, 13, 17, 18, 23, 26, 27, 30, 31
Best Days for Career: 8, 18, 22, 23, 27, 28

Retrograde activity among the planets gradually increases this month. By the 29th 60 per cent of the planets will be retrograde – a huge percentage, and the maximum for the year. So, patience is needed now. It's good to understand what's happening and not create problems where none exist. This is just cosmic weather, not bad luck. You're not a bad person and you haven't been born under a malevolent star.

You're still in a yearly love and social peak until the 23rd. There is more socializing at home and with family members. The family seems involved in your love life. Family connections too. The love life is still very strong, but it is less frenetic than it was last month. The New

Moon of the 16th occurs in your 7th house and will clarify love and social issues as the weeks unfold – until the next New Moon. The 16th is an especially good love and social day. The 14th and 15th bring some disagreement with the current love, but things smooth themselves out by the 16th.

On the 23rd your 8th house of regeneration becomes powerful. Love becomes more about sexual magnetism than anything else. Good sex covers many sins in a relationship, but it's not enough on its own to hold things together. Singles need to look deeper. A strong 8th house brings prosperity to the spouse, partner or current love, but there are delays involved. His or her financial planet, Mercury, goes retrograde on the 23rd.

Power in the 8th house tends to tempestuousness. The cosmic purpose of this is personal transformation and this is the reason behind it. Transformation rarely happens while one is on the beach drinking pina coladas. Sterner measures are often needed. The cosmos forces deep and hidden patterns to surface that have been holding you back, and by revealing them you have the opportunity to change things. A crisis, used correctly, is the best agent for personal transformation.

A strong 8th house often provokes psychological encounters with death. The cosmos brings events to your attention that force you to look at where you're going. The purpose is to gain a deeper understanding of life. It is not about punishment, but education.

September

Best Days Overall: 6, 7, 16, 17, 25, 26
Most Stressful Days Overall: 4, 5, 11, 12, 18, 19
Best Days for Love: 2, 3, 4, 5, 11, 12, 13, 14, 21, 22, 25, 30
Best Days for Money: 1, 4, 5, 9, 10, 14, 15, 19, 23, 24, 27, 28
Best Days for Career: 5, 15, 18, 19, 24

Retrograde activity is still at its maximum extent for the year until the 16th, so keep in mind our discussion of this last month. Even after the 16th retrograde activity is high – 50 per cent. So work towards your goals slowly and methodically. Time and time alone will straighten things out. No use trying to rush things. Practise the 'art of the possible'.

Your 8th house remains powerful until the 23rd. So, focus on renewing yourself – work on giving birth to the person that you want to be. It won't happen in a month, but you can make progress towards it. The New Moon of the 15th occurs in your 8th house, bringing a good romantic and erotic day. More importantly, it will bring clarity to issues involving the current love's finances, interest, tax, insurance and estate issues as the weeks unfold. It will also clarify your efforts at personal transformation.

This month is a good time for undergoing detox and weight-loss regimes and for decluttering the life of extraneous things – possessions and mental and emotional patterns that no longer serve you.

Health and energy are reasonable this month but will improve even further after the 23rd. Mars will be in your 9th house all month and the Sun enters in on the 23rd. A good period for students (both at college level and below). There is focus on the studies and this tends to success. Travel opportunities can occur, but with so many planets retrograde still it might be wiser to plan a trip rather than to take one. It is also a great period for religious and theological studies – all kinds of insights will come to you.

Love seems happy this month as well. Until the 23rd it is sexual magnetism that is the paramount attraction. But after then there is a need for philosophical compatibility – a compatibility of 'worldview'. Singles are attracted to those from foreign lands and to highly educated types of people – the professor, the worship leader. You like people you can learn from, mentor types.

October

Best Days Overall: 3, 4, 22, 23
Most Stressful Days Overall: 1, 2, 8, 9, 15, 16, 17, 28, 29
Best Days for Love: 3, 4, 9, 10, 11, 20, 21, 24, 28, 29
Best Days for Money: 1, 2, 7, 11, 12, 17, 20, 21, 24, 25, 28, 29
Best Days for Career: 2, 12, 15, 16, 17, 21, 29

We have two eclipses this month, which guarantees that the month ahead is eventful – full of change and excitement.

The first is a solar eclipse on the 14th and the second a lunar eclipse on the 28th. Of the two, the latter will probably have the stronger effect on you. However, if the solar eclipse hits a sensitive point in your personal Horoscope – the one cast specifically for you, for your exact date, time and place of birth – it can be powerful indeed. So it would be a good idea to reduce your schedule over both these periods.

The solar eclipse of the 14th occurs in your 9th house and affects college-level students or those applying to college (postgraduates too). There can be changes in educational plans, disturbances at the school or college, and sometimes changes of school. There are upheavals and shake-ups in your place of worship and dramas in the lives of fellow worshippers and worship leaders. More importantly – and something that will have a long-term impact – your religious and theological beliefs get tested. This testing will go on for a few months. Some of your existing beliefs will be discarded, some will be amended and fine-tuned. These changes will affect the way that you lead your life.

Every solar eclipse tests your current relationship. As we've said, you go through this twice every year, so you know how to handle it. Sometimes repressed grievances surface so that they can be dealt with – often a person is not aware of their existence. Sometimes there are dramas in the life of the beloved and this causes the testing. The beloved needs to redefine him or herself – it is an identity crisis at the root of the problem. He or she will change the image in the coming months.

The lunar eclipse of the 28th occurs in your 4th house of home and family. This shakes up the family circle – again, in a good way. Good things – moves, births, etc. – can be just as stressful as negative things. There can be changes in the health regime and job changes as well. Those who employ others can experience staff turnover these days (and in the coming months).

November

Best Days Overall: 1, 9, 10, 11, 18, 19, 27, 28
Most Stressful Days Overall: 4, 5, 6, 12, 13, 25, 26
Best Days for Love: 2, 3, 4, 5, 6, 8, 9, 12, 13, 18, 19, 23, 27, 28
Best Days for Money: 3, 7, 13, 16, 21, 22, 25, 30
Best Days for Career: 8, 12, 13, 17, 26

Health and career are the main headlines this month. Health seems very stressed (part of it is because of the demands of the career). So, very important to get enough rest. Since you seem successful this month, it might be a good idea to schedule in some massages or other health treatments – more so than usual. Enhance the health in the ways mentioned in the yearly report. Health and energy will improve after the 22nd when the short-term planets start making harmonious aspects to you.

Last month you began a yearly career peak, and this goes on until the 22nd of this month. You're in a successful career period. The outer, day side of your Horoscope is as strong as it will ever be this year – though it's still not dominant. Your challenge will be to balance home and family duties with the career obligations. There are no rules about this. Everyone finds their own way. But from your Horoscope, you're probably swinging back and forth between the home and the career. The New Moon of the 12th occurs in your 10th house, making it an even stronger career day than usual. It brings success. It is also an excellent day for love and for job-seekers.

The Sun, your love planet, is in your 10th house until the 22nd. This gives various messages. It shows that love and romance are high on the agenda and, in certain cases, could be read as the actual career – the actual mission – for the month. Those already married or in a relationship see their mission as being there for the partner and friends. Those who are single see their mission as finding Mr or Ms Right. Another way to read this is that much of your socializing this month is career related and that you enhance the career by social means – by attending or hosting the right parties or gatherings. Singles are attracted to people of power and prestige, to people above them in status, to people who can help them career-wise. These opportunities will happen.

Be more mindful on the physical plane on the 10th and 11th – drive more carefully. Be more patient with siblings and sibling figures on those days as well.

On the 22nd, as your 11th house becomes powerful, you enter a happy period. The cosmos impels you to do what you most love to do – network, and be involved with friends, groups and group activities.

December

Best Days Overall: 7, 8, 16, 17, 24, 25
Most Stressful Days Overall: 2, 3, 9, 10, 22, 23, 29, 30
Best Days for Love: 2, 3, 9, 11, 12, 18, 19, 21, 22, 28, 29, 30
Best Days for Money: 4, 10, 14, 18, 19, 22, 28, 31
Best Days for Career: 5, 6, 9, 10, 15, 23

A happy month ahead. The planetary power is still in your 11th house of friends – your favourite house – and you're expressing your natural gifts and talents: you're involved with friends, groups, group activities and trade and professional organizations. You're studying more deeply science, technology, astronomy and astrology. The 11th house is a beneficent house so all these activities go well. The New Moon of the 12th occurs in this house – making it an especially good day for these activities. This New Moon is also a great romantic day. Issues involving science, friends, technology, astronomy and astrology will become clearer as the weeks unfold. Your questions will be answered, and doubts assuaged – all naturally and normally.

Health is good this month. The New Moon of the 12th is also good for health and can bring job opportunities as well. You have more energy for health regimes and pursuing a healthy lifestyle from the 12th to the 27th as the Moon waxes. From the 1st to the 12th and from the 27th onwards are good times for detox regimes – getting rid of what doesn't belong in the body.

Love also seems happy. Your love planet is in your 11th house until the 22nd, and your involvement with groups, friends and organizations can lead to romance. Sometimes a friend decides to be more than that. Sometimes friends play Cupid. On the 22nd the love planet moves into your spiritual 12th house and love becomes more spiritual, more idealistic. Many of you are searching for the 'perfect love' – the ideal love. Anything less can make you feel dissatisfied. Love opportunities happen in spiritual settings after the 22nd – the yoga studio, at a spiritual lecture or seminar, prayer meeting or charity event. With your love planet in the 12th house the message is stay in love and your contact with the Divine will be strong.

Finances are starting to straighten out, at last. The two planets involved in your finances are both moving forward now. Saturn started to move forward on November 4 and Neptune, your financial planet, moves forward on the 6th. So stuck deals or projects are getting unstuck. The only problem is that your financial planet receives stressful aspects until the 22nd, which indicates that there is still more work involved in earnings – more challenges to deal with. But after the 22nd all of this settles down and earnings come more easily.

Pisces

THE FISH

Birthdays from
19th February to
20th March

Personality Profile

PISCES AT A GLANCE

Element – Water

Ruling Planet – Neptune
  Career Planet – Jupiter
  Love Planet – Mercury
  Money Planet – Mars
  Planet of Health and Work – Sun
{ *Planet of Home and Family Life* – Mercury
  Planet of Love Affairs, Creativity and Children – Moon

Colours – aqua, blue-green

Colours that promote love, romance and social harmony – earth tones, yellow, yellow-orange

Colours that promote earning power – red, scarlet

Gem – white diamond

Metal – tin

Scent – lotus

Quality – mutable (= flexibility)

Qualities most needed for balance – structure and the ability to handle form

Strongest virtues – psychic power, sensitivity, self-sacrifice, altruism

Deepest needs – spiritual illumination, liberation

Characteristics to avoid – escapism, keeping bad company, negative moods

Signs of greatest overall compatibility – Cancer, Scorpio

Signs of greatest overall incompatibility – Gemini, Virgo, Sagittarius

Sign most helpful to career – Sagittarius

Sign most helpful for emotional support – Gemini

Sign most helpful financially – Aries

Sign best for marriage and/or partnerships – Virgo

Sign most helpful for creative projects – Cancer

Best Sign to have fun with – Cancer

Signs most helpful in spiritual matters – Scorpio, Aquarius

Best day of the week – Thursday

Understanding a Pisces

If Pisces have one outstanding quality it is their belief in the invisible, spiritual and psychic side of things. This side of things is as real to them as the hard earth beneath their feet – so real, in fact, that they will often ignore the visible, tangible aspects of reality in order to focus on the invisible and so-called intangible ones.

Of all the signs of the zodiac, the intuitive and emotional faculties of the Pisces are the most highly developed. They are committed to living by their intuition and this can at times be infuriating to other people – especially those who are materially, scientifically or technically orientated. If you think that money, status and worldly success are the only goals in life, then you will never understand a Pisces.

Pisces have intellect, but to them intellect is only a means by which they can rationalize what they know intuitively. To an Aquarius or a Gemini the intellect is a tool with which to gain knowledge. To a well-developed Pisces it is a tool by which to express knowledge.

Pisces feel like fish in an infinite ocean of thought and feeling. This ocean has many depths, currents and undercurrents. They long for purer waters where the denizens are good, true and beautiful, but they are sometimes pulled to the lower, murkier depths. Pisces know that they do not generate thoughts but only tune in to thoughts that already exist; this is why they seek the purer waters. This ability to tune in to higher thoughts inspires them artistically and musically.

Since Pisces is so spiritually orientated – though many Pisces in the corporate world may hide this fact – we will deal with this aspect in greater detail, for otherwise it is difficult to understand the true Pisces personality.

There are four basic attitudes of the spirit. One is outright scepticism – the attitude of secular humanists. The second is an intellectual or emotional belief, where one worships a far-distant God-figure – the attitude of most modern church-going people. The third is not only belief but direct personal spiritual experience – this is the attitude of some 'born-again' religious people. The fourth is actual unity with the divinity, an intermingling with the spiritual world – this is the attitude of yoga. This fourth attitude is the deepest urge of a

Pisces, and a Pisces is uniquely qualified to pursue and perform this work.

Consciously or unconsciously, Pisces seek this union with the spiritual world. The belief in a greater reality makes Pisces very tolerant and understanding of others – perhaps even too tolerant. There are instances in their lives when they should say 'enough is enough' and be ready to defend their position and put up a fight. However, because of their qualities it takes a good deal to get them into that frame of mind.

Pisces basically want and aspire to be 'saints'. They do so in their own way and according to their own rules. Others should not try to impose their concept of saintliness on a Pisces, because he or she always tries to find it for him- or herself.

Finance

Money is generally not that important to Pisces. Of course they need it as much as anyone else, and many of them attain great wealth. But money is not generally a primary objective. Doing good, feeling good about oneself, peace of mind, the relief of pain and suffering – these are the things that matter most to a Pisces.

Pisces earn money intuitively and instinctively. They follow their hunches rather than their logic. They tend to be generous and perhaps overly charitable. Almost any kind of misfortune is enough to move a Pisces to give. Although this is one of their greatest virtues, Pisces should be more careful with their finances. They should try to be more choosy about the people to whom they lend money, so that they are not being taken advantage of. If they give money to charities they should follow it up to see that their contributions are put to good use. Even when Pisces are not rich, they still like to spend money on helping others. In this case they should really be careful, however: they must learn to say no sometimes and help themselves first.

Perhaps the biggest financial stumbling block for the Pisces is general passivity – a *laissez faire* attitude. In general Pisces like to go with the flow of events. When it comes to financial matters, especially, they need to be more aggressive. They need to make things happen, to create their own wealth. A passive attitude will only cause loss and missed opportunity. Worrying about financial security will not provide that security. Pisces need to go after what they want tenaciously.

Career and Public Image

Pisces like to be perceived by the public as people of spiritual or material wealth, of generosity and philanthropy. They look up to big-hearted, philanthropic types. They admire people engaged in large-scale undertakings and eventually would like to head up these big enterprises themselves. In short, they like to be connected with big organizations that are doing things in a big way.

If Pisces are to realize their full career and professional potential they need to travel more, educate themselves more and learn more about the actual world. In other words, they need some of the unflagging optimism of Sagittarius in order to reach the top.

Because of all their caring and generous characteristics, Pisces often choose professions through which they can help and touch the lives of other people. That is why many Pisces become doctors, nurses, social workers or teachers. Sometimes it takes a while before Pisces realize what they really want to do in their professional lives, but once they find a career that lets them manifest their interests and virtues they will excel at it.

Love and Relationships

It is not surprising that someone as 'otherworldly' as the Pisces would like a partner who is practical and down to earth. Pisces prefer a partner who is on top of all the details of life, because they dislike details. Pisces seek this quality in both their romantic and professional partners. More than anything else this gives Pisces a feeling of being grounded, of being in touch with reality.

As expected, these kinds of relationships – though necessary – are sure to have many ups and downs. Misunderstandings will take place because the two attitudes are poles apart. If you are in love with a Pisces you will experience these fluctuations and will need a lot of patience to see things stabilize. Pisces are moody, intuitive, affectionate and difficult to get to know. Only time and the right attitude will yield Pisces' deepest secrets. However, when in love with a Pisces you will find that riding the waves is worth it because they are good, sensitive people who need and like to give love and affection.

When in love, Pisces like to fantasize. For them fantasy is 90 per cent of the fun of a relationship. They tend to idealize their partner, which can be good and bad at the same time. It is bad in that it is difficult for anyone to live up to the high ideals their Pisces lover sets.

Home and Domestic Life

In their family and domestic life Pisces have to resist the tendency to relate only by feelings and moods. It is unrealistic to expect that your partner and other family members will be as intuitive as you are. There is a need for more verbal communication between a Pisces and his or her family. A cool, unemotional exchange of ideas and opinions will benefit everyone.

Some Pisces tend to like mobility and moving around. For them too much stability feels like a restriction on their freedom. They hate to be locked in one location for ever.

The sign of Gemini sits on the cusp of Pisces' 4th solar house of home and family. This shows that Pisces likes and needs a home environment that promotes intellectual and mental interests. They tend to treat their neighbours as family – or extended family. Some Pisceans can have a dual attitude towards the home and family – on the one hand they like the emotional support of the family, but on the other they dislike the obligations, restrictions and duties involved with it. For Pisces, finding a balance is the key to a happy family life.

Horoscope for 2023

Major Trends

A lot of changes are happening this year, Pisces, as the long-term planets are shifting positions. The cosmic chess board is being rearranged and you're playing a new game.

The most significant change is Saturn's major move from Aquarius into Pisces, your own sign, where he will stay for the next two and a half years. This happens on March 8. This affects your health and energy. Health is not up to its usual standards this year, so you will need to rest and relax more. More on this later.

Saturn's move into your sign has other implications, too. It signals a more serious attitude to life. You're forced to take on more responsibilities. Many of you feel older than your years – even young Pisceans are thinking of old age. It can induce a pessimism – a tendency to depression. Everything looks black (even though it isn't really the case). And while this transit is excellent for managing things, it isn't that great for love. (More on this later.)

In spite of the above, you're in a very prosperous year. Jupiter is moving through your money house until May 17, expanding earnings and the financial horizons. On May 17 Jupiter moves into your 3rd house of intellectual interests and communication for the rest of 2023. The mental faculties are very much enhanced by this transit and students will do well in their studies. It will be a good time in which to take courses in subjects that interest you and, in some cases, to teach courses.

Pluto, the ruler of your 9th house, your religious planet, is beginning to change signs. This will be a two-year process. This year and next year he will hover between Capricorn and Aquarius, your 11th and 12th houses – energizing both these areas. In 2025 he will enter Aquarius for the long haul (twenty years, approximately). This will start a revamping of your whole spiritual life and attitudes.

Venus will spend an unusual amount of time – over four months – in the sign of Leo, your 6th house, this year, from June 5 to October 9. Thus, there will be a focus on health – a preoccupation with it. Perhaps surgery is recommended. (More on this later.)

Your major interests this year are friends, groups and group activities (until March 24 and from June 12 to the end of the year); spirituality (until March 8); the body, image and personal appearance; finance (until May 17); intellectual interests and communication; and health and work (from June 5 to October 9).

Your paths of greatest fulfilment this year are finance (until May 17 and from July 18 onwards); and intellectual interests and communication.

Health

(Please note that this is an astrological perspective on health and not a medical one. In days of yore there was no difference, both these perspectives were identical. But these days there could be quite a difference. For a medical perspective, please consult your doctor or health practitioner.)

Health needs watching this year, especially for those born early in the sign of Pisces (February 19–27). All of you will feel the effects of Saturn's move into your sign, but these people will feel them most strongly.

Saturn by himself is not enough to cause serious problems with your health, but when the short-term planets join him in making stressful aspects, things can get dangerous. Your vulnerability is increased. We will cover this in more detail in the monthly reports.

When Saturn is in your sign it is like walking uphill. You expend more energy to cover the same distance than you would if walking on level ground. The normal activities of life require more than the usual energy, and so you shouldn't be alarmed if you can't do as many push-ups or walk or jog as many miles as you usually do. This is natural. Respect the limits of the body and heed its messages.

There are many things you can do to enhance your health and energy. Give more attention to the following areas – the vulnerable areas of your Horoscope this year (the reflex points are shown in the chart opposite). These are where problems are most likely to happen, so keeping them healthy and fit is sound preventive medicine.

- The feet. These are always important for Pisces as your sign rules the feet. Regular foot massage – see the chart above – should be part of your regular health regime. You not only strengthen the feet but the whole body as well. You boost your overall energy levels.
- The heart is another area that's always important for Pisces. And this year, from March 8 onwards, it becomes even more important. The important thing here, as our regular readers know, is to avoid worry and anxiety – the feeling that you're carrying the burdens of the whole world on your shoulders. Cultivate faith. Meditation will be a big help.

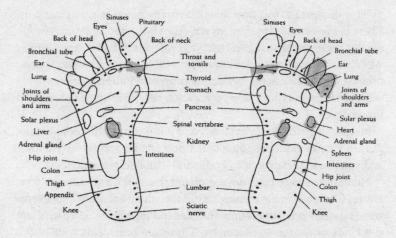

Important foot reflexology points for the year ahead

Try to massage all of the foot on a regular basis – the top of the foot as well as the bottom – but pay extra attention to the points highlighted on the chart. When you massage, be aware of 'sore spots' as these need special attention. It's also a good idea to massage the ankles and below them.

- The neck, throat, kidneys and hips become important this year, from June 5 to October 9, as Venus camps out in your 6th house. The neck and hips should be regularly massaged. Tension tends to collect in the neck and needs to be released. Hip massage will not only strengthen the kidneys and hips but the lower back as well.

Your health planet, the Sun, is a fast-moving planet who travels through your entire Horoscope during the year. So, there are many short-term health trends that depend on where the Sun is and the kinds of aspects he receives. These are best covered in the monthly reports.

Home and Family

Your 4th house of home and family isn't prominent this year – it is not a house of power. Only short-term planets move through there this year, and their impact is equally short term. So, the year ahead seems quiet with regard to this area. It will be pretty much as it was last year. There is a feeling of contentment with the status quo, and you have no need to make major changes. Next year will be a different story. Jupiter will move through your 4th house in 2024, bringing moves, house renovations and perhaps the acquisition of additional homes. This year, however, is more like a preparation year. The stage is being set for next year.

Mercury is both your love planet and family planet. He does double duty in your Horoscope. You like the home to be beautiful – artistic – and you like to socialize from home and with family members.

Mercury is a very fast-moving planet. He will move through your entire Horoscope in the coming year. Thus, there are many short-term trends in the home and family that depend on where Mercury is and the kinds of aspects he receives. These are best dealt with in the monthly reports.

Mercury goes retrograde four times this year (most years it is only three times) – from January 1–17; April 21 to May 14; August 23 to September 14; and December 13–31. These are times to avoid major decisions to do with the home or with family. Instead, they are times for gathering facts and gaining clarity. There are no quick fixes in family matters over those periods – only time will resolve things.

If you're planning on renovating the home or doing major repairs, January 1 to March 26 would be a good time. If you're just redecorating or buying objects of beauty for the home, April 11 to May 7 seems good. May 21 to June 21 is especially good for emotional healing and for making the home healthier.

A parent or parent figure could have moved last year. If not, a move for this person can happen next year. It seems happy. This parent or parent figure seems very active in your financial life and in a beneficial way. Siblings and sibling figures are prospering this year (and next year too), but a move is not likely (there's nothing against it, however). Children and children figures in your life have had a stormy romantic period for many years, but home and family life tends to the status quo. Grandchildren, or those who play that role in your life, are also having a stable home and family year. The good news is that they become more optimistic – less depressed – from March 8 onwards.

Finance and Career

Last year was a terrific career year and this year you get the results of this career success – financial prosperity. Jupiter, your career planet, is moving through your money house, enlarging and expanding it. Not only is his transit bringing extra earnings – windfalls and the like – but also happy and enlarging financial and business opportunities. The financial horizons expand. New vistas and possibilities open up to you. Assets you already own increase in value. As we've mentioned, a parent or parent figure seems very supportive and active in your financial life. Bosses and authority figures in your life are favourably disposed to your financial plans. Pay rises – official or unofficial – can happen. If you have any issues with 'officialdom', this is a time to resolve them – civil servants seem favourably disposed to you.

You are not known for your managerial skills, Pisces. By nature, you are 'free flowing', intuitive types. But with Saturn in your 1st house from the beginning of March you have excellent managerial skills – more so than usual. This is good for business.

Venus, as we mentioned, spends much time this year (over four months) in your 6th house of work. This suggests that a happy job opportunity will be coming to you.

Your financial planet, Mars, is relatively fast moving. He will travel through seven signs and houses of your Horoscope this year. So, there will be many short-term trends in finance that are best dealt with in the monthly reports.

Mars spends over four months 'out of bounds' – an unusually long time. This happens from January 1 to May 4, and again from December 22 to the end of the year. Thus, this is a year where you go outside your normal orbit in business and finance. Usually there are no answers to be found in your normal sphere and you must search in new places. You're someone who 'thinks outside the box' when it comes to finance.

As we said above, you're coming off the back of a very strong career year. This year, you seem sated with status and prestige, and want money. Career success is measured in terms of earnings – not in status and prestige. The more you earn the more successful you feel you are. You might sacrifice a prestigious post or venture in favour of something more mundane, but which pays more. On May 17 your career planet Jupiter moves into your 3rd house. This indicates that career is now boosted by good communications – good advertising and sales skills. Also, your knowledge of your industry (and in general) is very helpful. Superiors respect your brains.

Those who work with their intellect – teachers, writers, marketing people and so on – should have a good career year.

Love and Social Life

The year ahead is not an especially strong love year. For a start, your 7th house is not prominent. Basically, it is empty. Only short-term planets move through there and their effects are short term. Secondly, your 1st house of self is ultra-powerful, and *all* the long-term planets are in the Eastern sector of self in your chart. Love doesn't seem that important. The year ahead is a 'me-oriented' kind of year. And thirdly, Saturn is in your sign. This can make others feel that you're cold and aloof. Now you're really not like that, but it comes across unconsciously. It's as if you've taken a drug – a Saturn drug – and these vibrations emanate unconsciously. Happily, this last issue is easily dealt with: make it your mission to send love and warmth to others. You'll find that you don't need to be cold to be a good manager. And it will improve your love life.

Singles will most certainly date and have relationships this year, but marriage doesn't seem indicated.

Mercury, your love planet, is not only very fast moving but he is erratic in motion. Sometimes he speeds through the sky; sometimes he slows down; sometimes he is still; and sometimes (four times this year) he goes backwards. This is how your love life and love feelings behave. There's nothing wrong with you. You're just mercurial. It's your nature. So, there are always short-term trends in love that depend on where Mercury is at any given time and the kinds of aspects he receives. These can only be discussed in the monthly reports.

As we've said, Mercury will retrograde four times over the year, so there can be more dramas and delays and confusion in love than usual. These retrogrades happen from January 1–17; April 21 to May 14; August 23 to September 14; and December 13 to the end of the year, and are times to avoid making major love decisions, one way or another, and to gain clarity in this area. Get the facts. See where things can be improved. Then, when Mercury moves forward again, you can take the appropriate action.

Though romance is not a major focus this year, friendships (Platonic relationships) will be active and basically happy. Saturn, your planet of friends, in your own sign signals the devotion of friends. You don't need to do anything special to attract friends – they find you. Just go about your daily business. Some of these friends can be over-controlling, but they seem to mean well.

Self-improvement

With Saturn in your sign after March 8, you will start a two-and-a-half-year relationship with the cosmic drill sergeant. He is stern and seems tough on the outside, but it is tough love. His object – depending on your age – is to get you fit for service, for your life's work. And he is very thorough. He will throw more and more responsibility on you – but not more than you can handle. He might take you to your breaking point but not beyond it. He will reveal your physical limitations. He will 'road test' your image and personality. And, through all this, he will help you get the body into the shape that you want. It is good to know our physical limits. This way we won't set unrealistic goals.

If this transit is handled right, you will emerge in better physical shape – with a better personal appearance – than when you began. This is a great period for losing weight and for regulating the appetite. It is also good for exercise regimes (though these should be in moderation).

While this is going on there is a tendency to pessimism. Everything looks black. But there is light at the end of the tunnel. Meditation is especially helpful (it is always good, but especially now) to help you overcome depressive feelings. You will learn that these feelings are only feelings – not reality. You are more than your feelings. There is a place in your soul that is above all these feelings – above the whole material world – untouched by it. This is the place to seek refuge. You will come back more optimistic, more refreshed, more ready for the battle of life.

It would also be useful, as we have mentioned, to make it a spiritual project to project love and warmth to others. Gloominess, aloofness, coldness is not helpful in your love and social life. You would tend to feel isolated and alone. But this meditative project will dispel such coldness and there will be better relations with the spouse, partner, current love and friends in general.

There is another important spiritual lesson to be learned during Saturn's stay in your sign. This involves learning to love – to enjoy – the challenges, responsibilities and tests that arrive. Eventually you will see that there is no reason to face our challenges with gritted teeth. Does that make you better able to handle them? No. Why not face them with faith, confidence and a 'can do' spirit? Why not be happy as you overcome them? And you will.

Month-by-month Forecasts

January

Best Days Overall: 6, 7, 14, 15, 23, 24
Most Stressful Days Overall: 1, 2, 8, 9, 21, 22, 28, 29
Best Days for Love: 1, 2, 3, 10, 11, 12, 13, 18, 19, 21, 22, 28, 29
Best Days for Money: 3, 4, 8, 12, 13, 16, 17, 21, 22, 23, 30, 31
Best Days for Career: 8, 9, 16, 23

You begin your year with much of the planetary power in your 11th house of friends – a beneficent house. The month ahead is basically happy. Health is good. There is only one planet, Mars, in stressful alignment with you (although the Moon will sometimes be stressfully aligned for brief periods). All the other planets are either in harmonious aspect or leaving you alone. You can enhance the health with back and spine massage until the 20th and with ankle and calf massage after then.

Mars, your financial planet, is retrograde until the 12th. So, avoid making major purchases or investments until after that date. Mars will be in your 4th house all month, indicating that you are spending more on the home and family, but you can be earning from here as well. Family and family connections are important financially.

Mars is 'out of bounds' this month. (Next month he moves even further 'out of bounds'.) In financial matters you're exploring outside your normal sphere (and will be going even further outside it soon). There are no answers to be found in your normal orbit and you're forced to search elsewhere. Sometimes it is necessary to 'think outside the box' and this is one of those times.

Love is complicated this month as your love planet, Mercury, is retrograde until the 17th. The normal social grace is not up to its usual standard. Avoid judging the love life now – avoid making major decisions in love. Wait until after the 17th. Romance might be complicated, but the overall social life seems happy and active. These social activities are more Platonic than romantic, and more about friends, groups and group activities. They can, however, lead to romance – after the 18th.

The New Moon of the 11th occurs in your 11th house. This adds to the social nature of the period. It is a fun kind of day. A good love and social day for children and children figures. Any issues involving friends, organizations, astrology and astronomy will become clearer as the weeks progress.

February

Best Days Overall: 2, 3, 12, 13, 20, 21
Most Stressful Days Overall: 1, 7, 8, 14, 15, 27, 28
Best Days for Love: 2, 3, 7, 8, 11, 12, 13, 18, 19, 22, 27, 28
Best Days for Money: 1, 4, 5, 9, 10, 14, 15, 18, 19, 22, 23, 27, 28
Best Days for Career: 4, 5, 14, 15, 22, 23

On January 20 the Sun entered your 12th house of spirituality and will stay there until the 18th of this month. Spiritual healing is always powerful for you, but these days even more so than usual. Whether you're a patient or a healer, you'll be getting interesting results. The power of the spirit to heal is infinite and unlimited. In general, you're in a more spiritual kind of period this month – especially until the 18th. Your cosmic attunement is stronger than usual. The dream life is active and revelatory. There are all kinds of supernatural experiences happening.

Health is good this month and will get even better from the 18th. On that day the Sun, your health and work planet, moves into your own sign and you begin a yearly personal pleasure peak. This is a time to enjoy all the pleasures of the body and the five senses – to pamper the body. Also good for getting the body into the shape that you want. A happy job opportunity comes to you after the 18th. If you're a free-lancer, a happy assignment comes to you. The personal appearance shines. You have magnetism and charisma. Venus has been in your sign since January 27 and remains there until the 21st. So there is beauty, glamour and sex appeal to the image (especially from the 14th to the 16th).

Mars is still in your 4th house this month (and is even further 'out of bounds' than last month). You're still spending on the home and family (this is a good time to make repairs or renovations in the home) and earning from here as well. Perhaps you're setting up (or expand-ing) your home office. The home is as much a business as a home.

Love is improved over last month. Mercury is moving forward and your social confidence is good. Until the 11th you seem conservative in love matters – cautious. After the 11th you seem more experimen-tal. With your love planet in Aquarius from the 11th onwards social magnetism and confidence soars. Mercury is in his most powerful and exalted position, so the social grace is unusually strong. After the 11th spiritual compatibility is important in love. Romantic opportunities happen in spiritual venues.

The New Moon of the 20th occurs in your sign, signalling a happy day. There is more personal pleasure. Health, already good, improves even further. Your personal healing power is also improved. This New Moon occurs right on Saturn, your planet of friends, so it is a good social day as well. Children and children figures in your life have romantic opportunities (much depends on their age). Issues involving your appearance and image will clarify themselves over the coming weeks – until the next New Moon.

March

Best Days Overall: 1, 2, 11, 12, 19, 20, 28, 29, 30
Most Stressful Days Overall: 6, 7, 13, 14, 26, 27
Best Days for Love: 4, 5, 6, 7, 11, 12, 21, 24, 25, 31
Best Days for Money: 4, 5, 9, 10, 13, 14, 17, 18, 21, 22, 28, 31
Best Days for Career: 4, 5, 13, 14, 21, 22, 31

An eventful month, Pisces. Saturn moves into your sign on the 8th, bringing more responsibilities to you and a more serious attitude to life. This transit will affect the health as well – and for a couple of years it will need much more attention. Right now, those born early in your sign – February 18–21 – will feel this strongest. But eventually all of you will notice this. One of the problems here is too much of a good thing. It is good to take more responsibility and be more serious about life – but there is a tendency to overdo it. One can become overly pessimistic, always looking at the dark side of things. One can feel older than one's years. Even children often think of old age under this kind of transit. Certainly, it will affect the love life. People can take you to be too cold, aloof and distant. So, lighten up a bit. Project love and warmth to others.

You're still in the midst of a yearly personal pleasure peak until the 20th. Although Saturn in your sign tempers it a bit, it is still happening. Saturn's position means that you're entering a good period for disciplined exercise regimes and weight-loss programmes. Saturn in your sign tends to weight loss.

Women of childbearing age are less fertile now. Pregnancies can happen but they seem more complicated these days.

On the 20th the Sun enters the 2nd money house and you begin a yearly financial peak. For some of you – depending on your age – this will be a lifetime peak. Jupiter, the planet of abundance, has been in your money house since the beginning of the year. Now he is further energized by other planets, so the month ahead is super prosperous. Some of you will inherit money, some can be named in a will, some of you will get new cars or communication equipment, some can be lucky in a speculation. The cosmos has many ways to prosper you. The New Moon of the 21st occurs in the money house and brings financial increase – a great financial day. It brings luck in speculations as well. It is a fun day. Job opportunities can come. In the coming weeks the financial life will become clearer. Your questions and doubts will get resolved.

Love is happy this month. Your love planet Mercury enters your sign on the 3rd and stays there until the 18th. Love pursues you. You only need to show up. If you're in a relationship, the spouse, partner or current love goes out of his or her way to please you. On the 19th, Mercury moves into your money house and romantic opportunities occur as you pursue your financial goals or with people involved in your finances. Just be careful of jumping into relationships too quickly.

April

Best Days Overall: 7, 8, 16, 17, 25, 26
Most Stressful Days Overall: 2, 3, 4, 9, 10, 22, 23, 24, 30
Best Days for Love: 1, 2, 3, 4, 12, 13, 14, 21, 22, 23, 30
Best Days for Money: 1, 7, 8, 10, 16, 17, 18, 19, 25, 26, 28, 29
Best Days for Career: 1, 9, 10, 19, 28, 29

You've been experiencing a huge financial peak, so it is understandable that a course correction could be necessary. A solar eclipse on the 20th occurs right on the cusp of your 2nd and 3rd houses, impacting the affairs of both. As far as eclipses go, this one is generally mild in its effects. However, if it hits a sensitive point in your Natal Horoscope – the one cast for your exact date, time and place of birth – it can be strong indeed. So, it would be a good idea to reduce your schedule over the eclipse period.

The eclipse's impact in the money house shows a need to change the financial thinking and planning. The events of the eclipse will show you where your thinking has been amiss, allowing you to make the corrections. These should work out well.

The impact on the 3rd house shows that siblings, sibling figures and neighbours are affected – they have personal dramas. Students can change their educational plans or schools. There are shake-ups and disruptions at their school. Cars and communication equipment can behave erratically, and often repairs or replacements are necessary. It would be a good idea to drive more carefully at this time.

Pluto, the ruler of your 9th house, is directly hit by this eclipse, meaning that there are shake-ups and disruptions at your place of worship. There are dramas in the lives of worship leaders. Your religious and theological beliefs get tested and, over the coming months, some will be discarded; others will get revised and fine-tuned. This is very important as it will bring changes to the way that you live your life.

Every solar eclipse affects the job and health, because the eclipsed planet, the Sun, rules these things in your chart. So, there can be job changes – either within your present situation or in another one. There can be disruptions at the workplace; the conditions of work are changed. If you employ others there can be employee turnover – now and in the coming months. There will also be important changes to the health regime (very much needed now as Saturn is in your sign).

May

Best Days Overall: 13, 14, 22, 23
Most Stressful Days Overall: 1, 5, 6, 7, 8, 20, 21, 27, 28
Best Days for Love: 1, 2, 3, 9, 10, 17, 18, 19, 27, 28, 30, 31
Best Days for Money: 8, 14, 15, 16, 17, 24, 25
Best Days for Career: 7, 8, 16, 17, 24, 25

We have another eclipse this month. This time it is a lunar eclipse on the 5th. Again, it seems mild in its effects on you – but keep in mind our remarks of last month. If it hits something sensitive in your birth chart it can be powerful indeed.

This eclipse occurs in your 9th house and thus again impacts students – but here it is more college or postgraduate-level students (and those applying to college). There are changes of educational plans – perhaps changes of subjects. Sometimes people change schools. Sometimes the school you wanted rejects you and a better one accepts you. It is a good thing, but disruptive. Once again there are shake-ups in your place of worship and dramas in the lives of worship leaders. Once again, your religious and theological beliefs get tested – also your worldview. With both this month's and last month's eclipses hitting this area, there is obviously a strong cosmic need to reset your ideas here.

Every lunar eclipse affects your children or children figures in your life. So make sure they stay out of harm's way this period, and that they avoid stressful and risky activities. Many Pisceans are involved in the creative arts and this eclipse signals important changes in their creative life – and the way they approach their creativity.

A parent or parent figure has to make important financial changes. He or she can be experiencing a health scare, and in the coming months will change his or her health regime.

Uranus, your spiritual planet, is grazed by this eclipse. Happily, it's not a direct hit. There are spiritual changes happening as a result, but nothing too dramatic. There are shake-ups in spiritual or charitable organizations that you're involved with. You change or modify your spiritual practice and teachings. Guru figures in your life experience personal dramas.

This kind of eclipse often brings hyper kinds of dream activity, generally of a disturbing kind. But you should not take these dreams too seriously. It is just psychic debris stirred up by the eclipse.

June

Best Days Overall: 1, 2, 9, 10, 18, 19, 20, 28, 29
Most Stressful Days Overall: 3, 4, 16, 17, 23, 24, 25
Best Days for Love: 2, 6, 11, 16, 17, 21, 22, 23, 24, 25, 26, 27
Best Days for Money: 3, 4, 5, 6, 11, 12, 14, 15, 21, 22, 23, 24
Best Days for Career: 3, 4, 5, 6, 14, 15, 23, 24

Health needs a lot more attention this month (in fact since May 21). So, make sure to get enough rest. Enhance the health in the ways mentioned in the yearly report. With your health planet, the Sun, in your 4th house until the 21st good emotional health is very important. Watch the moods. Keep them constructive. A spiritual therapist can be a big help. Health will improve after the 21st, but emotional health will remain important. The diet becomes important after the 21st as well.

With your 4th house strong this month, your focus should be on the home, family and emotional wellness. Career issues can be downplayed. It is a time for building and strengthening the psychological infrastructure upon which a successful career rests. Thus, getting the domestic life and your emotional harmony in order will enable you to be more successful later in the year. The New Moon of the 18th also occurs in your 4th house, making it an especially good day for emotional healing and for fun in general. Issues involving the home and family will clarify as the weeks progress – until the next New Moon.

On the 21st, as the Sun enters your 5th house of fun and creativity, you begin another yearly personal pleasure peak. It's time to drop your cares and just enjoy life. Do the things that bring you joy. You'll find that many problems get solved just by this. Stop focusing on the problem for a bit and do something that's fun. When you come back to deal with the so-called problem – the answers are there. You'll also find that this is good health therapy. Joy is a powerful healing force – especially this month.

Jupiter entered your 3rd house of communication and intellectual interests on May 17 and will be here for the rest of the year. Thus, many of you will get new cars or communication equipment. Your communication skills are very much enhanced under this transit. Good communication skills seem vital for the career.

Your financial planet, Mars, will spend the month in your 6th house, indicating that money is earned the old-fashioned way – through work and productive service. Mars in Leo can make you more risk-taking and speculative in financial matters – so you need to be more careful about this.

Love is mixed this month. On the positive side, Mercury is moving quickly, which indicates confidence and someone who covers a lot of social territory. The needs in love change quickly as well – which can be a problem for those in relationships. Until the 11th love can be found in the neighbourhood and in educational settings. You're attracted by a person's communication and intellectual skills. After the 11th, those things are important, but you also want emotional bonding – emotional intimacy. From the 27th onwards, emotional intimacy is still important, but you'd like someone who can show you a good time too. Love should be fun. (But when the tough times come, you or the current love will probably want out.)

July

Best Days Overall: 7, 8, 16, 17, 26, 27
Most Stressful Days Overall: 1, 2, 13, 14, 15, 21, 22, 28, 29
Best Days for Love: 2, 8, 10, 18, 19, 20, 21, 22, 29, 30
Best Days for Money: 2, 3, 4, 9, 10, 11, 12, 21, 22, 30, 31
Best Days for Career: 1, 2, 3, 4, 11, 12, 21, 22, 28, 29, 30, 31

Though Saturn remains in your sign, health is good this month. Those of you with birthdays from February 24–27 are feeling the Saturn influence most strongly. But the other, short-term planets are helping you out. Enhance the health with right diet, emotional harmony and just having fun until the 23rd. After the 23rd give more attention to the heart. Chest massage would be helpful. Spiritual healing is always good for you, but especially so on the 8th and 9th.

Your love planet Mercury went 'out of bounds' on June 25 and remains so until the 6th of this month. So when it comes to love (and sex) you're outside your normal orbit. You're attracted by people who are outside your orbit as well.

Until the 11th love is mostly entertainment – fun – and not too serious. After then there is still a desire for fun but you also like people who serve your interests. This is romantic. The person who can fix your car or computer allures you. On the 29th Mercury enters your 7th house and you seem more serious about love. But Mercury in Virgo can make you (or your current love interest) too fussy – too hypercritical – in love. This needs to be avoided.

You're still in the midst of a yearly personal pleasure peak until the 23rd and fun remains the dominant theme of the period. There is also more involvement with children and children figures. The New Moon of the 17th occurs in your 5th house and adds to the fun – an especially enjoyable day. Children and children figures in your life seem more devoted to you. Issues involving children and your personal creativity will be clarified in the coming weeks – until the next New Moon.

Mars is still in your 6th house until the 11th. So, money comes from work and productive service. Your work creates your luck. On the 11th your financial planet enters your 7th house of love and stays there for the rest of the month. So social contacts are playing an important role in finance now. You spend on your social life but earn from it as well. Much of your socializing is business related. An opportunity for a partnership or joint venture can happen as well. The good thing about the financial planet in Virgo is that you're more analytical about finance. You're on top of all the details. You're more conservative, less speculative, than you were last month.

On the 23rd the Sun enters your 6th house and stays there for the rest of the month. You're in the mood for work now. Those looking for work have many job opportunities. And even if you're already in work, there are opportunities for overtime and second jobs.

August

Best Days Overall: 3, 4, 12, 13, 22, 23, 30, 31
Most Stressful Days Overall: 10, 11, 17, 18, 24, 25
Best Days for Love: 5, 6, 7, 8, 14, 15, 17, 18, 24, 25, 26, 27
Best Days for Money: 5, 6, 7, 8, 17, 18, 26, 27, 28
Best Days for Career: 7, 8, 17, 18, 24, 25, 26, 27

Planetary retrograde activity gradually increases this month until we hit the maximum extent for the year on the 29th – 60 per cent of the planets travelling backwards. So, patience is needed this month. Rushing will not make things happen quicker. Only time will do the trick.

Your health planet the Sun never goes retrograde, and he is in your 6th house of health until the 23rd. So, the focus is on health. This focus will stand you in good stead for later when health becomes more stressful. This transit is also good for those of you looking for employment and for those who employ others. There are good job opportunities and good candidates for jobs. The New Moon of the 16th occurs in your 6th house, making it an even stronger day for job-seekers and employers. It is also a fun kind of day. Children and children figures in your life have a nice payday (official or unofficial). This New Moon will have effects long after it happens, and health and job issues will clarify as the weeks progress.

On the 23rd the Sun moves into your 7th house and you begin a yearly love and social peak. Normally this aspect is good for love. But now it seems a lot more complicated. For a start, your love planet, Mercury, goes retrograde on the 23rd, which means that the two planets involved with you – your image and personal desires – are both retrograde. There are romantic opportunities, but you don't know what you want. Furthermore, you seem to be attracting people who also don't know what they want. So you're just drifting along here. There is another issue to consider as well. Although the Western, social sector of your chart is as strong now as it will ever be this year, it is far from dominant. The Eastern sector of self is still stronger than the social sector. So, although you're trying to be social, your primary interest is yourself and your goals. This is not conducive to romance.

Health needs watching after the 23rd as well. Make sure to rest and relax more – especially those born from February 22–24. Listen to the messages the body is giving you. If you're tired, rest. If you're exercising and feel pain or discomfort, take a break. Try not to push the body beyond its limits. Enhance the health in the ways mentioned in the yearly report. After the 23rd abdominal massage will be helpful.

Though there are many retrograde planets this month, Mars, your financial planet, is moving forward, so finance doesn't seem affected. Until the 28th Mars will be in your 7th house of love and, like last month, much of your socializing seems to be business related. Good social grace helps the bottom line. Likeability can be more important than your actual abilities or the quality of your product. You like to do business with friends and like to socialize – to befriend – those you do business with. On the 28th Mars moves into your 8th house of regeneration. This favours tax and insurance planning and, if you're of the appropriate age, it is good for estate planning.

September

Best Days Overall: 8, 9, 10, 18, 19, 27, 28
Most Stressful Days Overall: 6, 7, 13, 14, 15, 21, 22
Best Days for Love: 2, 3, 4, 5, 11, 12, 13, 14, 15, 21, 22, 23, 24, 30
Best Days for Money: 2, 3, 4, 5, 13, 14, 15, 23, 24, 29, 30
Best Days for Career: 4, 5, 14, 15, 21, 22, 23, 24

You're still in the midst of a yearly love and social peak this month, but love remains complicated. Review our discussion of this in August's report. However, your love planet Mercury starts to move forward on the 15th and so brings some improvements here. There is more clarity. The social confidence and judgement are improved. Mercury has been in your 7th house since July 29, and he will remain here all this month as well. This would indicate more socializing with the family and from home (remember that Mercury is your family planet too). Family and family connections seem involved in your love life. More clarity in love comes from the New Moon of the 15th, which occurs in your 7th house – an especially good social day. In addition, love and relationship issues will clarify themselves in the coming weeks – until the next New Moon. Your questions and doubts will be dealt with.

Mars, your financial planet, began his solstice on August 27 and it goes on until the 2nd. So there has been a pause in your financial life – a healthy pause – and then a change of direction. This pause should not alarm you.

Mars will spend the month in your 8th house of regeneration and this gives many messages. You're very involved in the prosperity of the spouse, partner or current love. In fact, with the prosperity of others full stop. In a sense you're like the mutual fund manager who only prospers in so far as his clients prosper. As you focus on the prosperity of others, your own prosperity will happen naturally.

Your financial planet in your 8th house is a good period to use spare cash to pay off debt – however, if you need to borrow, it is good for that too. If you have good business ideas, this is a good month to approach outside investors. On a deeper level, this is a period to purge your finances and possessions of all that doesn't belong there. Get rid of possessions that you don't need or use. De-clutter your home or storage units. Get rid of financial waste – redundant accounts or subscriptions or phone plans that you don't use (obviously, not what's needed).

Health still needs attention, but you'll see big improvement after the 23rd. In the meantime, enhance the health with more rest and abdominal massage. Massage of the small intestine reflex will also be good. After the 23rd, hip massage and massage of the kidney reflex will be beneficial (the reflex points are shown in the yearly report). Safe sex and sexual moderation seem important after the 23rd.

With the Sun, your health planet, in your house of regeneration after the 23rd there is a tendency towards surgery. Perhaps you see it as a 'quick fix' to a problem. Perhaps it is recommended to you. However, detoxes often achieve the same thing (albeit more slowly) and should be explored.

October

Best Days Overall: 6, 7, 15, 16, 17, 24, 25
Most Stressful Days Overall: 3, 4, 11, 12, 18, 19
Best Days for Love: 1, 2, 9, 10, 11, 12, 20, 21, 24, 28, 29
Best Days for Money: 1, 2, 3, 4, 11, 12, 15, 20, 21, 24, 25, 26, 27, 28, 29
Best Days for Career: 1, 2, 11, 12, 18, 19, 20, 21, 28, 29

Retrograde activity eases up this month but is still substantial – 40 per cent of the planets are retrograde from the 11th onwards.

Two eclipses this month guarantee an eventful kind of month, with many changes. Though these eclipses seem to be mild in their effects on you – so far as eclipses go – it won't hurt to relax and reduce your schedule anyway. For, if either eclipse hits a sensitive point in your personal Horoscope – the one cast for your exact date, time and place of birth – it can be powerful indeed.

There is a solar eclipse on the 14th and a lunar eclipse on the 28th. The solar eclipse on the 14th occurs in your 8th house and impacts the finances of the spouse, partner or current love. Important changes are needed. This eclipse can bring psychological encounters with death – sometimes near-death experiences, close calls. The thousand-eyed angel is letting you know that he's around. This is not punishment but more about education. There is a need for a deeper understanding of death – a need to lose the fear of it. In some cases, this is a love letter from the cosmos, a reminder that life is short and can end at any time: stop being frivolous and get down to the reason you were born.

Every solar eclipse affects the job and the health regime. So, there will be important changes to the health regime in the coming months. Job changes are also happening, which can be within your present situation or with a new one. There are probably disturbances or dramas at the workplace.

The lunar eclipse of the 28th occurs in your 3rd house of communication and impacts siblings, sibling figures in your life and neighbours. They experience personal dramas and should reduce their schedules at this time. Students below college level are also affected. They make changes in their educational plans, and sometimes change schools. There can be disruptions at school. Cars and communication equipment will get tested and often repairs or replacements are necessary. (This is a good year to get a new car.) It would be a good idea to drive more carefully over the period of the eclipse.

Every lunar eclipse impacts children and children figures in your life, and this one is no different. They should take it nice and easy and avoid risky, daredevil-type activities at this time.

November

Best Days Overall: 2, 3, 12, 13, 21, 22, 29, 30
Most Stressful Days Overall: 1, 7, 8, 14, 15, 27, 28
Best Days for Love: 2, 3, 7, 8, 9, 18, 19, 23, 24, 27, 28
Best Days for Money: 2, 3, 7, 12, 13, 16, 22, 23, 24, 25
Best Days for Career: 7, 14, 15, 16, 25

Retrograde activity decreases further this month. By the end of the month only 30 per cent of the planets are retrograde. Things are starting to move forward. Blocked deals or project are getting unblocked.

Health has improved since October 23. Saturn is still in your sign and is always a factor, but the other short-term planets are in harmonious aspect. After the 22nd, though, health will again need more attention. Enhance the health with more rest, as always. But thigh massage and massage of the liver reflex will also enhance health after the 22nd.

Your 9th house, a beneficent house, became powerful on October 23 and will remain so until the 22nd of this month. College-level students should do well in their studies. Those involved in the legal field or having legal issues should also do well. This period brings religious and theological insights as well. Some of you might be travelling to foreign countries – or the opportunity comes for foreign travel.

On the 22nd, your 10th house of career becomes powerful and the focus shifts to the career. There is much progress happening, although with Jupiter, your career planet, still retrograde progress can be slow – but it is happening. In addition, with Jupiter retrograde, career opportunities that come to you – and they will – need studying carefully. Don't just jump at them. You're working hard in the career. The demands are great. Perhaps you need to fend off competitors – to defend your turf. But your good work ethic is a big help.

Finances are good this month. Until the 24th Mars is in your 9th house, expanding earnings and bringing good fortune. It is still beneficial to detox the financial life and the possessions – this will make room for the new and better that wants to come to you. On the 24th Mars crosses your Mid-heaven and enters your 10th house. This transit is also good for finance. It shows that it's a priority – on top of your agenda. The financial planet in Sagittarius tends to expand earnings as well. Bosses, parents and parent figures are kindly disposed to your financial goals. A pay rise (official or unofficial) can happen.

Love, too, seems happy, although you don't seem sure what you want. Mercury is in your 9th house until the 10th, signalling romantic opportunities at school or religious functions. Perhaps in foreign countries or with foreigners. After the 10th Mercury enters your career house and you pursue career goals by social means. Likeability is more important than your professional skills. A good part of your socializing now is career related.

December

Best Days Overall: 9, 10, 18, 19, 27, 28
Most Stressful Days Overall: 4, 5, 6, 11, 12, 24, 25, 31
Best Days for Love: 4, 5, 6, 9, 14, 18, 19, 22, 28, 30, 31
Best Days for Money: 2, 3, 4, 11, 12, 14, 20, 21, 22, 29, 30, 31
Best Days for Career: 4, 11, 12, 14, 22, 31

The month ahead is successful – you're in the midst of a yearly career peak – but health needs a lot of attention. Now, it's not just Saturn stressing you, but many short-term planets are joining the party. Rest and relax more. Certain things, like the career and extra responsibilities of a personal nature, can't be avoided. However, keep your focus on the important things in your life and let lesser things go. As the saying goes, 'don't sweat the small stuff'. There should be some improvement after the 22nd. In the meantime, massage of the liver reflex and thigh massage will be powerful until the 22nd. After then, back and knee massage is beneficial. This is a good period to schedule more health treatments or massages. Spend more time in a health spa if possible.

Love is complicated this month. Your needs in love change. Also, your love planet goes retrograde again on the 13th and stays that way for the rest of the month. Mercury spends a day this month in your 10th house, moves into the 11th house on the 2nd and travels back into your 10th house on the 24th. This is typical of Mercury's erratic behaviour, but it means that you swing between a desire for friendship with the beloved and a desire for power and prestige. You're not sure what you want.

The New Moon of the 12th occurs in your 10th house of career, adding to your personal success (but also stressing the health and energy). Children and children figures seem successful that day as well – and they seem to be helping your career. There is more fun as you pursue career goals. The good part of this is that career issues will become clearer as the weeks unfold. Questions will be answered, and doubts assuaged – all very naturally and normally.

Your good career reputation is important in finance. It brings client referrals and perhaps pay rises (official or unofficial). You still have the financial favour of bosses, parents, parent figures and the authority figures in your life. Perhaps more importantly, with your financial planet at the top of your Horoscope in your 10th house, it shows financial focus.

Mars has spent many months 'out of bounds' this year. This month – on the 22nd – he once again goes 'out of bounds'. In financial matters you're going outside your normal sphere.